Bridge to Grace

Bridge to Grace

Finding life and peace in the midst of death and chaos

JEANETTE DUBY

Dedication

This book is dedicated to my lovely daughter, Nicole.

You continue to amaze me daily with your love for life and our Lord. You walk beside me through the difficulties of life and never fail to support me.

Always remember that One greater than us loves you. He will always look after you, so never fear my darling daughter. In those moments when life gets hard, remember you are never alone.

Stay true to who you are and allow God to handle the rest. I am eternally grateful for your love. I love you!

Mom

Special Thanks

To the friends who supported me while I worked on this project, thank you is simply not enough. God knew what He was doing when He sent you to help. He brought all the pieces together from editing to art work, and everything in between.

Some of you spent countless hours reading rough drafts. Others endured multiple text messages and emails with questions and ideas to ponder. I am thankful for your sacrifice.

I am also thankful for all those who prayed over this project. Your prayers are appreciated. This has truly been a labor of love!

To God be the glory for this work. May He use this to reach those who are hurting and to bring them back to Himself.

May He continue to bless you always!

Jeanette

Table of Contents

Introduction

Introduction

The bridge to grace is lined with love. Its members, its structure, its beams all embody love. Love seeps from the crevices. Its strength is like no other. It supports the weight of the broken, the hurting and the lost. It stands strong against the powerful winds of change and is not easily moved.

God is love. He loves us and He pursues us with that love. And when I experienced His love, I was able to share that love with others. I appreciate the love God has for me. I appreciate what Jesus has done for me on the cross at Calvary. It was love that led me. It was love that shaped me. It was love that saved me. It was love that led me to grace, God's grace.

So whether you are standing at the foot of the bridge, in the middle of the bridge or you're almost across, keep moving forward. God's open arms are waiting for you.

For the sake of writing this book, I have left out personal names unless they are deceased. I approached this story from my perspective, my memories, and my notes of what happened. The story was written based on my own experience.

My prayer is that this story will change someone's life – perhaps, your life.

CHAPTER ONE

Rough Road Up Ahead

It was HIV. The test came back positive. Human Immunodeficiency Virus – a very long name for a little-known disease. That's what the family doctor said. Joe's doctor was a longtime family friend and also my parent's doctor. My dad had been a patient of his for a very long time. When he didn't see the doctor in the office, he saw him in the hospital. Today was no different.

My mother was celebrating her birthday in a hospital waiting room, husband and son both going under the knife. That birthday would forever be etched in her mind.

Dad was recovering from having his leg amputated just below the knee as a result of an infected sore on his foot from diabetes. My baby brother, now almost 21 years old, was having an infected cyst removed from the inside of his upper thigh. They would send the cyst to the lab for testing.

The cyst had been growing for quite some time. Joe didn't know what it was, just that it shouldn't be there. He finally had the doctor look at it. Doc said the only way he could diagnose it properly was by doing a biopsy and removing tissue sample-for the lab to analyze. That meant cutting into it. I know, that's gross. I am sorry if you are getting squeamish already. I'm just telling you what my brother told me.

Doc took a sample from the cyst in my brother's thigh and sent it off for testing. I don't know if he suspected HIV based on Joe's lifestyle or if it looked suspicious, possibly cancer or both. I wasn't there for the procedure or the results of either one. But word made it back to me - Joe had tested positive for HIV, and my father had made it through the surgery fine.

Here we were, August 1990, nine years after the 1981 discovery of HIV/AIDS. In under a decade, HIV/AIDS had raced to the top of the list in the medical community as the number one deadliest disease.

Looking back, I am glad the doctor tested for HIV as bad as that sounds. I appreciated his diligence. Without it, my brother would have continued with no proper diagnosis, perhaps falling ill sooner than later and who knows, ultimately succumbing to the disease. Not to mention the risk his family would have faced with the unknown exposures as any one of us could have contracted this new disease.

Now that we knew, as for me, I was scared of the disease, scared of him and scared for myself. When confronted with a situation like this, my mind tends to go to the worst case scenario, and this would be no exception. Before I knew it, most of my family and friends had contracted the deadly disease and died. I imagined myself dying at a young age. I imagined everyone else dying at a young age. I started to imagine the guy's condition down the street was now my condition. I see his deterioration, and I imagine myself in his shoes, and I panic. That's how insecure and naïve I was. I didn't know any better. My mind took off on a marathon run and wouldn't be back for a while.

I wasn't there the day Joe received the terrible news, so I cannot speak for how he initially handled it. But knowing my brother, I can picture him pacing the room frantically, nervously rubbing his chin, feeling the razor stubble between his thumb and index finger as he digested the awful, life-changing news. I can imagine his mind going from one extreme to the next, searching for an exit. *Where can I escape? Is this a terrible dream? Maybe the doctor is wrong. Was it the night I threw caution to the wind?*

I am sure by now he had heard about HIV/AIDS in his circle of friends. It was taking the nation by storm, and no doubt was the subject around the bar top. In smoke-filled rooms around the country, HIV/AIDS became a popular and serious topic of conversation. The once carefree attitudes of some would now take on a different feel. Now one would have to be purposeful in their conversations without coming right out and asking the important, yet somewhat uncomfortable question – *Do you have HIV? Um, say…. Have you been tested for HIV lately? You haven't been around anyone who tested positive, have you?*

One would have to wonder if the other person was being honest. Could they answer the question with certainty? Was the risk worth it?

I am sure it played in Joe's mind a time or two or three his demise and imminent death. After all, the medical reports on the news were pretty negative. The outlook was pretty grim for someone with HIV.

Joe had already seen what death looked like and the toll the virus played on his friends. He had seen close friends grow weaker each day, with no hope in sight. They eventually became so weak, experiencing dramatic weight loss, while watching their T-cell count plummet. Some quit eating and drinking fluids as a result of losing their appetite. The dying process for many of the AIDS patients was at times a very lonely one.

I imagine many fathers were devastated and couldn't handle watching their sons die. Some fathers had struggled with the news of their sons being gay. Many were already shunned and banished from family and friends for their lifestyle choice. And now this.

Many died alone, surrounded only by *their* kind to comfort them and hold their hand. AIDS is a non-discriminatory disease. It is ruthless and unfeeling.

In my mind, we saw modern day leprosy step onto the world scene. And as in Bible times, people with leprosy were forced to live outside their tribes, outside the cities because people feared contracting leprosy from them. Leprosy itself was considered unclean. Therefore, anyone with leprosy was considered unclean, and so they were banished from society. HIV/AIDS had the same effect. People banished HIV/AIDS patients no matter their life-style to outside the city gates. There they would all gather and plead for help. Some would perish before the help arrived.

I think back to those first days after finding out about Joe's diagnosis, and I admit, all be it shame-fully so, I was afraid for my own life. I was afraid to be around him. I was afraid to touch him. I was even afraid to use the same silverware from the drawer in the kitchen. I didn't know enough about the disease at the time to take the chance.

Joe was a fabulous cook, but I didn't want the food he prepared. I was fine if he ate off paper and plastic so we could throw it away.

Don't touch me. Don't touch my food, don't offer to cook me anything even though experts in the medical community say heat kills the virus. By all means, don't use my toothbrush or get your toothbrush near mine. Don't kiss me goodbye on the lips or my cheek. Don't hug me. Oh and forget sitting on the toilet in the same house. Now that he had a diagnosis, I surely didn't want to sit on the same toilet as my brother. I didn't know enough about the disease. I couldn't take the chance.

I had shunned my brother in every way - hugs, food, even the bathroom. Only I didn't realize it at the time. I was just thinking of myself and my future.

They said when the virus hits the air, it dies. I'm sorry, but after everything I had heard and learned in the short amount of time, it had been enough for me to conclude I'd rather not take my chances. I couldn't comprehend a virus is floating in the air and dying. To me, it had space to float around and eventually land. Did that mean when someone infected with the virus sneezed, their germs floated into the air and died? Was there any way to have all their germs go airborne so they could die and the infected person be saved? Can we use bleach? Can we scrub it out? Can we apply some color to it, so we know it's HIV when we see it show up on hard surfaces? How do we know it dies when it hits the air? How do we know, just how do we know? Have you tested it? How have you tested it? Did you throw some up in the air and watch it fall back down and call it dead? They were questions I had no answers to – not yet.

I didn't feel they knew enough and what little they did know, was deadly. I still had my whole future ahead of me, whatever the future would entail. Can we say selfish? Can we say I was thinking about no one else but myself at the time? Can we say panic? Yes, we can.

People diagnosed with HIV not only had to accept their new future, some as a medical experiment, but they also felt the exclusion, the shame, the confusion and the sudden banishment from friends, family, employers, and society as a whole.

Following is some information on HIV/AIDS:

HIV is a virus spread through certain body fluids that attack the body's immune system, specifically the CD4 cells, often called T-cells. Over time, HIV can destroy so many of these cells that the body can't fight off infections and disease. These special cells help the immune system fight off infections.

Untreated, HIV reduces the number of CD4 cells (T-cells) in the body. This damage to the immune system makes it harder and harder for the body to fight off infections and some other diseases. Opportunistic infections or cancers take advantage of a very weak immune system and signal that the person has AIDS.

What Is HIV?

HIV stands for human immunodeficiency virus. It is the virus that can lead to acquired immunodeficiency syndrome, or AIDS, if not treated. Unlike some other viruses, the human body can't get rid of HIV completely, even with treatment. So once you get HIV, you have it for life.

HIV attacks the body's immune system, specifically the CD4 cells (T-cells), which help the immune system fight off infections. Untreated, HIV reduces the number of CD4 cells (T-cells) in the body, making the person more likely to get other infections or infection-related cancers. Over time, HIV can destroy so many of these cells that the body can't fight off infections and disease. These opportunistic infections or cancers take advantage of a very weak immune system and signal that the person has AIDS, the last stage of HIV infection.

No effective cure currently exists, but with proper medical care, HIV can be controlled. The medicine used to treat HIV is called antiretroviral therapy or ART. If taken the right way, every day, this medicine can dramatically prolong the lives of many people infected with HIV, keep them healthy, and greatly lower their chance of infecting others. Before the introduction of ART in the mid-1990s, people with HIV could progress to AIDS in just a few years. Today, someone diagnosed with HIV and treated before the disease is far advanced can live nearly as long as someone who does not have HIV.

What Is AIDS?

This is the stage of HIV infection that occurs when your immune system is badly damaged, and you become vulnerable to opportunistic infections. When the number of your CD4 cells falls below 200 cells per cubic millimeter of blood (200 cells/mm3), you are considered to have progressed to AIDS. (In someone with a healthy immune system, CD4 counts are between 500 and 1,600 cells/mm3.) You are also considered to have progressed to AIDS if you develop one or more opportunistic illnesses, regardless of your CD4 count.

Without treatment, people who progress to AIDS typically survive about three years. Once you have a dangerous opportunistic illness, life expectancy without treatment falls to about one year. ART can be helpful for people who have AIDS when diagnosed and can be lifesaving. Treatment is likely to benefit people with HIV no matter when it is started, but people who start ART soon after they get HIV experience more benefits from treatment than do people who start treatment after they have developed AIDS.

In the United States, most people with HIV do not develop AIDS because effective ART stops disease progression. People with HIV who are diagnosed early can have a lifespan that is about the same as someone like them who does not have HIV.

People living with HIV may progress through these stages at different rates, depending on a variety of factors, including their genetic makeup, how healthy they were before they were infected, how much virus they were exposed to and its genetic characteristics, how soon after infection they are diagnosed and linked to care and treatment, whether they see their healthcare provider regularly and take their HIV medications as directed, and different health-related choices they make, such as decisions to eat a healthful diet, exercise, and not smoke.

You now know a lot more about HIV/AIDs than I ever did, and I had a family member living with this horrible disease. I had no familiarity with the medical world, having spent most of my time either working or hanging out with friends. We didn't have social media then. You got a busy signal when you called someone's home phone. You wrote letters with your hands, using paper and pen. You paid bills with checks. You licked a lot of envelopes, and you looked for the newspaper at the end of your driveway every morning. Life was different. People spoke to each other around the dinner table, in coffee shops, and in the grocery store lines.

CHAPTER TWO

Love Broke Through

New diseases and world news were never on my radar or my television. I was 24 then, living on my own, and having fun most nights with my best friend Jennifer and our friends at the local pub. Occasionally someone turned the television on in the pub so we could all watch the local news.

More times than not though, we fed the juke-box with coins so we could hear our favorite songs. Night after night, we solved the world's problems over a few suds and hot wings only to resolve them all over again the next night. For some reason we never discussed HIV. My brother being gay or not wasn't a concern for me then. Wings, cold beer and a fast game of darts was all I worried about in those days.

I remember meeting Jennifer for the first time. I was working at this same pub which was located in a small town west of Palm Beach as a short order cook back in 1988. I'd been working there for about two years when Jennifer started working there as a bartender in the evenings. She was a very beautiful young woman, 22, when she started. Everyone loved her. She had big Farrah Fawcett style hair, always perfectly plastered in place, big hazel greens eyes, and the most adorable smile. Her smile was so contagious with dimples that could melt any man's heart. Every day she wore scrunchy socks with tennis shoes, white shorts, and a cute top. Her favorite lipstick color was pink, and she never went without it. She loved people.

Most days when I finished my shift, I'd stay and enjoy a few rounds with the fellas. Over time, Jennifer and I became fast friends. When the bar got too busy, I'd jump in to help serve beers. The patrons fell in love with us. Most of them were quite older, so they treated us like their daughters. We didn't mind because we knew if anyone became belligerent, all our adopted dads would come to the rescue.

As time went by, we eventually became room-mates, renting an apartment together on the edge of town. We stayed up many nights talking, laughing, and crying together about our young lives. We cried over broken relationships and fears. We laughed at the silly stuff we saw each day at the pub. We spent many hours talking about our hopes and dreams. She spent many hours talking about her son who lived with his father. He was five years old at the time.

Jennifer gave me a very valuable and special gift. She taught me how to hug and say I love you. That may sound strange, but I didn't grow up in a home where love had been freely expressed in words or physical expression. I don't recall experiencing that kind of emotion very much. We didn't say I love you too often, and we weren't ones to hug or kiss goodbye from what I remember. My dad's father, my grandfather, never experienced or learned how to show love or other emotions from his father or mother. Grandpa's mother died at a young age. When she died, great grandpa put his three young sons in an orphanage in Cook County, Illinois and headed out west. He never came back for the boys. The emotional attributes of the family dynamic were missing from our home.

I remember the first time Jennifer came up and threw her arms around my neck and said those three little words, "I love you, Duby."

What? You love me? I was very uncomfortable because I wasn't used to someone showing emotion that way. We loved from a distance in our house. Love in this form was a foreign concept, and I was naïve.

Jennifer sensed I wasn't comfortable and asked me what was wrong. I explained my family history and how it wasn't something we did often in our home. She told me there was nothing wrong with expressing emotion. Hugging someone felt good and saying "I love you" to someone you cared about was natural. Lots of people express emotion in this manner all the time.

Her family had always expressed love to each other in this fashion. It was something she grew up doing. I noticed she hugged everyone and the more I saw her hugging the people we knew, the more I realized this was who she was. She loved people, and she told them she loved them. It would take me a while, but I would utter those same words back to her and hug her in return. The awkward feelings were starting to subside, and I was coming to the realization lightning wouldn't strike me if I hugged her or anyone else at the pub. I learned over time to love it. And I did love everyone there. They were special people, and I knew they loved me too. I learned to hug people and to tell them you love them feels good. It's still something I love to do today.

It felt so good, I started hugging my family and friends and telling them I loved them too. I especially made it a point to hug my father, and his first reaction was very similar to mine; he was a little uncomfortable. It was the first time I could recall us embracing as father and daughter and saying those words to each other – *I love you.*

I made it a point for the rest of his life to tell him how much I loved him and hugged him every time I saw him. I began to see a change in him. He like me came to cherish the hugs and the words of endearment. Our relationship as father and daughter moved to the next level. I will always be grateful for the wonderful gift Jennifer gave me, a gift I shared with my father.

The day finally came when Jennifer moved out and rented her own apartment. It was the first time she had ever lived on her own. She was so excited to have her own place. I was very happy for her because I knew how long she had waited and how hard she had worked to save up enough money.

She still came to my house to visit, and we would sit around and catch up on the week.

I remember one particular occasion we made some popcorn, grabbed a few drinks and watched the movie, "Beaches" together. I remember us crying together as we watched the story of two lifelong best friends portrayed by Bette Midler and Barbara Hershey.

Hillary (Barbara's character) got very ill and died, leaving behind a child. I still remember Jennifer and me crying and saying we hoped that would never happen to us. We would always remain lifelong friends.

On November 27, 1989, my self-indulged world turned upside down.

Jennifer, just 24 years old, was killed in a drunk driving accident. She had only lived in her new apartment a few months. Whenever I hear the theme song from the movie, Beaches, *"Wind Beneath my Wings,"* I remember the night we watched the movie, just three short weeks prior to her death.

She and her new boyfriend of a few weeks had invited me to spend the day with them and then go to the local bar that night, our favorite cowboy joint. We all loved country music and line dancing. We would spend the day at the beach, grab food and what not. It all sounded good, but I didn't feel like going. I respectfully declined, saying I was too tired, but honestly, I didn't want to be the third wheel in a brand new relationship. I'd been there and done that too many times.

They went to the beach, soaking up rays and quenching thirsts with some Bud Lights. In the afternoon, they grabbed some dinner and finished the night at our favorite local country bar. To end a banner day, they enjoyed a little line dancing, a little romancing, and a little too many chilled flip tops.

At or around 3 am, they started the drive back to his place. He lived west of town, about

25 minutes or so from the country bar. The road back then was fairly desolate, not many people driving in the wee hours of the morning. Cruising home, radio playing their favorite country songs, they sat close to each other, holding hands. The remnants of her perfume collided with the smoke from her Marlboros.

He was a tall, stocky fellow, cute in tight jeans and a flannel shirt. His cowboy boots were worn on the edges, scuffed across the top. He was just the way she liked her guys.

She was wearing her pink lipstick, dressed to kill with her cowboy boots on. Jennifer and I used to laugh and say we were a bunch of concrete cowgirls. We never rode horses or roped any cattle. Heck, we never shoveled manure, but boy we sure did love a guy in tight Wranglers and a flannel shirt.

A little fuzzy and tired from the long day, my friend and her new beau were confident they could make it home. The night wasn't over. Daybreak would come in a few hours and so would breakfast.

Authorities figure he was driving about 55 miles per hour when he fell asleep behind the wheel of his old red pickup truck and drove straight into a concrete support pole that held up the Florida Turnpike. You can imagine the enormity of the concrete pole, and you can imagine the size of an F150 pickup truck heading straight for it at such speed. The old Ford was no match for the pole.

They were there for a long while. Jennifer lay across his lap as a result of the impact. So much for the seatbelt, if she was wearing one. Hunched over the steering wheel, he didn't move. They were both passed out from the impact and the alcohol.

Engine fluid spewed out onto the ground, filling the crevices of the grassy space around the bottom of the pole. Crumpled metal hugged the concrete post. Shattered glass like sun rays blanketed the dash. All was quiet except the hissing of radiator fluid misting the cool night air and the crickets high in the trees across the highway.

Finally, a lone car drove by and saw the mangled mess, stopped and called 911. They peered inside the truck window and saw two lifeless bodies. There was no groaning, no movement. It was dark and eerie out. It was about 4:30 in the morning. Dew was settling in now in anticipation of the rising sun.

The people who stopped were afraid to open the truck door and check for a pulse. The ambulance would be there soon enough to get the two of them out and access their condition. Eventually, both were taken by ambulance to separate hospitals west of town.

My phone rang about 5:30 in the morning. It was a police officer asking if I knew this girl.

"This is officer Troy with the Palm Beach County Sheriff's. Sorry to bother you at this time, but is this Jeanette Duby?"

Groggy from sleep and trying to focus on who was talking to me, I confirmed, "Yes, yes it is. Can I help you?"

"Ma'am, do you know a Jennifer Jones Babcock?"

"Yes."

"Ma'am, I need to get her parents contact

information. Would you happen to know how I could reach them?"

"Officer, can you tell me what's going on?"

"Ma'am, do you have a phone number for them? I need to get in touch with them right away?"

"Sir, they may not speak to you. I have their number, but I'm not sure if it's still correct. Can you please tell me why you are asking for this?"

"Ma'am, Jennifer has been in a terrible auto accident, and I need to contact her parents right away."

"The number is..... Sir, can you tell me what hospital she is in?"

"Palms West."

"Thank you, sir," and with that, I hung up.

I started walking around the apartment frantic not knowing how to process what I just heard, but I knew I needed to get down to the hospital as soon as possible, especially if they couldn't contact her parents.

I was living with a new roommate at the time. He heard the phone ring and wondered who was calling at that hour. I didn't have time to make small talk but told him to hurry up and get dressed. I was driving to the hospital if he wanted to go.

The two of us raced to the hospital, paying very little attention to speed limit signs. It was still dark outside, and there wasn't a lot of traffic on the road. The hospital was west of town in a somewhat rural area, not far from their intended destination.

When we arrived at the hospital, Jennifer's

father was already in the waiting room pacing slowly back and forth, hand to his chin, unsure of what to do next. Her mother stayed home. Her parents struggled with her partying lifestyle and tonight would justify their concerns. They had raised her as a Jehovah Witness, and even though she wasn't living that way anymore, they still were. Her mother couldn't bring herself to come to the hospital and see her daughter. Her father, despite the strict tenements of their faith, had given the hospital full authority to do whatever they needed to do to save her life.

A half hour later, as we stood waiting impatiently in a cold, dimly lit waiting room, an emergency room doctor came through the doors, blood down the front of his gown, asking for Jennifer's family. He moved toward us as we identified ourselves.

"How's she doing?" her father asked.

"Is she going to make it?"

The look on the doctors' face said it all.

"I'm so sorry to have to tell you this sir, but Jennifer didn't make it. I'm afraid she passed away a short time ago. We're very sorry. We did everything we could to save her."

My best friend passed away from multiple internal injuries. Doctors tried a few times to stop the internal bleeding so they could take her into surgery, but each time, the bleeding would start again, and they couldn't get it under control long enough to wheel her into surgery. Her injuries were fatal. I didn't get to see her or say goodbye.

Her father stood up after the doctor walked

away and pointed his finger in anger at me and said, "This is all your fault! If you hadn't talked her into moving out of our house and becoming part of this world, she would still be alive!"

An uncomfortable silence filled the air as he walked away. I said nothing in response. Anything I had to say would have inflicted further injury to a grieving man. It wasn't true, but it didn't matter. He saw me as the reason; I was the problem.

A nurse came through the same doors a few minutes later and escorted all of us to a little room so we could have some privacy. I will always remember what she said when she closed the door after us, "I'm sorry, but Jennie didn't make it."

Jennie? Her name was not Jennie! It's Jennifer! I lost it when she said those words. For some reason, it hit me the wrong way. The nurse didn't know her. She didn't know what her friends called her. Her name wasn't Jennie.

I stormed out of the hospital with my tired roommate lagging behind.

Meanwhile over in the other hospital, her new boyfriend of two short weeks lay there with a broken wrist. It would be his third DUI. This time he would go to jail for vehicular manslaughter and lose his license for a long time.

We were not invited to her funeral since her family didn't like me or the people she hung out with. To this day, I have no idea where they laid her to rest.

Everyone needed some closure, so a few friends and I held a funeral service ourselves down by the lake on the edge of town. A couple of hundred people turned out to remember Jennifer and everything she meant to us. I had wonderful support there between my parents, friends from work and friends from the bar. We even had a priest come and say a few words as we released a white dove into the air in remembrance of her. It was a very nice tribute.

Her father ended up attending the service which to me said volumes. I knew he loved and missed his baby girl. Perhaps he didn't feel quite as angry with me as he did a few nights before. After all, Jennifer was independent, and she made her own decisions. She was strong willed and a risk taker. Beautiful, but stubborn.

We took all the flowers down to the crash site. The evidence of crumpled metal and busted concrete pieces still lay on the ground. Knowing she laid there for a few hours unable to help herself brought tears to my eyes. We erected a wood memorial and placed it in front of the concrete pillar. Folks who knew her stopped and signed their names in remembrance. A few days later the wood memorial disappeared.

I was depressed because the life I knew was now forever changed. I wandered around for several months trying to find my way, trying to figure out my future. I had become accustomed to hanging out with the same people every day after work. They had become family to me. But since her death, those people now looked at me with pity. Many of the older guys were grieving the loss of their adopted daughter. I couldn't handle their grief or the unintended pity when they looked at me. I couldn't handle listening to all the old stories, so I moved on from them too and found another job shortly after her death.

For months after Jennifer's accident, I was angry with God. All of sudden, God was on my radar. He hadn't been there while I was out having a grand ole time with all my friends. *God who?* I didn't want to talk to Him because I knew what I was doing wasn't right. There are times when you choose to ignore what you know to be true and correct for the sake of satisfying those sinful ways in yourself. And that was me. I was having too much fun to be worried about what God thought about my life. Besides, I believed in my heart at a young age Jesus died on the cross for my sins, so I had my ticket to heaven. What was the harm in living how I wanted? Oh now I know, plenty.

I was mad at God because now I couldn't do the things I was doing before she died. I was mad because I couldn't go out and sin. Really? But it was because I realized how I was living was not honoring to God. Let's face it, getting drunk all the time and doing who knows what when I was drunk was not honoring to God. I'll call it what I believe it was – sin.

"Let us behave decently, as in the daytime, not in orgies and drunkenness, not in sexual immorality and debauchery, not in dissension and jealousy. Rather clothe yourselves with the Lord Jesus Christ, and do not think about how to gratify the desires of the sinful nature." Romans 13:13-14

For the next six months, I walked around aimlessly. I hung out at a dear friend's house most days after work so I wouldn't go out. I gave up drinking. I decided the accident was too close to home. Besides, when I drank I got more depressed, so I knew drinking wasn't the answer.

My friends convinced me to go to counseling. I reluctantly went, but the counselor made me mad during the first session, about ten minutes in when she told me Jennifer was stupid. The session abruptly ended. In hindsight, she was right - they were stupid for driving drunk, but when you're grieving the loss of your best friend, stupid is not what you want to hear despite it being the truth. *Let's discuss that point when we're on the tenth visit, shall we?*

I think one of the hardest parts about her death was having to return all the Christmas presents I had already purchased and having to explain to the cashiers why I was bringing them back. I remember my dear friends going with me. I remember walking into JC Penney's to return the clothes and hair dryer I had bought for her. I could hardly bring myself to explain to them why I wanted my money back. As I stood there trying to explain, tears running down my face, my friend stepped up to the counter and explained what happened. The cashier apologized for my loss and refunded all my money, and we left the store.

Jennifer grew up as a Jehovah Witness and never celebrated Christmas or her birthday until she met my friends and me at the pub. She celebrated them for the first time with us. She thoroughly enjoyed the celebrations and of course all the gifts and attention.

I had already bought her some things I found on sale and wrapped them. I was so excited to see her celebrate her second Christmas. But that wouldn't happen. There's nothing quite like having to unwrap gifts and take them back to the store – not because you didn't like what you got or already had one, but because the recipient was deceased. I couldn't see giving them to someone else. How do you tell someone you bought their gift for someone else, but because they died, I thought I'd give it you instead? I just couldn't.

My dear friend would walk the neighborhood with me most nights. She knew I was still grieving and she and her husband were very supportive during that time. But one night, she chose not to walk with me. It was still daylight, and I decided to walk anyway.

I can still see the day so clearly in my mind. I was walking down the street in their subdivision. They lived in a small subdivision, quaint and quiet. Trees lined the roads in the neighborhood and acted as a tree canopy, especially around the lake near their home.

I was walking out of their subdivision, headed to the sidewalk that ran along the main road. I headed toward our usual walking path which lasted about forty-five minutes or so depending on how fast we walked. Sometimes we ran the route.

As I was walking along, I felt a very light tap on my right shoulder. I turned around, but no one was there. I chalked it up to a big bug and kept walking. Again, I felt a light tap on my right shoulder, and I turned around. Again nothing and I kept walking. Again, the same light tap and I quickly spun around, and there was nothing to see, but there was something to hear.

I heard a still small voice say, "You don't know

what I have done for you. You have been so mad at me all these months, but you don't realize what I've done. I saved you. I have plans for you. It could have been you in the truck that night. It could have been you driving. It could have been you who died or you who killed someone. It could have been you, Jeanette."

"For I know the plans I have for you," declares the Lord, "plans to prosper you and not to harm you, plans to give you a hope and a future." Jeremiah 29:11

He had knit me in my mother's womb.

"For you formed my inward parts; you knitted me together in my mother's womb." Psalm 139:13

For the first time since the accident, the little small voice was right. It could have been me. For the first time, it finally hit me that it could have been me who died that night. I could have ended up a vegetable, in jail, or who knows what. It could have been me who was responsible for her death. Jennifer had she lived could have been a vegetable for the rest of her life. There was no guarantee she would have come out whole again.

For the first time, my anger towards God for what happened to Jennifer dropped me to my knees in the middle of the road. I had selfishly thought about it over and over, never once considering it could have been me. I didn't go out that night like all the other nights. So many nights we drove home from the bars impaired, and we always made it home safely. I had been watched over and protected so many times. And here I was angry at God because I thought He caused it. I thought He didn't love me. I thought God didn't care. It was just the opposite, He did. I was wrong, and I was sorry.

A few years ago, the Lord gave me the lyrics and the beat to a song. I tape recorded what the Lord gave me so I would always remember. The words describe what happened that day in the middle of the road all those years ago. The Lord pulled me out of the miry clay and set my feet on solid ground.

Happened one day

25 years ago

I was out walking on my own

I couldn't see it,

honey, I was blind,

not really knowing what to find.

Then it happened

On one bright day

Someone tapped me on the shoulder to say

I have a plan for you

You don't know what I've done

I have saved you

I'm the Father's, Son

I died on the cross for you

So you could have my life

Now I made a way

For you to be alive…"

Have you had this happen?

Have you seen the signs?

Do you know the Savior?

Are you alive?

My walk that day took on a whole new meaning as I pondered over and over again what God had revealed to someone like me who hadn't been interested in what He had to say. *What did it all mean? What was the plan? Why me?* I wouldn't come to understand what plans He had for me till many years later.

It's hard to explain how one goes from being mad at God to accepting what happened and moving on. It was as if I had been released from the depth of the grief because I realized this was so much bigger than selfish me. I still carried a broken heart especially for her son who was just six years old at the time of her death. She had left behind a beautiful little boy, and his future was now up in the air. I eventually lost touch with him.

Nine months after Jennifer's death, I received news of my brother's horrible diagnosis. If Joe was struggling with his health, I never knew.

CHAPTER THREE

It Will Not be Easy

As far as I knew, HIV was a newly discovered disease. All I remember is when someone was diagnosed with HIV; it was a pretty quick and painful death sentence. How long the infected person lived depended on how far the disease had progressed in their body and how they took care of themselves.

And just to be clear, HIV wasn't exclusive to gay men or the gay community then, and it still isn't now. It was determined others could contract the disease as well. People like women who slept with infected men, drug addicts who used dirty needles, people who received contaminated blood transfusions, people who had dental procedures done by HIV positive dentists, infected people mishandling food products, and mothers who transmitted it to their babies. It's what I remember from the nightly news.

Some HIV patients died quickly. By the time they figured out what it was, the disease had overtaken their immune system beyond anything the newly released medications could repair. For others, it came down to a lifestyle change and a daily regimen of the newly released drugs. I don't know all the ins and outs of the development of the new medications to combat HIV/AIDS, but eventually, my brother began a serious regimen of drugs which became commonly known to me as the "cocktail." He explained to me the "cocktail" was a combination of drugs used to combat HIV.

Life was a whirlwind now. So many things are happening at the same time. I was still grieving the loss of my best friend. My father lost his leg below the knee, and my baby brother was diagnosed with HIV.

According to doctors, HIV would eventually lead to what they called full blown AIDS. The new developments about the disease continued to escalate in intensity. I think it's pretty normal to feel panic over something so scary especially when everything you hear about it is so negative. It's bad enough getting the flu. You can fix that, get over it in a few days and move on. There was no fixing this according to the medical community. There was no cure. Instead, to my little brother, it was a death sentence. To the rest of the family, it was a heartbreaking situation.

Finding employment was difficult. The newest question on most applications – Do you have or have you contracted the HIV Virus (Human Immunodeficiency Virus) /AIDS?

How would you answer the question?

You need money to live. But you knew if you tested positive for HIV, you ran the risk of infecting another person(s) and not getting the job. Google didn't come out until September 4, 1998, so we still couldn't research it to find out more about the disease. For our family, we had to rely solely on what little information Joe and the doctor were giving us.

I believe when you find yourself in a situation like Joe found himself, your mind has a difficult time focusing on everything the doctor is telling you.

Once the doctor started sharing specific details with Joe about his new disease, he got stuck on one specific thing, and everything else the doctor said went in one ear and out the other. He didn't hear the rest. The rest of the information, whatever it had been, was just as important.

Joe wasn't the only person in the world who struggled with remembering medical details about their diagnosis. I have been around plenty of people in similar situations, whatever the diagnosis, and it just happens. Their minds start swirling. Dreams change, life runs before their eyes and what they once envisioned for themselves suddenly takes a back seat to the newest curve in the road. Fear, worry, and anxiety take the place of joy, happiness, and even routine life.

I've always believed it's very beneficial for someone getting test results or going through surgery to have someone there with them who cares so they can catch the information the sick person misses. Too many times, the patient returns home and wonders what the doctor said a short time ago. Family members and friends call and ask questions, and more times than not, it seems the patient doesn't have all the answers. That in itself causes more anxiety and leads to frustration.

Let's face it; it wasn't an easy time for my brother. It wasn't an easy time for my parents or me. What did it feel like to have my baby brother contract such a deadly disease? Let's just say I wished we had the cure back then, but we did not.

For the next several months, Joe spiraled out of control. He lost ground and lost all hope of surviving. He convinced himself he wouldn't make it six months. He was already planning. His mind was racing, and he saw no hope in sight.

CHAPTER FOUR

Memories of Yester Years

I never knew my brother to date girls. He had friends at school like everyone else, but girls didn't seem to be his thing. I just figured he couldn't get a date. Perhaps he was too shy. Maybe it was because of his red hair and freckles. He was such a cute little boy when he was young. The red hair and freckles against his pale white skin were the perfect match for his baby blue eyes. He and I were both born with red hair, freckles, and blue eyes. I had friends who desired to connect the dots on my pasty white arms; there were so many freckles. Joe's was the same way. I always thought those features gave him low self-esteem. I know they did me.

What I didn't realize is that he wasn't into dating girls. He had plenty of friends who were girls, but he was attracted to the guys. He never told me. I never had a reason to ask. It wasn't obvious to me, maybe because I didn't stick around the house much. Being in high school and out with my friends all the time, I was never home. I was three years older than him, so we never ran in the same circles. He was my baby brother, so we didn't have much in common.

I do recall when we were young. One of my favorite memories was the fruit battles in the alley behind the houses across the street. Oh, those were the days. Friends versus foes, boys against girls, it didn't matter. Rotten oranges, lemons, limes, and grapefruit adorned the rocky, sandy alley. Fruit trees lined several backyards in the neighborhood. Open yards were an invitation to pick fruit from the trees. It was also an open invitation to gather all the rotten fruit on the ground and take our battle positions. The home-owners didn't care – less to mow over. Metal trash cans transformed into towers of steel fortresses. The round metal lids were our shields. They held up well against ripe lemons zooming toward their intended target at 50 miles per hour from the opposing side. The resounding noise from an injured target confirmed a hit.

We imagined ourselves as soldiers on the front line of the army; shield in hand, shoeless dirty feet, standing behind our flimsy metal fortresses, and flinging rounded artillery at the enemy just twenty-five short yards away. The summer air was warm and humid. When we felt brave enough, we'd distract the opposing side with a few reck-less rounds into the trees and send forward a brave warrior armed with enough fruit to knock down the enemy's fortress and pummel the resistance. They were no match for the up close and incoming fruit salad.

Rotten oranges and rotten grapefruit were the best. When you succeeded in hitting the enemy with rotten fruit, everyone in the neighborhood knew it from the pulp residue all over their clothes. They smelled fruity fresh but looked awful. We spent many summers fighting in the fruit wars. Memories of picking fruit for battle will always bring a smile to my face.

I remember babysitting Joe and our other brother. My two brothers were so annoying, just fifteen months apart. Little brothers do things purposely to provoke you, and my brothers were no exception. It's no wonder I spent a lot of time away from the house when I was a teenager. They always did something to annoy me, and I usually lost my temper. I dreaded my parents going out and leaving me to babysit. Do you know what it's like to have younger siblings who choose to get your goat on purpose because they think it's funny? My brothers loved to get my goat.

Have you ever run around your dining room table chasing two boys so you could beat them senseless when you caught them because they did stupid things to you? Haven't you? You ought to try it. Oh wait, never mind. You'll get upset with yourself because you can't catch them unless one of them trips and falls. There is the off chance you can gang up on them while they are asleep, but by then your parents are back, and you're already in bed. Fortunately for them, by morning or at least lunch, the irritation had been forgotten until next time.

When we weren't chasing each other around the dining room table, we were playing outside. We spent many a day climbing trees and jumping from the neighbor's rooftops onto old mattresses or bales of hay down at the local golf course. The park down the street had the perfect hill. It was the tallest mountain I had ever seen in South Florida besides the garbage dump. We spent many hours rolling down the side of the mountain, bumping into each other as we rolled out of control. No one ever got mad. Dizzy at the bottom, we ran sideways back up the hill just to roll down again. Its funny how you intend to roll straight down and end up rolling sideways all the way down.

Skateboards and pogo sticks, bicycles and roller skates – we had them all. I remember the stilts we used to walk on and the unicycle I wanted so desperately – *I had to have a unicycle!* I was the only person I knew who had a unicycle in five square miles, maybe even a hundred. *My brothers were not allowed to ride it!* I rode the unicycle like a champ – in my mind. I don't think I ever rode the unicycle more than two feet on my own. It was so frustrating and dangerous. I never enjoyed my "must have, I'm going to die if I don't get one" unicycle.

The days we spent on the neighbor's trampoline were memorable as well. The constant stream of impatient jumpers lined the sidewalk in their backyard. To allow everyone a chance, we played a game.

"You start!"

The first person up – sit. "Next."

The second person – sit knee.

The third person – sit, knee, sit.

The fourth person – sit, knee, sit, back.

The fifth person – sit knee, back.

"Hey, you're out. You missed the sit!" we exclaimed. "You're out!"

The sixth person – sit, knee, sit, back, reverse back.

The first person again - sit, knee, sit, back, reverse back, stomach!

Oh, from reverse back to stomach! The game just got serious.

The second person - sit, knee, sit, back, reverse back – didn't have enough momentum to get to the stomach – "You're out!"

And on and on we'd go till we got a winner and then we'd start all over again.

I loved the trampoline and always wished we had our own, so we didn't have to wait for our friends to wake up. My dad, however, was happy someone else had the liability and the noise at their house instead of ours. When I turned 21, I bought a trampoline and kept it at my friend's house since I was living in an apartment.

When we weren't running around the neighborhood, jumping on things or riding bikes, we played with cars. I'm not referring to Tonka toys or matchbox cars. I'm talking about real cars with real drivers. We did stupid stuff like stringing fishing line from one side of the road to the other. We'd hide in the bushes and wait for a car to drive by, ultimately driving through the fishing line as if it was the finish line to a marathon run. Laugh. We thought it was the funniest thing. We'd string up more line and wait for another unsuspecting victim to snap our line. There was something about the ping of snapped fishing line that tickled us.

I remember when we used to take wood logs and fashion them as arms and legs inside an old pair of pants and a long sleeve shirt. We found something round to imitate the head. We placed our wooden human alongside the road and waited in the bushes for cars to drive down our street. More than once, cars slammed on their brakes thinking it was a human being lying next to the road. We'd snicker as we watched them get out of their cars, walk up to the wooden dummy and shake their heads in disgust. There were a few who used choice words I had only heard my father use.

We played dodgeball, kickball, football, baseball, and kill the man with the ball.

We built tree forts, swam in the neighbor's pool and ate dinner at friend's houses. We flew kites and paper planes. We made the old neighbors mad when we went into their yards. We drank out of garden hoses. We ate fruit directly off trees. We stayed outside till dark every night. Curfew was 9 o'clock. We rode our bikes to the local 7-11. We rode down to the local mall. We walked to and from school or rode our bikes. We never worried about anything or anyone. Life sure was different back then.

CHAPTER FIVE

For the Love of Cars

Joe was the rebellious type. I don't know if he was a rebel at heart all along or if the news propelled his persona, but he was rebellious.

Joe loved cars. It didn't matter what kind, color, or size. He loved cars. He also loved detailing cars. I haven't met another person on this planet that could clean a car like Joe. He used q-tips to clean engines and the insides of cars. Q-tips are very good for cleaning dirt and grime in those little nooks and crannies a rag can't reach. He would clean every inch of a car if the owner wanted him to, depending on what they wanted to pay for the job. He was fascinated with cars. I don't remember him being someone who could fix them per say, but I do remember he was quite the auto detailer. Detailing cars was something he could do. No one asked him about his medical condition or whether he would pass an HIV/AIDS test. They were more interested in how many cars he could detail in a day and how good a job he could do.

Joe could lose himself in the detailing of a car. All his worry, all his anxiety seemed to fade away like the dust on the manifold. He didn't have to think about his situation as he washed soap from the hood. His focus was making those cars shine. By the time he finished, the sun had bounced off the chrome bumpers like the Fourth of July. No smudges, no dirt, no grease – so polished you could see yourself in the reflection, slick and clean. Like new – that's what they wanted, like new.

I remember the personal struggle Joe had with cars and there are a few stories that will always and forever go down in the history book of my baby brother and cars – someone else's cars that is.

I remember when the local credit union repossessed my brother's car. That little car was his pride and joy, and this would inflict another blow. He failed to make his payments and they had no choice but to repossess his little pride and joy.

I remember the car so well. It was a little white, two-door Pontiac Fierro with black interior. My brother loved the car and was devastated when they repossessed his baby. I remember him trying to get it back, but I can't remember if he succeeded. He would have had to steal it back and I couldn't locate a police report to confirm.

Joe's escapades continued for the next several months on into years. Yes, years went by, and Joe was still around. He hadn't died six months after learning his diagnosis. He hadn't succumbed to the disease. He hadn't suffered the same painful death so many guys he knew had before him. Six months turned into nine months, turned into two years, turned into five years and Joe was still living with HIV. He also struggled with thrush, which is a painful bacterial infection inside your mouth.

I still remember the infection spreading to his lips when it was bad. Some days the fatigue and weakness were too much.

He had blown past all the medical forecasts for someone in his condition, but he had not escaped watching several of his friends die slow, painful deaths as a result of the disease. Joe was still on this earth and couldn't understand why.

Every day with Joe still around was a mixed blessing. On the one hand, I knew the personal struggles he faced daily, and I wanted him to be free of them. He struggled with eating and sleeping. He struggled with making good choices and listening to sound advice from those he loved. He was an active soldier on the battlefield of his mind. The self-inflicted chaos was difficult to manage.

On the other hand, he was my baby brother, and I hoped he would beat it. I hoped the diagnosis was wrong and one day perhaps he'd learn through new blood work he had been misdiagnosed, and he wasn't HIV positive. Oh but then, he'd have a huge mess to clean up.

I remember the time Joe found himself in Virginia. I don't know how he got there or why he went, but I have a pretty good recollection of how he got back to Florida.

Auto trains traveled up and down the east coast all the time. A retiree state like Florida invites many senior adults from the north to winter down here in our lovely state, especially South Florida where it is nice and warm. I lived in some of the hottest weather in South Florida. I don't recall many cool days under 75 degrees. The humidity in

Florida is awful. The only consolation to living in the South Florida heat is its proximity to the coast. Ocean breezes from the nearby coast help cool things off, but it is still hot. We joked that we could cook eggs on car hoods it was so hot. Many senior adults take advantage of the auto train instead of spending long hours behind the wheel driving to and from their northern abodes.

While Joe was in Virginia, it just so happened an auto train full of nice cars was headed south, specifically to West Palm Beach, Florida where he lived. For whatever reason, and how he found himself in this situation, I don't know, but Joe decided the quickest and cheapest way to get back to West Palm Beach was to hitch a ride on the old auto train.

Now you may be asking how he did that. Well, think about it for a minute. Here's a train heading back to Florida and its carrying cars. Cars are what Joe loved. Why pay money to ride on a train made to carry people when you could hitch a ride on an auto train? Better yet, why go through the hassle when you could ride in comfort inside a brand new car for free? Sure, you missed dinner and the chit chat amongst strangers, but the radio provided decent company when you got tired of listening to the whistle blow at each railroad crossing.

If memory serves, it was a Jeep, not sure the model, but it doesn't matter at this point. He rode the auto train, inside a car all the way from Virginia to Florida. When the train reached its final destination in West Palm Beach, a car dealership, they started offloading the vehicles and parked them in the car lot.

Joe being the helpful person he was, helped them drive the car he had been sleeping in, right off the carrier and right off the property. They would not see him again. To my knowledge, they never caught him or got the car back.

"Thou shall not steal." Exodus 20:15

He was brazen like that. He had no fear. Besides, he had HIV and was going to die soon. What's a little time in jail when you're sick with a virus everyone is afraid they'll contract? He'd tell the judge he was HIV positive and they would probably freak out and let him go.

I also remember the time he owned a junker car. It was old, beat up and maroon if I remember correctly. I don't remember the make or model, but I do remember the struggle he had with it working properly.

The year was 1995. Joe's car was having mechanical issues. He took it to the local car dealership and asked them to repair it. He convinced them to give him a rental car while they serviced his car. Not knowing his background, they gave him a rental car to drive. The car rental place never saw the car again. The dealership making the repairs to his car now had a car to dispose of because he never came back and picked it up. Rumor was he drove to California, but I can't confirm either way.

This time someone went the extra mile and filed a criminal case against him. The courts ruled in their favor and found Joe guilty of two counts of grand theft. They filed a judgment against Joe for $4,600.

As his family, what could we do? We had no control over him, and we never knew his exact location. He was an adult, and everything he did was now solely on his record.

By now, Joe had proven he could not be trusted with anything. Not with anything I had, or the family had. He was a risk, not only health wise but now materialistically - he wasn't trustworthy, and he wasn't honest. I found myself not only watching what I did around Joe, but now I had to watch my possessions too.

California seemed to be Joe's place to escape to every time he did something unlawful or grew tired of the status quo. I guess California was a safe place for him to run and hide from everything. I suppose he found other people who shared the same lifestyle, lived with HIV and were struggling to make ends meet. I believe he found acceptance there. No one knew his background. He could hide among the people like a flea hides in a dog's coat. He managed to make lots of friends there, but couldn't support himself and live out there permanently. He always came to back to Florida.

CHAPTER SIX

Regrets

It hadn't been very long since Joe's HIV diagnosis when he made a bold, yet very desperate decision. One day, he walked into my mom's place of employment, which was a community bank at the time. She worked behind the scenes in the accounting division.

Joe strolled past the receptionist, smiling and waving to familiar faces as he walked to the back where my mom sat. Everyone knew whose son he was so they waved with a warm smile, never questioning his intentions. "Aw, he's here to see his mother." How sweet they must have thought.

But Joe wasn't there for a lovely unexpected visit. He had ulterior motives. He continued to make his way back to our mother's work cubicle. Without any hesitation, he lunged for her purse and snatched it right off her desk and quickly made his way out of the building, leaving our mother confused and upset at the same time. Co-workers stood there in shock. They had just waved to Joe not even a few minutes prior. He said nothing as he raced past them. Her son had just robbed her in front of her coworkers. How embarrassing it must have been for her. Joe had no fear of anything or anyone, so he thought nothing of walking into the bank. Besides everyone knew who he was; he was the son I'm sure she had discussed numerous times.

My father had just had his leg amputated and was home recovering. On this particular day, a home health nurse had come to the house to care for his wound.

I received a frantic call from my mom telling me what had just happened. I remember telling her not to worry; I would leave work right away and drive as quickly as I could over to my parent's house. She had a feeling he would go there first. My parents lived in a small condominium subdivision for retirees. All the buildings looked the same - one story, concrete buildings with beautiful landscape adorning the front of each unit. Palm trees swayed in the breeze as they caught the ocean air. They lived about ten miles from the Atlantic. They owned a corner unit across the street from the community clubhouse. It was very convenient to the pool.

Mom was right. When I pulled up to their house, there sat my brother's car carelessly parked on the concrete sidewalk in front of their door, engine still running. The driver door was wide open. He didn't plan to stay long. I pulled my car up next to his car, threw it in park, and jumped out. As I was running toward the front door, my brother came out with his arms full of stuff.

My father had frantically followed behind him in his wheelchair, yelling at him to stop. The nurse wheeled him over to the front door and stopped his chair at the threshold. As my brother hurried to jump into his car, I ran after him and attempted to grab my mom's purse from the back seat. I didn't care about the stuff he had just thrown in the front of the car - most of it was his stuff anyway. But I did want my mom's purse back. As I reached into the backseat of the car to grab it, my brother pushed me to the ground. I can still see the front yard. I can still see the anguish on my father's face as he sat helplessly in the doorway.

I tried several times to get back to his car to grab the purse, but each time he wrestled me to the ground. It was back and forth, back and forth. I remember so vividly my father sitting in his wheelchair, his new stump bandaged up, other leg dangling, and hands on the frame of the doorway helpless as his daughter was getting the crap beat out of her by his son. He could do nothing to help me. The nurse could do nothing to help because she was caught behind his chair, frozen and unable to come outside. Everything happened so quickly; she didn't know what was about to ensue.

My brother eventually made it to the driver seat, threw his car in reverse, and nearly ran me over as he shut his car door. He sped away with my mom's purse and whatever else he took from their home. Dad couldn't do anything but ask if I was ok. The look of despair on his face was heartbreaking. He couldn't help his daughter. He couldn't prevent the attack. He couldn't stop him from taking things from the house. He couldn't do anything from his wheelchair, except watch it all unfold.

After catching my breath and realizing I was ok, I motioned for the nurse to take dad back inside and called mom to tell her I was unsuccessful. Dad and I talked for a bit about what happened. By now, he was tired and so was I. There was nothing else we could do.

"A foolish son is a grief to his father and bitterness to she who bore him." Proverbs 17:25

Joe drove to North Miami where some of my family still lived at the time. For some reason, maybe he felt a little guilty over what he had done, he drove over to my aunt's house and dropped my mom's purse on her doorstep and drove away. I don't know how long the purse had been there, but some time later that day, my aunt called my mom, perplexed I'm sure, and told her she didn't know how it happened, but she had her purse. Puzzling. She found it on her front door step. I hadn't told anyone what happened earlier that morning. All he took from her purse was some of her makeup and money. Joe was infamous for applying mascara to the top of his head to make his peach fuzz hair look fuller and darker.

Joe drove to California and stayed there for the next several months.

It wasn't long after that incident that our father passed away. He passed away one hour before the one year anniversary of Jennifer's death. I couldn't believe this was happening. First Jennifer, now my dad. I had just been to the florist the day before to get a memorial wreath for Jennifer's roadside memorial in remembrance of her one year anniversary. I had to go back to the same florist and order more flowers, this time for my father's funeral which would take place a few days later. The guy who owned the shop remembered me and gave me a small discount on the arrangements.

The sad truth is we didn't know how to reach Joe or exactly where he ended up. We didn't have contact information for him or a phone number for one of his friends we could call. We had no way to get in touch with him to let him know his father had passed away. My dad's funeral came and went without Joe's presence. I wondered how he would handle the news.

Sometime later, I heard a friend of his had found out about our dad's passing. Somehow he got word to Joe either directly or through a friend of his who knew him. Although I wasn't happy about Joe missing the service, I was relieved to know Joe was still alive, and that he had finally learned the news about what happened to our father.

Joe finally mustered up the courage to call home and confirmed it was in fact true. Dad was gone. It had been a few months since he passed and he had missed it. He had missed everything.

Regret is a pretty big word. It encompasses many scenarios in our lives. It defines those moments we wished we could do it all over again, but the opportunity to do so has left the building. It calls for action before it's too late. It screams you make a different choice before your chance is gone. But so often our pride and stubbornness prevent us from doing so. We want to think we're right. We want to think we made the right decision at the time, in that specific moment. Regret calls out into the streets and tells on all of us. Like a gossip, regret tells of the past mistakes we made of which we can never undo. Like a teacher, regret teaches us hard lessons about those mistakes in hopes that we never repeat them. Regret – such a powerful, yet sorrowful word. If only we didn't do things that caused regretful moments. If only we'd listen to the small little voice in our head that says, "Don't do it or you'll regret it." If only.

"If we confess our sins, he is faithful and just to forgive us our sins and to cleanse us from all unrighteousness."
1 John 1:9

I think about how Joe missed saying goodbye to our father. Joe had rushed past him in the living room while dad sat in his wheelchair, arms full of stuff trying to get out the front door. He ignored our father calling his name. He ignored me, well not entirely – physically, he went round and round with me, ignoring my pleas for help. He had beaten his sister in the front yard, in front of our disabled father.

My dad didn't know Joe had HIV. We never told him. Dad had his hands full with having just lost his leg. It was a lot to handle. He had been dealing with phantom pain in the foot and ankle ever since the surgery. He could still feel his toes move even though they were gone. It frustrated him. It depressed him. In his mind, he wasn't a whole man anymore. He was relegated to a wheelchair and even more dependent for help. He could do even less now then all the years he had been disabled following a work accident. One more thing on the downward spiral of poor health had claimed its place in my father's life.

Joe had missed saying goodbye to our father. But more importantly, he had missed apologizing to him for what he had done.

"Repent, therefore, and turn back, that your sins may be blotted out." Acts 3:19

He had missed those final moments in the hospital, watching dad struggle for every last breath. He had missed being there when he breathed his last. He had missed caring for him. He missed those long chats about nothing.

He had missed saying his final goodbye at the funeral. He had missed the family coming together to help my mom. It wasn't too difficult to explain where Joe wasn't. It was more difficult to explain where he was. Who knew?

Joe believed HIV would take him out and it's what he used to legitimize everything negative he did. He knew others had succumbed to the disease. But Joe was still alive and spinning out of control.

There are times when someone we love walks out the door, and sometimes it's the last time we see them alive. We don't know if the words we spoke, whether good or bad, will be the last words they hear us say. We don't know what the future holds. Only the Lord knows that.

"The heart of man plans his way, but the Lord
establishes his steps." Proverbs 16:9

Unfortunately for me, I can't claim to have
been around for my dad like my brother had been
in those early years. Joe got the award for being
there for him. Joe had eventually settled down to a
tolerable level and had moved back to my parent's
house. He helped care for dad which is why I am
still surprised he did those things to our father. I
don't know what anguish he felt coming back from
California after finding out his father was dead,
but I can only imagine he lived with a ton of regret.
I can imagine it was very painful regret.

How many times would he think back to those
dreaded days and wish he had acted differently?
How many times had he thought about calling
home during the months he was on the run? How
many times had he pictured our father sitting in
the doorway, helpless, and yelling his name? How
many times had he wished he would have turned
the car around? How many times had he confirmed
to himself it had been his only choice and was
justified? How many times had he cried himself
to sleep knowing he missed the chance? I still
tear up thinking about those days and how Joe
missed our father's continued deterioration –
how he missed the final curtain.

And sometimes I wonder how much pain my
father suffered not seeing his baby boy one last
time before he died. His last memory of Joe was
yelling his name as he drove away. He never saw
him again. Joe was his baby boy, his youngest child
of seven children he had, and despite everything

Joe had done, he still loved him.

My dad was a tough man. He was far from perfect as most of us are. I learned a lot about him in the last year which explains so many things about my childhood growing up. I had so many questions about my dad's side of the family. There were so many people I hadn't met who were blood relatives on my dad's side. I was 50 years old when I met most of my father's family for the first time. What a blessing it was to finally meet them.

Dad suffered some pretty big losses in his life early on. He lost his baby brother Bill in a freak accident, his mother, Dorothy, whom he dearly loved, his sister Dorothy, some say as a result of sickness, and his namesake, son, Raymond Jr. (13) from a ruptured appendix - all in a matter of a couple of years both right before I was born and shortly thereafter. His mother and son died within a month of each other a short time after I was born according to the death records I found.

I can't imagine the pain he felt losing his mother and child so close together.

I believe the amount of loss and grief he suffered caused a lot of the difficulties and depression in his life. Couple that with injuries that led to permanent disability and the inability to work outside the home to support his family. Those emotional and mental difficulties spilled over into our house and made for very difficult days. Now he didn't know if or when he would ever see his youngest son, Joe, again. Dad knew his own health wasn't good. He knew he was losing the battle. Each day dad waited for Joe to come home - each day passed – but he would never see him again. Another loss, another heartbreak.

Oh daddy, I love you and I'm sorry. Maybe if I hadn't tried to stop him that day, maybe he would have come back to you and mom sooner - just maybe you would have seen your youngest son again before you passed away.

CHAPTER SEVEN

There's Good News

There are many years of which I have no memories of Joe. We didn't spend any time together. Maybe it was because of our last encounter – something about me ending up on the ground. Maybe it was because I didn't trust him at all, and was afraid he would take advantage of me financially.

Joe spent a lot of years living on the streets of Palm Beach County. Despite everything, he found a truly compassionate man through a county program called "Comprehensive AIDS Program (CAP)." This program assisted people like Joe with their health and living situations. They arranged housing for Joe numerous times.

Somehow Joe always managed to sabotage his living arrangements. Court records show he had been formerly evicted from an apartment complex one time. I'm sure it wasn't the only time he was evicted. Still, his CAP worker would find him another place to live.

His CAP worker was a very compassionate and caring man. Joe became so well known to him, so much so he was like a son to him.

JC was his name, and he understood Joe like no one else. He tolerated him beyond what everyone else was willing. He had the patience of a melting iceberg in Alaska. He was slow to anger, quick to listen and slow to speak.

"My dear brothers, take note of this: Everyone should be quick to listen, slow to speak and slow to become angry, for man's anger does not bring about the righteous life that God desires." James 1:19-20

Joe quickly figured out how to push the limits of the program and his case worker JC. But somehow he always managed to get JC back on his side and convince him he would change. He promised he would change.

JC was a man with unending patience, but he was no fool. He had experience with people like Joe. He was working for a program whose mission was to help people like Joe. JC had heard and seen it all. Nothing Joe said was a new revelation to him.

It reminds me of a story I heard one time where someone said, "God isn't looking down at you and wondering how He's going to handle what you did today. He's not saying to Himself, "Gee I've never seen someone do that before. That's a new one for me. Let me get back to you."

I believe JC came into Joe's life for a specific purpose. I believe God led Joe directly to him. None of us could help Joe the way JC did. None of us could understand his behavior the way he did. None of us could look Joe boldly in the face and tell him he was wrong. Besides, Joe wouldn't listen to us anyway. We tried it already, and we were tired. None of us could love him without wanting to strangle him.

JC was the man who could reach into Joe's heart and pull those strings. God had equipped JC with compassion for the lost, the sick and those dying. He had equipped him to interact with HIV-positive people who saw their world's turned upside down overnight. JC saw the pain in their eyes, and he felt compassion. JC did not see color - he saw a human being who was made in God's image. JC was more like Jesus Christ in Joe's life than most.

> "As a father shows compassion to his children, so the Lord shows compassion to those who fear him."
> Psalm 103:13

Joe's behavior wouldn't change. He didn't know how to change. He didn't know how to live life honestly. He didn't know how to live without the daily threat of physically worsening and ultimately dying. He came to believe this was all life had to offer.

I don't pretend to understand how it must have felt to look at life through the HIV lens every day and wonder when the day would come. When would HIV become full blown AIDS? When would the T-cell count drop below 200? Would it be this doctor visit or the next? Would I still be able to get the medicines needed to combat the disease? Sadly, those same questions ring true today for many people. Will they be able to get the medicines they need to survive?

I imagine numerous thoughts went through Joe's head frequently. Thoughts like:

When would my condition go from bad to worse?

When would the cocktail of drugs stop working?

When would they gather around my bedside to say goodbye?

Would I have anyone surround my bed to say goodbye?

Joe didn't have many people left in his life because he had done so many things to hurt people, too many people, especially those who loved him. The irrational behavior was intentional. Some people would say that's no excuse for the poor choices and bad behavior. The diagnosis didn't give him the freedom to throw it all away and hurt people in the process. While true, I wasn't in his shoes every day, none of us were.

He was mad at himself. He was mad at the guy who told him HIV was no big deal. He was mad at himself for believing what this guy said.

He was mad at himself for being gay. He was mad at himself because he wasn't happy. He was mad at everyone for ostracizing him. He was mad because he couldn't get a job. He was mad because everyone changed the way they looked at him. He was mad because he couldn't make the money he needed to support himself. He was mad because he changed the way he looked at everyone.

He was running.

He was mad.

He didn't care about life anymore. There were

days he just wanted to die.

If HIV wouldn't take him out, then something else would, and he would do it. He would handle it himself. He tried multiple times to commit suicide, all to no avail. No death, not yet.

Over the years, I tried to reach out to him. Some days were more successful than others. I was changing for the better. I was starting to realize where real hope originated. I was starting to experience real love for the first time in my life. I had found the answer to what I was looking for, and it had been unexpected.

"So now faith, hope and love abide, these three; but the greatest of these is love." 1 Corinthians 13:13

Joe and I would connect here and there, but there was always a self-erected barrier between us, a boundary I had put in place to protect myself from being hurt again. I tried to be a big sister to him, but I still couldn't trust him. I knew how desperate he had become after years of living with the disease. I knew he had turned to alcohol and drugs among other things to cope. I knew he was hanging out in places he shouldn't be. I knew he was finding acceptance in those places.

I remember the time he went down to Miami and got high on crystal meth and ended up in the bushes, scared to death to come out. Meth had played a nasty trick on him. He had to be rescued and brought back home.

Drugs, alcohol, and homelessness had become

the norm for Joe. They had become his way of coping. What a dark and cold place it must have been for him. Part of me says he chose to go down that road. Another part of me says he wasn't capable of making a better choice. His mind wouldn't let him. And still another part of me says he ran as fast as he could and as far away from the Lord as possible. What was missing in his life and mine for that matter – a personal relationship with Jesus Christ, a daily walking with Him.

There's comfort in what you learn, in what you come to know. There's comfort in the normal you make for yourself. It may be damaging to our minds and our well-being, but we've grown accustomed to it. We've tailored it to fit. We've accepted it. It's become a part of the fabric of who we are. It couldn't be as simple as loving the Lord with all our heart, all our soul, all our mind and all our strength. Nah. It couldn't. Could it? And yet some take on the attitude of they just don't care anymore – whatever happens, happens.

Who am I anyway? I am no one.

What do I have? Nothing.

No one plus nothing = One big bag of nothing – or as I'd like to say – hopelessness.

I have a big bag of nothing, and the big bag has a big hole in the bottom. I have a big bag of hopelessness. The bag is so big; I can't see around either side or through it to see who is standing on the other side of it holding out their hands to me, arms open wide, waiting and wanting to love me. Joe couldn't see around or through his big bag of hopelessness. So, you go for what stands directly in front of you whether it's good or not.

Drugs and alcohol call your name like you're waiting in line for your turn. Addictive substances call out knowing you will answer, because you've answered the call so many times before. It's a wicked game of cat and mouse, and you are the pawn, the cheese, the bait. It has no discrimination. There's no cap on membership. All are invited to the party. It doesn't matter if you're well or sick. It doesn't matter if you are rich or poor. It doesn't matter who you are. Single, married, short, tall, man or woman. The call is the same. It claims to have all the answers to your problems. It will help you forget even if only for a little while. It will promise you a glorious, pain-free existence. It lies to you. It deceives you. It mocks you.

But can I tell you something my friend – there is one and only one who has all the answers. There is only one who truly loves you. There is only one who was willing to die for you and me. There's only one – and His name is Jesus. Don't stop reading now – the story gets better. I know some are tempted to stop here, but I encourage you to keep going. I triple dog dare you to keep reading...

"For God so loved the world, that he gave his one and only begotten son, that who so ever believes in him shall not perish, but have eternal life. For God did not send His Son into the world to condemn the world, but to save the world through him." John 3:16-17

Drugs and alcohol condemn you and trick you into believing they represent eternal pleasure, an eternal life on earth where all your problems simply slide down the storm drain of life never to be seen or heard of again – at least for the next hour.

They trick you into thinking they are the answer to your problems when in reality they make your problems worse.

The high you feel when the smoke is enough, and the drink has sent you into a land floating on air, almost whimsical, and is promise enough for you. The floor is light underneath your feet. The edges have become softer, fog-like, and your brain folds like a limp noodle. The pain is deadened for a time until it all wears off.

Reality hits! Reality hits in the form of an empty wallet, a hugged toilet bowl, a dirty ashtray, a stack of bills you can't pay and regret – oh, the regret. It's a slow ride into deception and a quick ride to destruction. When someone faces uncertainty, and everything looks grim, of course, drugs, alcohol and other crutch like substitutions look like the answer. They'll help you forget your problems. They'll drown your tears. They'll make you feel good for the moment. Oh, but my friend you need to know;

> "Be self-controlled and alert. Your enemy, the devil, prowls around like a roaring lion looking for someone to devour." 1 Peter 5:8

Moment by moment under their influence, you walk further and further into a darkness you can no longer describe. Once you're in there, you can't find the doorway to escape. You reach out your hands, grasping for anyone or anything to help you, but more comes. It's another hit. Another swig. More self-defeating talk with yourself. And before you know, you have fallen to your knees, your body rolled down to the floor into a fetal position, begging for an exit. The room encircles you like a ride on the merry-go-round. What looked clear and crisp now looks blurry. You see three of every-thing, and you can't make it stop. The voices are screaming in your head. Only you aren't enjoying the ride anymore. You want to get off the colorful horses that went up and down as the music played. It wooed you. It soothed you – but for a moment and a moment's gone.

You have moved away from the light of the world. You have moved away from Jesus. He holds out His hands to you, but you pushed them away.

Darkness doesn't like the light.

"When Jesus spoke again to the people, he said, "I am the light of the world. Whoever follows me will never walk in darkness again, but will have the light of life." John 8:12

The biggest lie the enemy tells you is there is no way out. You are stuck there forever, so why bother. The enemy tells you God couldn't possibly love you anymore because of everything you have done. *You blew it! You sinner!! Way to go! Bravo! You're use-less to God now – He can't and won't use you - ever! You're washed up! Face it! Join the rest of us; you'll be in good company. Come over here, and we'll com-fort you. You're too good for Jesus Christ anyway.*

He's perfect, and you're not! Get over it! You'll be fine tomorrow!

Lies!!! Lies!!! All lies!!!

Answer this question – Would someone who cares about you and loves you enough to die on the cross so you could live, say to you, "You're washed up, no good, useless, unloved, sinful, wasted, or unwelcome?"

A few of you might answer yes to that question because that's what you heard or experienced growing up. You may be repeating those very words to your loved ones now.

But here's the thing – here's the good news of the gospel which means good news - GOD LOVES YOU VERY MUCH!! He just does. There's no sugar coating it, making it flowery, and putting a pretty bow on it. He loves you very much, and I do not believe He would ever say those mean and hurtful things to you or about you. Those hurtful things are lies from the enemy – an enemy who seeks your soul – who seeks to kill and destroy you. He seeks to keep you eternally separated from God forever in hell.

My God isn't like that. The creator of the world who sent His one and only Son to die on the cross for you and me isn't like that.

How do I know that you ask?

Simple. I have seen God work in my life in ways which would require another book. There are no other explanations for all that He has done in my life and all I have seen. It's not my skill or luck or my own strength. I can say it now, but I'll be honest – I couldn't say it back then when I first found out about Joe's condition. Then and for many years following, I believed it was my skill or good luck, it was in my own strength.

Joe failed to realize that God was very well aware of his situation. God was waiting for Joe to call out to Him and ask Him for help. I don't know how long before Joe made the call to the Lord for help, but I do believe he reached out to God at some point.

I have never experienced what it's like to receive a diagnosis of a deadly disease that essentially bans you from all normalcies once people find out. It may be different today now that many are getting educated about HIV and other sexually transmitted diseases. Although, I did read an article recently that HIV is popping up in the schools.

Many teens are having unprotected sex, and the disease is finding its way among them. It is not unusual these days to have a middle schooler intimately describe the sexual intercourse taking place in the bathroom stall next to him or her. A good portion of society has accepted this behavior as the new norm. After all, we all did it in school too. Didn't you? Maybe you did, maybe you didn't. I didn't. I didn't have a boyfriend in school.

It makes sense to me. Society has moved the marker dramatically, and we have become unaffected by the shock. Many have become callous to the effects.

As of this writing, there is no cure for HIV/AIDS. It is still an active aggressor. I know this to be true because I send a monthly check to

Compassion International who cares for children with HIV/AIDS in other countries.

We don't hear much about it anymore in the news, but it doesn't mean it's non-existent. Who is educating our children about the threat of AIDS? Anyone? Even if the schools are educating them, are the parents following up, making sure they understand the risks? Don't let school be the only teacher.

It seems to be more of a norm. But forty years ago, it wasn't. We knew nothing about HIV and what we eventually learned scared us. It wasn't anything to play around with or chance, and it still isn't, yet we seemed to have dismissed it to some degree. The statistics and the number of deaths were horrifying back then. Research may show fewer people are dying from AIDS these days, but the one thing it still hasn't shown – a cure.

CHAPTER EIGHT

Big Changes on the Horizon

Joe spent a lot of time in and out of hospitals during his adult life since the diagnosis.

Pneumonia was the new norm for him and he became a regular visitor as a result of the disease. After all, when you contract HIV, your immune system is about as good as one ply toilet paper – not!

He contracted pneumonia more times than anyone else I know. Somehow he managed to overcome death's door again and again. They would nurse him back to health, and he would go right back to the streets or wherever he was living. There were several times I thought that round of pneumonia would be the last, but he always recovered.

Despite Joe's various attempts to end his life, he somehow managed to pull himself together each time after being required to spend a few days in the mental institution. The internal conflict was tremendously heavy.

As I write this, my eyes tear up, because I think that was the very first time I ever truly acknowledged how hard it must have been for him to live each day. What you don't know, you don't know. We can't be inside everyone's thoughts and emotions. We can't truly imagine the despair and the difficulty people face. It's the old saying, "Walk a mile in my shoes." Sometimes, I look at a situation, and I think - *No thanks. I'll pass. Keep your shoes.*

I take great comfort now in knowing God knew all along. He loved Joe. He knew how Joe was struggling. He knew his fears. He knew his pain. He knew his thinking and his reasoning. God knew everything about Joe, and He loved him still. He longed to have a relationship with Joe. I can't help but think Joe spent years thinking about his life and the choices he had made and where they led. Surely he spent countless hours replaying his life over and over again.

"The Lord is merciful and gracious, slow to anger and abounding in steadfast love." Psalm 103:8

In 1996, at the age of 30, I got married in July to a guy I thought truly loved me as much as I loved him, only to find out he loved someone else who was also married and had four kids.

We filed bankruptcy in 1997 and lost everything but the house. We separated in December of 1997 and in March of 1998, our divorce was final. Our daughter was one year old when we divorced.

I was heartbroken, embarrassed, and angry. I waited all those years before taking the plunge only to have my feelings trampled on like a herd of zebras running from a ferocious predator.

Some say turning 30 is the highlight of your life. I beg to differ. Turning 30 for me was awful, but the best blessing among the rubble was my daughter.

I remember the weeks following the separation. I walked the neighborhoods, pushing my daughter in her stroller looking for aluminum cans to buy my daughter some milk and baby food because I wasn't receiving any financial support from my soon to be ex.

The night before the recycling man came was the most fruitful night of the week for aluminum cans when everyone carried their recycling bins to the curb. I waited till after 9 o'clock at night to go through everyone's recycling bins. I was so embarrassed and afraid someone would yell at me for picking through their garbage.

Other nights I drove to the old country bar that had been my go to place for years when Jennifer was alive. In the wee hours of the morning, with my daughter fast asleep in her car seat, I climbed into the dumpster and ripped open trash bags looking for aluminum cans. I knew the trash bags were full of beer cans. Some still had the remnants of stale beer and cigarette butts. The odor was disgusting, but I needed as many cans as possible to get a few bucks and what better place than the bar dumpster.

I collected aluminum cans for weeks and drove them down to the local recycler every Saturday morning for a little money. Life was a whirlwind, and I didn't know how I would survive. I was doing my best to make it as a new mom raising my daughter alone. The problem that is so evident to me now is I wasn't seeking God's help. The blessings from

God would be recognized a few years later.

One of the blessings I came to realize later in my life was when I went to work at a little family owned insurance agency in Lantana, Florida. My husband and I were newly married, and I was six months pregnant. You can do the math. We worked for the same company. When we returned from our honeymoon, our boss fired me and a week later, he fired my husband. A nicer term would be staff reduction.

We both searched for work for three weeks to no avail. I struggled to find work because no one wanted to hire a pregnant woman who hadn't given birth before. It was my first child, and there was no guarantee I would make it to my due date of December 25 - yes Christmas Day. She was a week late and was born on New Year's Day. We missed the big tax benefit by seven hours.

I started panicking and became desperate, so I called a friend of mine who wrote insurance for my previous boss. I begged her for a job, any job. I didn't care if I had to wash toilets and windows. I desperately needed work and maternity benefits.

Later that day, I received a call back asking me to come in for an interview the next morning with the office manager. We met, and she hired me to work in their Personal Lines Department. I had no clue how to process insurance, but I was going to find out soon enough.

I will always remember the day the owners of the little agency returned from their vacation. Their office manager hired me while they were traveling.

That morning I was sitting at my desk working

on insurance policies when an older gentleman came in with his wife. Everyone welcomed them back and asked how they enjoyed their time away. After a few trips down memory lane and some photos, they excused themselves and started heading back to their office. Their office was located in the back corner of the building, and they had to pass by my desk to get there.

They were a cute couple, and you could tell he was a little older than her as evidenced by his dashing silver hair and a gray mustache. He was tall, slim and debonair. He had a little pot belly that sat over the waistline of his gray slacks. He wore suspenders and a blue button down short sleeve dress shirt. She was very pretty, hair feathered back, wearing comfortable looking slacks and a nice blouse. Her smile was contagious.

They walked by, and I waved to them as they passed. A few moments later, the man walked back and stood outside my cubicle. We briefly made eye contact. He looked me over from head to toe, stopping at my pregnant belly and then he looked up. We exchanged pleasantries after a brief introduction. I think he was surprised to see a pregnant girl sitting in one of his office chairs. After a few seconds, he walked away.

I worked there for almost three years.

They took me under their wing and helped me get a vehicle. They also helped me with my daughter and helped me pay for my divorce. It was like they adopted me as one of their children. They helped my daughter and me any way they could.

Who knew a pregnant girl would make such

inroads with such wonderful people, but God knew. They would play a huge part in my future as I still work in the insurance industry today.

I had to put my daughter in childcare two weeks after she was born because my husband didn't feel comfortable taking care of her. Thankfully, my new boss' sister watched children in her home, so my new born baby stayed with her during the day, but not for free. I still had to pay the weekly expense of a daycare which as some of you know can add up very quickly, especially when there are five weeks in a month. It's a real drag on the budget. My husband was trying to find a job but was unsuccessful. Thinking back on it now, I wouldn't give him the gold medal for effort when it came to job hunting. Finding a sugar momma who had some money and a petite frame— yes. He never went back to work, but instead found other things to do with other people. In case you are wondering – I have forgiven him.

I sure wish when this first started with Joe, I had known God better. Maybe I would have recognized sooner the Lord's hand in my life and all He was doing to provide for me. It would be a while before the realization would come into focus.

By now, Joe had struggled through life with HIV for over ten years. He was now 31, and I was 33.

One of the markers you watch closely with someone who is HIV positive is their T-cell count.

I was always interested in Joe's T-cell count because that would tell us what was going on and how he was progressing or more importantly if he was declining. If the number fell below 200, it wasn't a good sign for him. The T-cell count became a very important measure throughout Joe's life.

To combat the disease, doctors put together what they call "a cocktail" of drugs which work hand in hand to help treat the condition and at the very least stave off the worst part - AIDS. As long as Joe took this cocktail faithfully, he would be good, not cured, but better than not taking it. I can't speak for all those years, but I think Joe missed a few cocktails because of his behavioral choices.

I also can't speak for how well the cocktail of HIV drugs worked when mixed with alcohol and other street drugs. I don't know. I can say his ability to make good choices did not improve, and his desire to quit using street drugs didn't diminish entirely.

Joe was finally diagnosed with AIDS if memory serves me correctly, sometime in 2004, several years later after contracting HIV. The HIV finally turned into AIDS or what they called "full-blown AIDS." His T-cell count finally dropped below 200. We were now facing the most dangerous part of the disease. Things started to get dicey from here.

I had always wondered when the day would come or if it would come at all. I must admit part of me wondered from time to time if Joe had AIDS. So many years had passed. He had outlived so many people with similar diagnosis. So many of his friends had died from the disease. There were some days I wondered if the diagnosis was accurate. I couldn't help but question the validity of the diagnosis. *Are they sure they read the report correctly? Are they sure they read his report correctly? Maybe they confused him with someone else?*

But with the new diagnosis came even more sickness and trips to the hospital wherever he happened to be living. He had made additional trips to and from California and out west, one time going to New Mexico where he spoke at a conference about his life in hopes of discouraging others from reckless behavior. For a guy on social security disability, he sure did have the where with all to travel out west. I don't want to know the details of how he made those trips happen.

Depending on where he was, it wasn't unusual for him to be in a hospital a few days. Each time I wondered - *Would this be it? Would we finally get the call to come and bring him home?*

And each time, he walked out of the hospital to live another day, another month, another year.

I remember the time I went down to West Palm Beach to see him after learning he was in the hospital again with another bout of pneumonia. I lived in Orlando at the time. We were much later into the AIDS progression, so each new bout of pneumonia was more serious than the last. He had been living somewhere close by with several people. I tried to find the house but was unsuccessful. I wanted to see what the placed looked like and where he was living. When I couldn't find it, I went on to the hospital and spoke to the visitor's desk. I gave them his name and asked for his room number. Searching their system for Joe's information, the nurse said, "Joe was released a short time ago." My heart sank.

Had anyone picked him up? Had he walked out? All I could think was my brother had no car, had just been released from the hospital, and was walking the streets of downtown West Palm Beach alone.

I drove up and down the streets trying to find him and was unsuccessful. I even went into the nearby pharmacies because his floor nurse told me they had given him a prescription to get filled. I thought I would surely find him at the drugstore down the street, but he wasn't there. I asked the pharmacist if they were filling a script for Joe Duby and they weren't. He hadn't shown up yet to fill the script. When I lost all hope, I drove back down the street I thought he might be living on, but still no sign of Joe. Wearily, I drove the three hours back home - without seeing Joe.

There were times we would talk on the phone. But as we talked, all too often, we would end up fighting over something stupid, because he always wanted something from me – money. And I was always reluctant to give it to him. He always wanted to borrow money. Borrow is the term we often use when folks ask us for money, but we mean give. We know we will never get it back.

Joe always had a story as to why he needed it. He was shrewd and good at deceiving people. He was good at telling stories and pulling on your heart strings. He struggled to tell the truth. Desperation does that to folks I suppose.

I knew his history all too well, and I couldn't bring myself to send him any money. I was a single mom trying to support my daughter and me. I didn't have money to throw his way, only to be used for heaven knows what.

Instead of agreeing to send him money directly, I tried to talk to him about the way he was living. Everyone in his situation wants someone to tell them how they should be living, don't they? Uh... yeah – NO! Those conversations went south faster than a drag racer on the Indy track and of course always ended up in a big screaming match, because he didn't want to listen. *Just give me the money!!*

It required big changes – changes at the time I didn't fully understand. It would be a while before I understood grace.

CHAPTER NINE

Merry Christmas Everyone

I remember one Christmas, I had my family, including my brother Joe over to my new home for the holidays. I lived in Orlando at the time, and they had all traveled up from Palm Beach County to see me. Joe drove his car and spent a few days with us. We were getting along at the time, and he was somewhat stable. It was a pleasant change of pace for us.

The most memorable Christmas I have ever had in my life was that year. Merry Christmas!

Joe had heard there was a popular gay bar down off Highway 441. Always looking to keep life exciting and off center, Joe decided Christmas Eve night to head downtown to this club. We all knew it would be a late night, so we chose not to wait up for him. He was a big boy. He could find his way back to my house.

Early Christmas morning, Joe got arrested for running a stop sign outside the gay bar in their parking lot.

Court records show he was given a breathalyzer and tested above the legal limit. Court records also show he was in possession of some cannabis and some drug paraphernalia. The judge set bond at five hundred dollars in Orange County.

Wonderful! Merry Christmas! Oh and Happy New Year too!

Why not? He lived in Palm Beach County and would now have to go to court two and half hours away.

Anyway, my phone rang about 5 am Christmas morning. It was him asking us to bail him out.

"Net, I accidentally ran a stop sign in a parking lot."

From his slurred words, I could tell it was about more than running a stop sign. He got the old one time "collect call to your momma" call. Gee color me surprised that Joe's in trouble again and on Christmas morning when we're supposed to be having a nice morning, opening gifts, spending time with family, and enjoying each other's company. We were looking forward to spending time together since we hadn't been able to do that for so long. So much for the Christmas ham and yams. So long Christmas cookies. So long Tourtiere pie! (Ground pork pie in case you're wondering that we eat it for breakfast. It's a long time family tradition at Christmas.)

By now, the whole house is up, and we're searching for a bail guarantor. Have you ever searched for a bail bondsman on Christmas morning? Haven't you? Oh, you celebrated Jesus' birth instead? What a novel idea. That's what we should have been doing, but we were looking for a man with a different plan.

We finally found one on the advice of the jailer. The bail bondsman was a real jerk and told us to go back to sleep. Merry Christmas to him too! There was no happy, well-meaning intention there. He wasted no words. I suppose it was a good thing at five in the morning. According to our new found friend Mr. Grumpy, the bail bondsman, Joe wasn't going anywhere for a while. His advice – "go back to sleep and call me in a few hours!" I sensed he was upset we woke him up over a jolly run to the bar down the street from his office.

Merry Christmas to us. Bah humbug! Any anticipated excitement quickly left my home. And once again it had become all about Joe and his poor choices. Instead of planning breakfast and sitting on the floor covered in Christmas paper, we were strategizing. *How do we get Joe out of jail? How much is this going to cost my mother? We still have to get his car from the tow yard. How much will that cost? When can we get his car back? Who's going to go pick him up? Who's going to pick his car up? Was it better to leave him in jail and teach him a lesson? How is he going to get back to West Palm Beach now that he has been arrested for a DUI?*

Questions, questions, questions. Joe's arrest was my Christmas present from my lovely brother. Coal in a stocking or a big fat nothing would have been more appreciated. For the first time in my life, I was trying to maneuver my way through the court system. I had no idea what I was doing. I had never been arrested or helped anyone post bond.

Once again Joe thrilled us with his antics, and one could say selfishness. He always kept it exciting, even on Christmas morning when the excitement was supposed to be a colorful tie, a nice dress, or fun toys for the kids. Once again Joe cost someone money – mainly my mother.

After some strategizing, due diligence and wrangling with our new friend, Mr. Grumpy, we eventually bailed him out of jail. We also retrieved his car. He had already faced the judge that morning, entered his plea, got himself a court date and would return to court in a few months where they would pronounce him guilty of driving under the influence (DUI). He would also lose his license for six months. He was required to attend DUI School, serve a hundred and fifty hours of community service and be on probation for one year. I'm not sure how one does community service without a license, but hey there's the city bus. In the process, the court transferred his case down to Palm Beach County where he could participate in all the court appointed requirements.

Joe couldn't spend much time in jail due to his illness for fear of catching a cold as a result of his weakened immune system, so he never spent very long in the jails. He usually bailed out pretty quickly; especially when they found out he had AIDS. He never got what he rightfully deserved. Do any of us ever get what we rightly deserve? No.

Out of the many years of stealing cars, license plates (he stole the little stickers for his license plates from other cars), money, makeup, and who knows what else, he never did much time. Somehow he always managed to get away in the eyes of the public.

He did not, however, get past God.

"The eyes of the Lord are in every place, keeping watch on the evil and the good." Proverbs 15:3

God can see everything we do even in the dark. He knows everything. Joe was no exception just because he was gay and sick. God loved him still and desired for him to turn from his sins and live in right relationship with Him.

"Be not wise in your own eyes; fear the Lord, and turn away from evil." Proverbs 3:7

Joe's the only person I know who stole cars. He's the only person I know who rode an auto train back from Virginia inside a car and then drove it off the car carrier.

He's the only person I know who survived several suicide attempts and some nights in the mental ward.

He's the only person I know who survived getting pneumonia several times while HIV positive and lived.

He's the only person I know who survived drugs, getting high, and being strung out in the bushes.

He's the only person I know who survived all those years living on the streets of Palm Beach County.

He's the only person I know who survived getting HIV and then AIDS for over fifteen years and counting.

Joe was the only person I knew with AIDS.

My experience with someone who had AIDS may not be the same as everyone else's, or they may be very similar. All I know is this was my experience, and it was a difficult one.

"But when one turns to the Lord, the veil is removed."
2 Corinthians 3:16

CHAPTER TEN

New Beginning

Let's back up a bit if you don't mind.

My daughter and I moved up to Orlando from West Palm Beach in August of 1999. I had been laid off from the insurance agency. The lovely owners retired and sold the business and moved north. The new owner kept me on for three months and then gave me the boot. I searched for work for several months to no avail.

I had a friend in the insurance industry who worked for a big insurance company. She suggested I seek employment in the Orlando area. Several of the big name insurance carriers are located in Central Florida. I took her advice and eventually landed a job in an independent insurance agency. The story behind all of that is for another book because it was amazing how God moved in my life during that time. One little admission here – I didn't know God was moving. I was still in the dark about His movement's years after He had tapped me on the shoulder that day in the middle of the street. I failed to connect all the dots.

I started attending a little Baptist church in the Winter Park area at the invitation of the only person

I knew in town. I had attended a Catholic church my whole life until I moved out of my parent's house at eighteen. From eighteen to about twenty-five, I went to church very little. Most of the family on my mother's side is Catholic. As I mentioned earlier, I did not meet most of my father's family until July of 2016 at the yearly family reunion. It had been over forty years! Meeting them answered a lot of questions and filled a few gaps in my heart.

Anyway, back to the story! We had been going to church almost every Sunday, all the way back to when my grandma was alive. She always made sure we were going Sunday mornings. God rest her soul, she was an amazing woman. I love and miss her dearly.

I was hit or miss on the church thing for some years after moving out. I would go occasionally, especially Easter and Christmas, (yes I was guilty of the C & E) but my mind was elsewhere and with others. God wasn't on my radar. I didn't see Him on my radar until I started attending that little Baptist church in Winter Park.

I remember my first Sunday there. My friend asked me to arrive at 9:30 so I could attend Sunday school with her. I had never been to Sunday school before. I thought school was Monday through Friday. They did Sunday school first and then church. Ok. I'm just along for the ride at this point. I don't know what's going to happen and when - I'm just following the program. If anything appeared to be strange and uncomfortable, I'd quietly excuse myself.

Being divorced at the time, I assumed they would lead me to a singles class. I had heard they had classes for various ages. My friend who was married attended class with her mother. They were both in a class of senior adult ladies over sixty years of age. Since they didn't have a class for singles, she had me follow her to class and sit in with these older women. They were excited to have new, young blood. I was shy then, not wanting to talk, so I did the best I could to respond when called to answer. Other than that, I sat and listened.

There was something about the group of women that touched a heart string in me. I can't explain it, but there was an easiness in the room I had never felt before. Maybe they reminded me of my dear grandmother who I missed so much. She had died a few years after my dad. I lost three people dear to me in a matter of a few short years.

From Sunday school, we went to church and sat in the balcony area. I wasn't into shaking hands with strangers, even though everyone appeared to be nice and friendly. I was new in town, my daughter and me, so I wasn't quite comfortable with the new surroundings. It felt different than the church I had grown up in as a child. It was very clean looking and bright, the walls white and the pews were maroon. The only similarities were the stained glass windows and the big cross that hung on the wall.

For the next hour, I sat there amazed by everything.

We stood and sang several songs. We shook hands, although in the balcony, very few. Then the guy who was speaking, the pastor, told us to open our Bibles to study God's Word. I grabbed the Bible from the pew holder in front of me because I didn't have a Bible of my own.

The preacher started reading the Word of God, and then he started preaching, and my hair stood on edge. The preacher was on fire and so passionate about the Scriptures. He even cried as he explained what Christ did for us. I didn't know what was happening, but I could feel a sense of comfort I hadn't felt before in church. It was peaceful and inviting. His tears moved me. I hung on every word. I still remember his name after all these years, Pastor Glen Owens. He would forever leave an indelible mark on my life. What was apprehension when I arrived soon turned into excitement and a new hunger for more.

I went back the next Sunday and the Sunday after that for the next year and a half.

The senior adult ladies in the Sunday school class were very instrumental in leading me to a personal relationship with Christ. They understood I had accepted Him into my heart when I was young, but they knew I didn't know anything about walking in a daily relationship with Him. And so they taught me through the lessons each week. They nurtured and cared for me.

One of the women in the class took a special liking to me and treated me like her granddaughter. Her name was Doris Jones. When I first met her, she was in her seventies and a very prayerful woman, totally devoted to the Lord and His work. She amazed me with her frequent trips overseas through Campus Crusade for Christ.

She traveled several times with the Jesus Film folks to the ports of Spain. She would stand at the shipyard docks and greet people as they disembarked from boats, longing to hand them information about the Jesus Film. She loved traveling and sharing the gospel. She made a positive impact in my life with her love and dedication to the Lord. She started referring to me as her granddaughter. Eventually, she moved to California to be with her family. She used to mail me her monthly newsletter for years which always contained lovely pictures of her with family and news on the progress of the Jesus Film. She'd sign it, "Hugs and kisses from Grandma Doris." Jesus' love was very apparent in Doris Jones.

I also remember one evening being invited to my Sunday school teacher's house. She was entertaining missionaries in from another country. I can't recall from where, but I remember being so intrigued by people who were voluntarily living in another country to spread the gospel. I had not been exposed to anything like that before.

For some time before this evening, I had been experiencing a little more stress than normal. In all the Sunday school lessons, I had learned how perfect Jesus Christ was. There was no other perfect person on the earth. He had been the only one and still is. He was sinless and yet faced the same temptations we all do. I learned I had to be more like Him. My old self had to die to new self.

In my wee little brain, that equated to being like Jesus in every way – perfect and without sin. And so my new endeavor was to get to the place of perfection. No more sin, not now, not ever. If I'm to be like Christ, I must be sinless.

Do you have any idea how hard that is? It's

excruciatingly difficult. Oh sure, you can sin a lot less than you do now and you can keep moving towards less and less each day, but to be truly sinless daily is impossible. Besides the Bible says something about that:

"All have sinned and fallen short of the glory of God." Romans 3:23

Somehow, I had missed the word "all," in my aim to be perfect. The problem was I couldn't be perfect, and it was stressing me out terribly. So much so, my Sunday school teacher asked me what had been going on in my life recently.

She had noticed a change and wanted to know if everything was alright. As I stood in her driveway getting ready to enter her house, I started crying and told her I just didn't understand how she and the other ladies in the class were doing it.

"Doing what?" she asked.

"Being perfect," I cried.

"Perfect? Honey, we are far from perfect!"

"But, but you all seem…"

"Sweetie, we are not perfect. None of us are. Remember what the Bible says in Romans 3:23?"

"No."

"All have sinned and fall short of the glory of God. That means all, even us."

"Do you know how hard it is to try and be perfect like Jesus?" I asked.

"No. I never tried. It's too stressful!" And with that, she waved me on into the house.

I took a few minutes and dried my tears and tried to make myself more presentable to the new people I would meet soon. It was so interesting to listen to these folks talk about the customs of the country where they were ministering.

It was there in that little Baptist Church where I came to know the Lord and all He had done for me on the cross. We studied the Word of God more in-depth, and I saw the words in red, and we studied them.

I started praying on purpose for Joe and his situation. I didn't know where it would lead, but I just knew it gave me comfort I never knew before. I think before it was a hit or miss, if at all. I hadn't spent a lot of time talking to God about Joe. The truth is I hadn't spent a lot of time talking to God about anything. I believed God existed. I heard Him speak to me years before in the middle of the street, so I knew He was real. I also believed Jesus Christ died on the cross for me, but I had no idea what a personal relationship with Jesus Christ looked like and what it would come to mean to me.

It wasn't until I saw people reading from their Bibles, singing songs, and listening to a preacher so passionately preach the Word of God, that He got my attention. It was when I opened up the Bible and read the words for myself. When I read the red letters of the Lord Jesus in the gospel accounts in the New Testament, I finally understood there was more to this life than what I had ever envisioned for myself. It was there in that little Baptist church that I came to realize that the Jesus I asked into my heart when I was a little girl was the same Jesus who desired to have a personal relationship with me daily. He desired to love me, care for me, know me and guide me – the very things He had been doing all along, but I had been too blind to see it. I always chalked up all the good things in my life to luck and my own good doing. I had patted my own back, tooted my own horn, put myself on the throne in my life and threw flowers at my own feet.

I hadn't given credit where credit was due – Jesus. My eyes were opened to the truth that there is much more to religion than the ritualistic motions I had been going through during those younger years. It was more than my shallow prayers, flare prayers, and get me out of trouble prayers. No. It was much deeper. It was meant to go deeper – it has always been meant to go deeper. I realized I had been swimming in the shallow end most of my life. God was calling me to walk in deeper water; to be overtaken, but a hand was being outstretched for me to grasp. The question was – would I take His hand in mine and follow Him? Would I trust Him to lead me?

There's a real love which seeks to know and love us. There's a real creator who made us in His image. There's a real purpose for our lives. Oh, sweet Jesus! I finally found what I had been looking for all those years; I found the love of Jesus Christ! The dots were starting to connect, but it would still be a while before I fully understood what it looked like in my life.

"The Lord is not slow to fulfill his promise as some count slowness, but is patient toward you, not

wishing that any should perish, but that all should
reach repentance." 2 Peter 3:9

Prayer for Joe continued to increase. I shared
with my new friends the plight of my baby brother.
I would share with my Sunday school class what
had been happening with him, and they would pray
for him, my family and me for God's will to be done
in our lives. More people were praying for Joe, and
that gave me such hope to continue and take each
day as they came. With Joe, you never knew what
was around the corner.

For the next several years, Joe and I would
banter back and forth over the phone when I could
get in touch with him. There were times he managed
to call me.

As I mentioned earlier, the conversations usually
took the avenue of him wanting money. When you're
homeless, and you think your sister has everything
in the world, surely she can send you something to
help you make it through.

Every conversation started off the same way –
"How are you? How's my niece doing? How's she
doing in school? Listen Net."

And so once we got past the obligatory questions
and comments, the big question would come – "Can
you send me some money?" Or "I got this problem,
can you help me?"

All my years of experience with him taught
me that most of what he said was fabricated and
a means to an end, so admittedly I declined his
request multiple times. As an alternative, because

I wasn't a cold hearted monster, I would offer to send the money to his case manager JC. Remember the man I told you about early on with CAP which was Joe's case worker? Well, he was still in Joe's life after all these years. Of course he was! In my mind, the man was a saint sent by God himself. I knew I could call JC and get the real scoop on Joe's current living situation. If I felt inclined, I would send him money, and he'd be sure Joe got it. Joe never cared for my ideas much because they didn't play into his hands. But I knew better. I'd been down that road with him too many times before. Enabling is what I called it. An enabler I did not want to be.

I will say this though - Joe and I did continue to try and be sibling like to each other. I loved my brother, and I knew he loved me despite our bickering. I did have concerns and was heart-broken over the choices he made early in his life after the initial diagnosis.

Joe did manage to attend mine and my other brother's wedding. My brother and I didn't marry each other. We had a double wedding ceremony. We figured it was easier for the family to come into town one time, so we both married at the same time. It was a pretty cool event- two pregnant brides, and two grooms. Joe was at our wedding, and he looked good all dressed up. It's one of the few pictures I have of him in his adult life.

I always pictured my brother as a doctor. Yes, Dr. Duby who could care for his patients and make them well again. He would have made a fabulous doctor. Joe had such a caring and gentle heart for people when he was in his right mind. He was smart as a whip when it came to medical stuff. Part of me wonders if that was because of the immediate health care he would need over the years.

Joe was becoming more and more familiar with his disease and the necessary meds required. He became his own expert and knew the ins and outs of AIDS. When I think about it now, maybe the road we should have taken with him was to have him participate in some kind of AIDS study. There weren't very many people living very long with AIDS that we were aware. Joe could have been a case study which could have helped further medical research.

I remember Joe telling me one day when we were talking civilly to each other, which wasn't very often then, "Net, they could cure AIDS if they wanted to, but they don't want to. They make too much money off all the medicine."

None the less, Joe was a medical marvel, and he was good at medicine. He had been through enough poking and prodding by now to experience the ins and outs of the medical field. He had sat in waiting rooms for hours, observing the sick and dying and listening to their experiences. He had faced the uphill climb to get better many times, and he had suffered his share of defeats. He understood the medical field better than most patients. It's too bad he chose to listen to a guy who foolishly looked at AIDS as a kiddie game. This bad decision changed the course of Joe's life forever.

I spent so many years praying for Joe to change. I wanted God to swoop in on Joe's life and perform a miracle. I wanted Joe to change. I wanted him to make better decisions about life. I wanted him to accept responsibility for all the foolish choices he made over the years. I wanted him to apologize for all the pain he had caused. *Come on God, why can't this happen? Why won't Joe change so I can see he is a better man? Why does Joe refuse to see the route he is taking is a dead end? Why does he refuse to listen to reason? Why won't he take my advice? Why? Why? Why? What's wrong with him? Joe's choices were so frustrating. I have been praying for him for years to make better ones. Why won't he change? When I talk to him about Jesus, why does he blow me off? Why can't he see that Jesus is the answer? What is wrong with him? Doesn't he trust what I'm telling him? Can't he see Jesus in me and how Jesus Christ has changed my life? He needs Jesus in his life, and I've been praying he would see that and decide to quit going in the wrong way.*

I came to realize there was a much better question I needed to ask. The question was – C*ould Joe see Jesus in me?* The answer as painful as it was to admit – *No.*

All these years I prayed for Joe to come to know Jesus Christ better. I knew he believed Jesus died on the cross for his sin, but he was living anything but a life of following Him. I had been praying all those things, but behaving the same way in front of him I had always behaved. The two were not lining up. The problem was that Joe didn't see Jesus in me. He didn't see Jesus in me when we fought over the phone. He wasn't seeing Jesus in me when I saw him in person, granted those times were few and far between. My words weren't lining up with my actions. I was speaking the talk, but not walking the walk with him. I had managed to get the two to line up at church and around my friends, but when it came to my brother, the two weren't lining up. How could I expect him to draw near to Jesus when his only example was a very poor one at best?

It's in those moments you have two choices when you realize your error. You can choose to change it and make a concerted effort to get your walk and your talk lined up. Your other option is to dig your heels in and insist the other person you have been praying for change while you stay the same.

If I was going to see any progress, see any fruit in this relationship, I had to be the one to change. I knew who Christ was. I had forged a personal relationship with Him. If I was to reach Joe with the love of Christ, I needed to be the one to change how I approached him, how I prayed for him, and how I spoke to him. God would work on me for many months as I walked daily through the process. There was no guarantee it would work, but the one thing I believed was, either way, I'd be a better person in the end regardless of the decision Joe made to accept or decline Jesus' love for him.

Many people pray for those they love every single day, some multiple times a day. We pray they change. We pray they'll come to know Jesus personally. We pray they quit doing things that upset us. We pray our loved ones will do it our way. We pray our loved ones will see Jesus in us and want to be like us – notice I didn't say be like Jesus. But I believe all too many times, those loved ones look at us and don't see Jesus. I believe those praying people need to look in the mirror and see if they can see Jesus in themselves, in the way they talk and the way they live their lives. I don't discount how hard it is to do – I did it myself. When I looked in the mirror at myself, it wasn't a pretty sight. A pastor once said, "Sin not removed and pain not resolved will always hinder our attempts to think differently. Our strongholds are a stubborn pattern of thinking and resistance to God's Word."

When the Lord gets ahold of you, you go through a refinement process. It reminds me of a diamond in the rough. I always imagined someone taking a small hammer and a pick and chipping away at the hard surface encasing the beautiful diamond. With each tap, a little bit more ugliness gets chipped away.

Eventually and over time, the beauty of the stone begins to emerge, and before you know, you have exposed a very beautiful stone. It's the same way with us.

God takes His hammer and pick and begins to chip away at our hard exterior. Little by little, He chips away at our anger and jealousy. He chips away at the greed and envy. He continues to chip away at unforgiveness and hatred. He chips away at our low self-esteem and negative self-talk. He starts hitting tender spots like past pains and hurts. The pressure from the hammer creates sensitive areas that need to be addressed.

The chipping continues as He works through pride and selfishness. Little by little, we start seeing the rough edges smooth over as He begins to polish those areas. He chips away a little more at our doubts, our concerns, and our fears. He continues to polish those exposed areas. When He has reached the center, and the entire ugly exterior has been chipped away, He polishes and polishes until its beauty radiates like a rain drop glistening in the rays of the sun after a light rain shower. He holds it close to His heart. He has made it into a beautiful masterpiece. He has called it His own. And even when it was covered with a hard exterior and looked anything but beautiful, He still called it His own.

Over the years, I would be a rock God was chipping away on consistently. I would be a beautiful diamond He was trying to expose. I would be the one He was shaping and polishing. It would be a painful experience, but it would be worth it. God would clean me up so Joe could see Jesus in me.

There's an old song that goes like this:

"I have decided to follow Jesus.
I have decided to follow Jesus.
I have decided to follow Jesus,
no turning back,
no turning back.

Though none go with me,
I still will follow.
Though none go with me,
I still will follow,
no turning back,
no turning back..."

CHAPTER ELEVEN

Still Small Voice

The years would lead us to the beginning of the end for Joe who was now 39 years old.

In May of 2009, I learned of Joe having a huge tumor that started in his rectum and had moved up into the groin area. It was cancer, colorectal cancer. Now the roller coaster ride was getting more intense.

The surgeon told us they could remove the tumor in the rectum, but they would have to surgically attach a colostomy bag to his upper left side to replace output from the rectum area. He would probably never be without the bag. He opted for the surgery realizing he had no other choice except the inevitable and Joe now wanted to live.

While they were in there, they found another sizeable tumor just inside the pelvis area, tucked among the bone structure. The doctors were unable to get to it and determined they would have to treat the area with radiation once Joe was well enough to move forward.

He spent several days in the hospital after the surgery. Eventually, he heard the news about the other tumor.

One of the things I learned during the cancer diagnosis according to his doctor is lots of his AIDS patients die from cancer before they die of AIDS. He said, "It is very common in AIDS patients for cancer to appear."

He went on to explain, "Most gay men get cancer as a result of anal sexual activity. The main reason it progresses is that they feel something is wrong in that area, and rather than go to the doctor, they live with it, hoping it goes away. They are too embarrassed. By the time they get up the courage to see a doctor, because now whatever it is has progressed and caused more problems, it has advanced into something they wished they never heard of – colorectal cancer."

He went on to say, "Many will die from cancer because it usually spreads up the body and eventually kills them."

The doctor told me he has seen more AIDS patients die from cancer than the AIDS disease itself. It was quite a shock to learn some AIDS patients could have potentially prolonged their lives if they had sought medical help earlier. All these years I had been wondering when AIDS was going to take Joe's life, and now it appeared AIDS might not be the final victor. I never imagined cancer would come into play. As the doctor spoke, I couldn't help but think he was describing what my brother had experienced himself. Joe had to have known something wasn't right, and I wondered if he prolonged seeking medical help for it because he was embarrassed. As a result, he was now suffering the consequences of his indecision.

At about the time Joe was dealing with this

new diagnosis, I was dealing with female bleeding problems and seeing a gynecologist for treatment. My gynecologist told me the female problems were beyond repair. It wasn't going to get any better, and I needed to have surgery. A partial hysterectomy was the solution to my problem. While I was grateful I wouldn't have to deal with the pain and inconvenience of bleeding all the time, I was conflicted because my brother had been diagnosed with cancer. My bleeding problem could wait if need be. What to do, what to do?

I did the only thing I knew to do – pray.

I asked God what I should do, and then I waited for His answer. I had learned along the way a lot about God. I had learned more about God and His love since moving to Orlando than I ever had before in my life. Ten years had passed since I moved to the Orlando area and my relationship with the Lord was more present in my life than it had ever been before. I had continued to grow in my walk with the Lord, regularly attending Sunday school and church, Women's Bible studies, fellowship events and joining a prayer team. I was now teaching Women's Bible studies and Sunday school. I had been Children's ministry director for some years.

My faith had taken flight, and it was thrilling and exciting. I was making an impact in people's lives, lives God had put in my path. I was able to use my story and my experiences of what God had done in my life to reach other people with the gospel, the good news, and it was a fantastic feeling. I had an opportunity to pour into people what had been poured into me when I moved to Orlando and started going to the little Baptist church in Winter

Park. Sharing what God did for me was so much fun and admittedly still is today. I was seeing God's plan unfold before my eyes. I was living it out. He told me He had plans for me, but I never imagined anything close to this.

I made a lot of mistakes along the way, but God was gracious to me. I was growing in my faith and loved it. I felt His presence, and I was living my life wholeheartedly for Him. He had been chipping away on the old ugly stuff and making me into a beautiful masterpiece.

I have discovered being in a relationship with Jesus Christ was the ultimate relationship for me. It was the one thing I had been looking for all my adult life. I was no longer lonely. I didn't cry anymore because of loneliness. I didn't drink anymore because of loneliness. I didn't look for love in all the wrong places because of loneliness. I found the love of my life. I found the one who loves me for me. He doesn't ridicule me, call me ugly or judge me unfairly. He never puts me down or berates me. He loves me for who I am and for who I will become. He never leaves me alone. And His love is never ending. He calls me His. He knows me best and loves me despite my failings. It is still the best relationship I enjoy. As the picture on my bedroom walls says, "I have found the One in whom my soul loves."

Facebook post dated July 8, 2009:

Worked late tonight and didn't make a dent. For all of you praying for my brother, he is doing well considering the circumstances.

Facebook post dated July 12, 2009:

Sunday morning and all is well today. Know why? God is in control. All I have to do is be obedient to Him and His word. Now, if He would just get that denture cream over to my brother, my phone would ring ten fewer times today.

By now, Joe was living in a nursing home. He needed more care as a result of the surgery and cancer treatments. I was relieved because I knew he was in a safe place and finally off the streets. I knew they were transporting him to and from the treatment facility.

He still required the necessities while he stayed there, things like clothing and snack type foods and denture cream. I remember mom and me going to Wal-Mart and buying him a big black trunk for his room. We purchased sharpies, some food items, personal hygiene items, and some clothing. We had to write his name on all his clothes because when they went to the laundry, they needed to know whose room to return the clothes. If you didn't write their name on the underwear and socks, someone else ended up with them. It was the same for shirts, pants, and pajamas. We wrote Joe Duby on every tag. Writing his name didn't guarantee all his clothes would make it back to his room, but it certainly increased the chances. The black trunk was a great place to store his snacks and hygiene items so no one else could borrow them (steal them). Borrow is a nicer term. We bought a padlock for the trunk and gave Joe the key.

Wallets and watches were a real problem. Joe

couldn't seem to hold onto either one. They disappeared more regularly than anything else. He did manage to hold onto his cigarettes. Most days he smoked half the cigarette, saving the other half for later in the day. Saving half smoked cigs was pretty ingenious considering cigs were so expensive. Once we stocked up on everything we thought he could use, we felt comfortable leaving him there and checking in with the staff on his condition.

Now that he was situated, I could focus more on what I needed to do.

As I searched for the answer to my bleeding problem, one morning in prayer, I heard the Lord tell me in a still small voice, "Proceed with surgery now, because it will be September for Joe."

The Lord told me to go ahead with the surgery and get it done now because Joe would need me in September. It wasn't audible like we know sound, but it was the same still small voice I heard when he spoke to me on the street that day years before. I liken it to when your mind is completely empty; thinking about nothing and out of nowhere comes a comforting voice who speaks truth to you about something that is positive and not intended to hurt you. They were loving words of instruction and encouragement, and I believed as I do today they were from God.

I had to be well. I had to be available for Joe. I didn't know what it would entail or how involved I would be, but the Lord specifically told me to get the surgery done. It was clear as a bell. There was no denying God had spoken to me that morning. God spoke to me of all people. He answered my prayer. I knew He was able and I knew He cared.

So on July 21, 2009, I had a partial hysterectomy.

I have to tell you about my surgical experience because it is unlike any story you have probably ever read before.

I went in for the surgery, and as I mentioned had a partial hysterectomy - vaginally. It's probably way more than you wanted to know, but you had to know the surgeon didn't cut me across the belly, use stitches or staples like some women who have the same surgery. The doctor didn't see the need to cut me, and I was elated about it – if one could be elated over having surgery. Although, if you are a woman reading this, you might have been elated knowing you weren't going to have to deal with the monthly visitor, monthly friend, or whatever else you called the lovely thing called period EVER AGAIN. I can't find the word, "period" in the Bible.

"Just then a woman who had been subject to bleeding for twelve years came up behind him and touched the edge of his cloak. She said to herself, "If only I touch his cloak, I will be healed." Matthew 9:20

Other verses in the Bible refer to the monthly bleeding as menstrual bleeding. I don't know who coined the phrase, "period," but I would be done with the monthly bleeding and excess thereof – period!

After recovery, they wheeled me to my room where I would spend the next twenty-three hours or less recovering and then be released to go home - that was the goal anyway.

I was in some pain, but it seemed to be tolerable.

Sometime during the afternoon hours, the pain began to intensify, and I couldn't get full breaths. Each full breath I took was like a knife stabbing me in the chest. It hurt to breathe. It hurt to move. The culprit, so everyone thought was residual gas left in there from the surgery, and somehow it had lodged itself right behind my rib cage. My sweet daughter who was 12 at the time and a couple of dear friends came to visit me while I was experiencing the awful pain.

I had been complaining of the pain and trying to find a comfortable position, but there simply wasn't one to be found. You cannot breathe and find a comfortable position at the same time. After a few unsuccessful attempts at moving around, I finally managed to sit up in the bed.

The next thing I remember is opening my eyes to an older black nurse staring me in the face. She had been trying to get me to open my eyes and speak. From what they told me, when I tried to reposition myself, I guess because the pain was so intense; I passed out. My friends quickly escorted my daughter out of the room who were all now in shock, and this same nurse started slapping my face saying, "Come on Momma, wake up. Wake up, Momma. Come on Momma, wake up."

Apparently, I wasn't waking up, so she called code blue or red, whichever brings the crash cart in. My poor daughter watched as several nurses flocked to my room.

The nurse's slaps must have worked because I eventually woke up without the assistance of the paddles to my chest. My cheek was a little sore, and I was in a fog and didn't know what happened. All I knew was that a slew of people I didn't know were staring at me, and my daughter and friends were gone.

They told me what happened and checked my vitals. They determined it must have been a vagal response to the pain. Vagal, vagina, what's the difference at this point? I hurt then, and I still hurt when I woke up.

They were still saying it was gas leftover from the surgery, so they started me on a hot prune and grape juice concoction. Disgusting!! I had to drink eight ounces of this wonderful substance, slowly, each hour to help pass the gas. Slowly is all I could manage anyway because of the taste. I never drank warm prune juice before that day. I always thought it was for people a lot older than me who couldn't go to the bathroom on a regular basis. Don't blame me for those thoughts. Blame the commercials.

I hadn't experienced pain like that since being diagnosed with pleurisy back in 1989. In fact, the pain reminded me a lot of pleurisy.

Here's the thing - I didn't hurt down south near as bad as the stabbing pain underneath my rib cage. The pain was awful.

All evening I lay there as still as could be, while friends visited my room. When visiting hours were over, I tried to sleep, but I just couldn't get comfortable because I was in so much pain from the gas. And do you want to know the worst thing? I knew by morning I would have to get up and walk those halls to go home. I had to walk the halls for hours. Talk about torture. Walk the halls with the blessed hope you pass the biggest gas bubble right in front of the nurse's station and hope you don't mess yourself from all the prune grape juice. Now there's a sight – and smell. Talk about crop dusting. Now that's something to look forward to – yes? No.

Momma nurse who slapped me silly the day before came in bright and early the next morning and insisted I move to the chair. I was still in pain. She thought the change in position would help me pass the gas. Moving from the bed to the chair was so painful. I was afraid I'd pass out again. I could feel the anxiety rising up in me which added to the pain. I didn't want to pass out and hit the floor, bump my head, break a bone, or anything else. I wanted relief from the pain. Never in my life had I wanted to fart as badly as I did that morning, but I couldn't. I did manage to use a few choice words as I moved from the bed to the chair. Ramblings from the meds and all that warm juice let's say.

I sat in the chair for a while. Nothing. The sights out the window didn't help either. The noise from the television didn't help. Nothing helped. Breathing was still painful, and I was horribly miserable. It didn't look like I would get out in the allotted time.

Momma nurse came back in, asked me if anything substantial had happened, and I sadly told her no.

She helped me make my way back to the bed to rest. I couldn't take the chair anymore.

However, that didn't last long. It was now time

to move to the next level, pain or not. Another nurse came in shortly after and made me get up and walk. I had not so lovingly nicknamed this charge nurse, Nurse Ratchet. She had no sympathy for me or my pain. "Walk the halls!" she'd say. "Walk faster!" she'd say. "Keep walking Ms. Duby every hour. We need you to be up and walking the halls."

I'll tell you what I need ma'am – well I can't repeat it here.

And so I walked the halls.

Several hours went by, and the pain only intensified to the point of me barely being able to follow Nurse Ratchet's commands to "walk the halls!"

I had been drinking the juice concoction that was supposed to be breaking up the wretched gas and moving it out, but I wasn't having any success. I couldn't understand it. I couldn't pass a tiny toot! Something! Anything! Nothing!

I walked by Nurse Ratchet and told her I felt like I was dying from the pain and I was going back to my room whether she liked it or not. I was done walking the halls!

A short while later, another nurse came in to check on me. She went into the bathroom to check the plastic urine collection bowl and came back and asked me a question.

"When is the last time you voided?

"Voided? What does that mean?"

"Pee. When's the last time you peed?"

"Oh," to which I replied, "Hmm, I think it was before surgery yesterday. I had a catheter yesterday afternoon when I got out of surgery, but it was removed a short time after."

Ding! Ding! Ding!

Puzzled, she replied, "You haven't emptied your bladder since they took the catheter out?"

"No ma'am. I havent had the urge to go to the bathroom," I answered.

Uh oh. Houston, we have a problem. A pee problem. A big pee problem and Houston we don't need any gas, and we definitely don't need more hot prune juice or grape juice!

I hadn't used the bathroom on my own since the morning before surgery. I hadn't thought about it. I was still slightly medicated, so it never crossed my mind, nor did I have the urge to go. No one thought to check the pee collection cup, and no one asked. The pain was coming from my bladder filling up and not being relieved. The pain I was feeling wasn't gas pain at all! It was bladder pain from being so full of urine! My bladder was full of prune/grape juice and whatever else hadn't emptied from the day before.

I couldn't go. My bladder had temporarily shut down. Now what?

Straight cath.

Wait! What? Straight for what? Straight cath? What is that? That sounds painful! Yikes!

The nurse informed me she was going to have to straight cath me. Oh, joyous occasion! I didn't know what she was saying. If you don't know what that is, google it. Wait. To save you from putting the book down, allow me to describe to you what straight cath means.

Essentially they stick a straw like clear tube in a wee little hole in something you can't see from the outside of your body and drain your bladder. There you have it, the DRV of straight cath – the Duby Revised Version.

I can't believe this is happening to me. I sucked down - sipped warm, nasty prune & grape juice for hours only to further promote bladder dysfunction? Wonderful!

A few minutes went by, and the nurse returned with the necessary tubing. After getting into position, which is a real treat by the way – NOT, bare butt and showing my business to the whole world of one, she proceeded to stick the tube where the sun doesn't shine. Only one problem - she couldn't get anything to come out. She tried a couple of times – push tube in, pull tube out, push, pull, push, pull. Talk about an awkward experience. Each time the tube went in, it hurt because she wasn't hitting the intended target. Despite her many attempts, she was unsuccessful. Next thing I heard was, "I'll be back."

Oh, joy! I can hardly wait to go through that again!

A few minutes went by, and in walk two nursing assistants I had never seen before. They looked like they just came from high school. I'm being nice here because I think it was their first day on the job.

"The first task on the board for today ladies – insert a plastic tube into this woman's wee little hole and break the gigantic urine bubble."

So here you have these two nursing chicks who looked like they just graduated high school come into my room to do this procedure. If I'm honest, they were a bit older than high school grads. They came in with the see through straw (plastic tube) and get this – you're going to love this as much as I did – one of them was carrying a household flashlight that looked like something from the maintenance closet. No joke! It was yellow and black and had grease all over the handle and rim of the light. I am not kidding!

I should have told them right then and there to get the heck out of my room and take that nasty thing with them. I should have told them to send a different nurse, but I was still in shock over everything happening, and I was in so much pain, I just wanted to pee. I wanted the embarrassing procedure to be over.

Lesson learned here – just because a nurse or doctor comes in with a greasy flashlight in their hands doesn't mean you have to allow them to perform any medical procedures on you. You have the right to refuse service!

Sadly, I did not refuse service or throw them out of the room. The two nurses had me get back into the same embarrassing position again and together, yes I said together, one held the dirty flashlight shining up into you know where, while the other one shoved the plastic tubing up into you know where and attempted to get the pee bubble to explode. Here I lay, legs spread open with two women's heads rested on my bed, looking up where the sun doesn't shine using a dirty flashlight and guess what? They couldn't get anything to come out of the plastic tubing. In and out, in and out, by now I'm ready to shout - *Get out!* By now I am horrified, and the pain is intensifying because of the added stress! *Can someone please, who knows what they are doing shove this plastic tube in the hole correctly so I can get some relief??!!?!?!?!?*

I liken it to someone who tries to hit the vein in your arm with a needle to draw blood. After a nurse has poked you five times unsuccessfully, you're like, *Get out of here and send someone in here that can do the job!* By the time you get to this place, you have lost all generosity. Your witness has left the room. Has anyone seen Jesus lately? No.

At this point, I was beside myself in pain. I've been spread eagle for three different nurses with a dirty flashlight and plastic tubing trying to pop a big pee balloon, and they got nothing! Nada! Zip! They too said, "We'll be back." They must have heard me say, *Oh, no you won't! No thank you!*

I knew one thing – drinking more fluid and doing any walking was completely out of the question. About ten minutes went by which seemed like an eternity and in walks the nursing supervisor for the floor. *Oh, praise God!*

She asked me a few questions about my current situation. I wasted no time, pain or not, expressing my revulsion over what I experienced shortly before she came in. I proceeded to tell her what I had just been through and I wish I could have captured the look on her face. She was completely stunned to say the least. She apologized profusely and promised me those ladies would not be back in my room. She promised me she would speak to them about their choice of tools – their lighting choices.

She excused herself and within a few minutes returned. Yes, with another see through straw aka plastic tube, but no lighting tools in hand. I felt confident she may finally hit pay dirt.

I know, I know, move into position. I hadn't pulled my underwear up from the last two times. Third times a charm, right? If she couldn't do it, then I imagined it was off to surgery for some procedure. If it went that route, I wanted to be knocked out. I was over the total embarrassment of it all. My gynecologist never told me I would have to experience this. It's bad enough everyone is looking up your vagina to perform a surgical procedure, but at least I was asleep for that. This was something entirely different.

She promised me she would hit the mark. The other ones said the same thing so you can imagine my confidence was waned. To her credit, she did hit the bullseye on the first try. She popped the gigantic pee balloon! Let's celebrate!

If memory serves me right, I believe 1500 ccs of urine voided from my bladder through the plastic looking straw and into the urine collection plate.

Can I just tell you that I didn't know what relief from pain was until that moment? All the pain I had been experiencing in the last 23 hours had washed out through a little plastic tube. Let that be a lesson for you in the event you ever feel pain, and you haven't been to the bathroom in the last 23 hours. It's not always leftover surgical gas. Let someone else drink the prune juice.

I couldn't believe how much better I felt almost instantly. The nursing supervisor was my new hero. I could breathe with ease. No more stabbing pain with every breath. She then asked me to drink more fluid and try to go to the bathroom on my own. Great! More prune juice! Lady? She wanted to test my bladder to see if it would work on its own now that it had been relieved. She would return shortly to check on me. We had to determine if my bladder was going to work before I went home. If the bladder didn't come back on its own, I would have to stay and go through more tests.

Please work. Please work. Please work, oh I prayed.

Somewhere in those instructions, whether it is because I was so relieved or not paying attention, I misunderstood what she said. I drank a bunch of fluid and then called her back in. She went into the bathroom to look at the collection plate, and it was empty.

Puzzled, she reappeared and asked me why I didn't use the toilet to go to the bathroom. I told her I thought she was going to straight cath me again. She shook her head no. *Oops. My bad.* I misunderstood. I made my way into the bathroom and filled the pee collection cup. My bladder started working again. I guess it had gone into temporary shock after the surgery and no one had noticed, not even me. I was so grateful the pain had finally dissipated.

I was now free to go home. Discharge papers were under way. I would never see Nurse Ratchet or the flashlight twins again.

I was released from the hospital later that day. I was so relieved I wouldn't have to walk the halls anymore under the loving instructions of Nurse

Ratchet. She wasn't a very nice nurse. I was in legitimate pain, and she was unsympathetic. Perhaps it was routine for her to hear women complain from a little pain, but the pain was real. Throw in a full bladder about to bust, and you have the perfect storm.

Three days later, count them, three, I went back to the emergency room of the same hospital. I was so sick and in so much pain, but I didn't know why. Something was terribly wrong. I wasn't feeling good, and it had gotten progressively worse. I drove myself to the hospital and checked in at the ER desk. They asked me what was wrong and I told them what happened while I was in their hospital a few short days ago. Again, I wish I had a camera for the look on that girls face at the triage desk as I told her the horror story of the dirty flashlight.

She asked me what color my urine was and when I told her I could hardly see through it, she knew right away she needed to get me into a room.

I had a urinary tract infection and a severe one at that. Go figure. Hmmm, I wonder if it had anything to do with the tubing combined with the germs from the dirty flashlight. *Your Honor, Exhibit A – dirty flashlight! Exhibit B – Plastic tubing!*

They gave me antibiotic medicine by IV because the infection was so severe. Each person who entered my room heard the story of the dirty flashlight. I wanted everyone who worked there to know, so they didn't make the same mistake on someone else. Needless to say, they treated me like royalty. I couldn't imagine royalty ever feeling as sick as I did that day, but when you have a dirty flashlight and plastic tubing as the prequel to your story, royalty is what you get. Some of them still couldn't believe it was true.

They did blood work and confirmed it was indeed an infection. The medical staff surmised the three attempts to straight cath me with the plastic straw caused the infection. *You think?*

I was later told by the nurse in the ER that if someone attempts to straight cath you, they get one shot with one tube. If they miss, they must use a new tube. I can tell you that didn't happen with the first nurse who tried several times using the same plastic tube. In and out, in and out, in and out. The incorrect procedure had resulted in me getting a severe infection. It's no fun when you're already recovering from surgery. I was so sick. Meds, I needed meds.

After pumping meds through my IV for a few hours, I was released to go home. I had already started feeling a little bit better. I stayed on meds for the infection for several days and followed up with my doctor as I recovered from the surgery.

A few months later, I received a bill from the hospital for $200. I already paid everything for the year, so I didn't understand why I was receiving a bill from the hospital.

When I called the insurance company to find out why they were billing me $200, they informed it was for a penalty. I asked them to explain what the penalty was for. They explained that the hospital had failed to contact them and get my second day's stay in the hospital approved, and despite the insurance company paying a majority of the bill, which was very nice of them by the way, they were penalizing me $200 which the hospital was trying to collect.

Guess what I did? You bet! I told the insurance girl my nightmare about the dirty flashlight. You could have heard a pin drop on the other end of the phone. "Hello, are you still there?" I asked.

She advised me to call the hospital billing office and ask them to write it off for all the trouble they put me through. I immediately took her up on the advice.

I called and explained the whole thing again, and they were unwilling to write off the $200. Can you say medical malpractice? Admittedly, I threw the term around. I was beyond frustrated they would invoice me for something they were clearly at fault on - not calling to get my second day in the hospital approved. It wasn't because they caused an unnecessary infection, although the resulting infection cost me more money.

Now they were refusing to write off the $200 for an error they made. Because I had to stay in the hospital past the negotiated time of 23 hours for this particular procedure, anything over that must get approved by the insurance company whether or not your bladder is working.

The hospital didn't call and get approval, so they penalized me. Can you imagine if they did call and the insurance company said no? "Sorry, she can't stay there. You need to send her home, or she needs to pay for the second day herself." I guess it can happen.

It took about two years to get my point across that I wasn't willing to pay $200 when I had to pay out a bunch of money for additional prescriptions and doctor's appointments to get rid of an infection they caused. I pleaded my case to each bill collector that called. The female bill collectors sympathized with me. The men were grossed out by the story. They probably never looked at a yellow flashlight from their toolbox the same ever again. You may never look at a yellow flashlight the same either. I know I sure don't. I still have a yellow and black flashlight as a reminder of what happened. After all, it is a funny story now. It wasn't very funny then.

It took a good couple of weeks for me to get back on my feet. While I was recovering from the surgery and infection, my brother Joe was steadily progressing with cancer.

CHAPTER TWELVE

Painful Choices

After finding out Joe had cancer, he was put on special medication to help with the anxiety and pain of it all. The colostomy bag surgery had been painful and was hard to deal with each day. The medicines combined with cancer affected his ability to think clearly. Joe had no problem calling me for anything and everything every single day.

Night after night, I sat on the phone talking with Joe or my mom, listening to the two of them talk about each other. It went on for several weeks. As the weeks rolled by, it got uglier and uglier, and all I could do was sit and listen – sometimes for hours after long days at work.

I knew Joe was scared. I knew Mom feared for him and the thought of losing her baby upset her. I found myself caught in a very difficult position between the two of them, and it was taxing me tremendously. The situation was mentally, emotionally and physically exhausting me and something had to change. We were now at a point where something different had to happen. *Lord, a change needs to occur and quickly Lord.*

Joe soon made a decision that would hurt my mother very much. He removed her name from his health records as the main person of contact – and he put my name in her place. I was his new health surrogate. I became the main contact person for everything.

Talk about a jab to her heart. Talk about putting someone in a very difficult position. He just moved his chess piece into check, and the queen was wounded. He and mom just couldn't seem to get on the same page about his health or the decisions he was making whether it be about his bank account or the way he chose to live. He saw her as too controlling - trying to control his health, his money, and his life. True or not, that's how he felt. So Joe felt he had no other choice but to remove her as his health surrogate and appoint me in her place.

I didn't ask for the position. I didn't want the position. I didn't have the experience Mom had. She had all those years with my father. She knew the ins and outs of the medical community. I did not. But when your brother is dying, there isn't much you can say to decline such a request, so I reluctantly accepted knowing I would bear the brunt of her pain and frustration. At the very least, it would slow down the frustrating and sometimes angry phone calls from the two of them.

I had no idea what I was doing or going to do. The only concrete thing I knew to do was to give it over to the Lord. I prayed and prayed about it and asked God to guide me and give me wisdom.

"Consider it pure joy, my brothers, whenever you face trials of many kinds because you know that the testing of your faith develops perseverance. Perseverance must finish its work so that you may be mature and complete, not lacking anything." James 1:2-5

We had entered a whole new phase. Managing Joe's health was new to me. I would come to learn a lot more about his health, the health care system, nursing homes, AIDS and cancer in a very short amount of time. I learned very quickly what documents were required and what documents to sign and not to sign. I also incurred the painful injuries of being appointed his health surrogate, injuries that have left lasting emotional scars. The weeks and the months ahead were sure to be some of the most difficult days of my life. *O God, did I need you!*

"If any one of you lacks wisdom, he should ask God, who gives generously to all without finding fault, and it will be given to him." James 1:5

"Blessed is the man who perseveres under trial because when he has stood the test, he will receive the crown of life that God has promised to those who love him." James 1:12

I work in the commercial insurance industry. I have been in the commercial insurance arena since 1996. Health insurance is not my expertise. I write insurance for commercial properties.

Honestly, I didn't have to worry too much about

his insurance anyway. Joe's case manager, JC with CAP, was a big help there too. He knew the system well. He had been using it well for many years, and if we needed anything, I knew I could call him and he would help me out.

Joe had managed to maneuver through the Medicaid system pretty well. After all, he had been on it for many, many years since being diagnosed with HIV. He had been collecting social security disability since then too, so he had the system figured out. He'd been on Medicaid type insurance for almost twenty-two years. When I think about the life span he was given when he was first diagnosed compared to how long he lasted, I'm sure even the social security office didn't expect him to live that long. They weren't without their hiccups either. Social Security was notorious for overpayments, and my brother was equally notorious for keeping the extra money. But they never failed to figure out their error. To fix it, they'd hold his payments until they got all their money back. It would have been so much easier for Joe to return the overages when they occurred, but he always thought he could sail by and not get caught.

One of the benefits of becoming his health surrogate was our opportunities to talk more on the phone about details. I used these moments to start talking more about what Jesus had been doing in my life and letting Joe know I was praying for him along with many others I knew that were also praying for him. We had a few good conversations about the Lord which made me very happy. I could see the reception was starting to improve.

At the same time all this was going on, I was

still going to college on a part-time basis, taking two classes a semester since 2006. I was going for an AA degree in Divinity through a small college in North Florida under the suggestion of a former pastor of mine who is now deceased. What a sweet man. The pastor was so encouraging to me and saw something in me I didn't see in myself.

Not only was I trying to juggle single motherhood, work full time, and helping to manage Joe, I was going to college online. Fortunately for me, I was on summer break, so recovering from the surgery and dealing with Joe on a daily basis was working out ok.

I returned to school in early August. My job was very patient with me and understood the situation. I returned to work after being home three weeks for recovery. I lost a week because of the infection. But I was thankful a partial hysterectomy didn't require a longer recovery period. At least mine didn't. I would have been back to work sooner had it not been for the flashlight fiasco.

Joe still rang my phone every single day. Sometimes, he called me five to six times daily. He called and asked me the same questions, talked about the same things, told me he loved me and then hang up. Sometimes he was coherent, and I could understand everything he said. Many days he was not, and his words ran together in a string of mumbled sentences. I knew the meds for the pain and the anxiety, coupled with the AIDS meds, were affecting him. Depending on what time of day he called, I knew he either had his meds already or was about to. It didn't stop him from calling. He still had the wherewithal to dial my number every day.

I got to know the nursing staff pretty well at the nursing home. Joe was living there full time. It was so much easier to monitor his progress, get him to and from doctor appointments, and give him the medications he required. We didn't have to worry about him being on the streets or missing medicine or important doctor appointments.

Since being diagnosed with colorectal cancer and the doctor finding the huge tumor in the pelvis area, they chose to try radiation and chemo to shrink the pelvis area tumor down to a size they could later go in and remove. I always wondered if they intended to do that given the condition of his body.

Joe's first chemo treatment; well let's just say it was a quick one. What was supposed to take up to four hours, took about an hour. Joe became so good at medicine and treating himself over the years; he thought he might try his hand at giving himself the chemo drugs.

While at his first chemo appointment, all hooked up to the IV and ready to go, the nurse started the chemo drip and left Joe alone in the room for a while. She knew the drug typically took about four hours to run through the IV line, so she figured she would check in on him from time to time throughout the treatment. No big deal.

What she didn't know was Joe was impatient and crafty. He wasn't willing to wait four hours, nor did he think he had to, so Joe being Joe sped up the IV drip and somehow managed to get all of it to enter his body in about an hour. This drug required a four-hour injection rate combined with a saline solution. Joe changed the drip rate on both the drug and saline solution, so the drip was done in under an hour. His first chemo injection was complete. He was ready to go home.

The nurse came back in, not suspecting anything, after making her rounds to check on her other patients and was shocked and dismayed by what she found in Joe's room. She asked him what happened and he showed her what he did.

Joe found out that day he could have killed himself right then had he not altered the saline drip too. Going forward, Joe was not to be left alone with the IV drip anymore. He was on a watch.

The chemo started to take a lot out of Joe, but he stayed as positive as he could. The colostomy bag was still his daily companion. I settled on the fact it would be there the rest of his life. Joe had different thoughts about it. Joe convinced himself once he finished the chemo and radiation, the doctor would go in and remove the other tumor and give him his plumbing back.

A few months into the chemo treatments, they found out his bladder now had a hole in it. He was leaking fluid. The cancer had eaten a small hole in his bladder. It had continued to move north in his body and was now affecting his urine output. The reality of getting his plumbing back was gone. The cancer continued to spread despite the chemo treatment and putting him through more surgery didn't make sense. It was too taxing on an already weak system.

Those days were not fun at all. Mentally, I believe it set Joe back quite a bit because reality had hit - the cancer was making its way north, and nothing was stopping it. Not the chemo, not the radiation, not the drugs. The cancer had become the new aggressor in his failing body.

I remember Joe always telling me that when it came to fighting any kind of major illness like AIDS or cancer, you must keep your head in the game. You must make mental focus a priority or you will lose it. The moment you start to give up, he said, was the moment you started to lose the battle.

CHAPTER THIRTEEN

Time for Reinforcements

The daily phone calls from Joe continued, and I tried as best I could to manage his case from Orlando. Joe was still living in a nursing home in West Palm Beach. I continued to communicate with his caseworkers and nurses over the phone. We all had an open line of communication, and they kept me updated on everything that was happening. Some days they had good news and other days they did not.

There was always one thing I couldn't get past. It troubled me daily. So I took the liberty of bringing in one more important piece of the puzzle for Joe —a chaplain. I needed someone who could talk to Joe about Jesus.

He grew up in the same church I did, but I didn't know where he stood now as far as believing in Jesus Christ as his Lord and Savior. I used to feel confident, but at this stage of the game, my confidence wasn't as strong. After all, he had done many things in his life and he had been through many difficult things. I wasn't sure he believed anymore that God would forgive him; I wasn't sure he even gave God any thought anymore. A chaplain was the one person I needed to help me get to the bottom of this. I suppose I could have asked Joe directly, but when dealing with a family member who is ill, I have found it is best to get a third party involved.

My experience has been that sick people tend to tell outsiders more about where they are spiritually than they do their own family and friends. Joe knew where I stood in regards to Jesus. I had not made that a secret over the last ten years, especially in the last few years. He knew I valued my relationship with the Lord more than I did my own family. God first, family second.

I needed to know where he stood spiritually. I needed to know where he would spend eternity. In my mind, it didn't matter what Joe had done in the past. There was a very long list, but when I think about his long list of sins, was the length of his list any longer than mine? Different things, different sins, but sin is sin. It didn't matter that he was gay. What I wanted to know is if he had accepted Jesus as his Lord and Savior. I believed he had, but I couldn't say with hundred percent certainty. Secondly, had he ever asked for forgiveness of his sins?

I contacted the chaplain who was part of the hospice team assigned to Joe's case. We now had a hospice team that visited Joe in the nursing home to check on him, treat him, and do whatever else was required. They were not a twenty-four-hour service, but they had been called in to help provide care for Joe. Joe's case was a little more advanced than the nursing home staff could manage. He was too sick to go to an assisted living facility, and insurance was probably an issue there anyway, and he wasn't sick enough to go to a full-time hospice unit. The nursing home worked out fine for what we needed.

Chaplain Nino was his name. He was such a nice man, patient, nonjudgmental and caring. We spoke over the phone, and I explained what I was trying to accomplish. He understood what I was asking. He said he would love to visit Joe as often as I needed him to, or as often as Joe allowed. He checked his calendar for availability and set some time aside to visit Joe and have the discussion. He was a wonderful addition to the team.

Whenever Joe was feeling low, I knew I could call Chaplain Nino and ask him to go by and pay him a visit. He knew Joe was in a deep hole and needed help maneuvering around it. I was so thankful I could count on the chaplain to help me with Joe's spiritual needs. I needed another voice, a gentle voice, a spiritual voice, someone besides me who could talk to Joe and not judge him for who he was. I needed an unbiased person who could sit and listen to Joe share his feelings and his fears. After all, he was facing a giant he hadn't faced before. I needed someone who could encourage him with the Word of God. I had been finding my strength in the Scriptures, and I knew Joe could too.

It is one thing to battle HIV/AIDS all your life. You get the initial diagnosis. You're shell-shocked for a while. But you come to understand it. You finally manage to maneuver through it. Then to your shock and surprise, cancer pops up on the radar and the rules of engagement change. Cancer was a new twist to an already stressful life.

It's not easy to fight cancer when you have AIDS because the medications don't always work well together. In many cases from what I remember, you can make one disease worse than the other. It's a very delicate balance. There are some medications you are not able to take because they contradict each other.

The T-cell count was still relevant to me despite the cancer. I was still watching the T-cell count. Joe was continuing on the downward spiral. Despite all of that, Joe was still thinking and strategizing.

One day Joe called me to tell me he had a brilliant idea. His brilliant idea was something he felt was very important. We had been talking daily, so I thought we had provided everything he needed. What else could be so important?

"Net, I want to buy a car."

I coughed. "What did you say? Did you just say you want to buy a car?"

"Net, I want a car. I am going to buy a car Net."

"Joe, you do realize you are living in a nursing home?"

"Yeah so. Net I want a car, and I'm going to buy a car."

"Joe, what do you need a car for?"

"I want to drive around town. I want to go to The Lord's Place on Thursday nights."

"Joe, you don't have the money to buy a car. You need to hold onto what money you have in your account. We need that money to get you the things you need. You need those things the nursing home doesn't provide. You need denture cream, haircuts, extra food, cigarettes!"

With a little more excitement, he exclaimed, "Net, I'm buying a car! I have plenty of money in my account to buy a car. I found one I like. It is beautiful and in great condition!"

"How much is this beautiful car?" trying to hold back my frustrations.

"$1,495."

"Fourteen hundred dollars? Joe? Seriously? You don't need a car. What will you do when you run out of money because you have to buy insurance for it and a tag? You have to have a tag. What about gas? How are you going to afford the gas on $35 a month?"

"Net."

He always called me Net.

"Joe, what will you do if you spend all your money? We won't be able to buy you denture cream or cigs. What about your cigarettes? You know how much you smoke."

The nursing home would take all his money each month for room and board and nursing care and leave him with $35 to his name each month. Smokes back then cost anywhere from $2.50 to $3.50 a pack depending on the brand you smoked. Joe tried to smoke the cheaper cigarettes, but when you smoke almost two packs a day, $35 a month doesn't go very far. I knew cigs were a necessity for him too. He had been a smoker all his adult life, and it didn't change when he went into the nursing home. Being that he had transferred into a nursing home, the first three months were free on Medicaid, and then they would start taking his disability check and leave him with $35 a month in his account. So Joe had extra money sitting in his account, burning a hole in his sweat pants.

Denture cream was also a necessity for him. Several of his teeth had rotted or broke off from all the drug and alcohol use over the years. When he didn't have his denture cream, he couldn't eat much.

"Net, you there?"

"Joe, what will you do when you run out of money?"

The response I will always remember as long as I live, *"I will cross that bridge when I get to it."* And with that, he hung up. All that remained was the dial tone.

I had no financial ties to Joe's bank account. I couldn't control what he withdrew. I decided a while ago not to sign anything that tied me to him financially. I heard it was something you avoided if you didn't want to be saddled with any remaining debt they owed once they were gone.

I gave it a few minutes and tried calling him back. I managed to get him to answer his phone, but he still wanted the car. I couldn't talk him out of it. I tried using the rules of the nursing home. I tried using the cigs and denture cream. I tried using the unknown expenses. I said everything except, *Joe you are dying! You have cancer! You have AIDS! You're on a plethora of medication! You are out of it half the time! Joe, what am I going to do with the car when you're gone?"*

But I knew I couldn't say any of those things to him even though they were all true. Joe would do what he wanted. He always did. That's how he rolled.

Joe contacted his friend and asked him to help him get the car. He found this wonderful car, a beautiful white car with lush maroon cloth interior – so it had a few burn holes, but who's counting. I think it was a Chevy if memory serves.

Joe was living in a nursing home and was actively buying a beautiful used car. He even went as far as getting the driver of the nursing home van to drive him to the tag agency once he purchased this wonderful car so he could purchase the tag. I still question what was going through that guy's head.

Joe bought a tag! He paid extra for a special tag too – DUBYDOO. He bought a special tag for the beautiful used car he had to have while living in a nursing home. Who does this? Oh yeah – Joe!

He brought the new beauty back to the nursing home and there it sat.

Once a week his friend came to the nursing home and drove Joe in his own car to The Lord's Place. For those of you who don't know about The Lord's Place, here is a brief description of what they do from their website as of May 2017.

The Lord's Place transforms lives by providing solutions that break the cycle of homelessness for the most vulnerable and neglected in Palm Beach County. Our nonprofit has been serving men, women, and families in our community for over 30 years. Our innovative, compassionate, and effective services are constantly evolving to effectively eradicate local homelessness for good. - See more at thelordsplace.org.

Joe had been going to The Lord's Place for years. They helped him in a variety of ways. He met a lot of people there and made friends. He wanted to spend time there weekly despite his physical condition. He wanted to attend the recovery meetings. He needed it. He wanted it. Who was I to tell him he couldn't go to a place where he found comfort and loving support from those who knew him better than I did? His friend was willing to drive him there and hang out with him. It was some normalcy for him.

When I think about it, Joe was a thirty-nine-year-old gay man with AIDS, dying from cancer, living in a nursing home full of senior citizens, some twice his age, who had lived their lives and were now living their final days on earth. Any normalcy was good medicine. The Lord's Place for Joe was his normal. They were very caring people who loved Joe and didn't judge.

So now we have a car. I laugh as I write this – he paid for this one and didn't steal it. His decision-making process was improving if that was possible.

A beauty of a car now occupied a space in the nursing home parking lot. When I saw this car for the first time, I chuckled and remembered what he told me over the phone – *Oh Net, it's so beautiful!*

The shiny, pitted white exterior encased the beautiful maroon cloth interior with its cigarette burned maroon seats. It was a real beauty alright. The rust covered roof gave the car class, not to mention the empty liquor bottles and half-smoked cigarettes overflowing in the ashtray. The aroma was as original as the bar down the street. They always say beauty is in the eye of the beholder. In this case, the beholder was my baby brother who was drugged up half the time from his daily medication regimen. But he so was proud of his purchase. It made him happy for a bit.

He didn't care. He just wanted to feel like everyone else. He just wanted to experience the freedom he always had during his days on the run. Wheels could take him places his feet couldn't.

My biggest concern was always the risk he'd take driving himself somewhere. I always worried about the other drivers should he hit someone else and cause real damage or bodily injury. He did, in fact, get into two small fender benders with the car and thankfully no one was injured. His insurance canceled by the next due date for non payment of premium, so he had no insurance to pay for any damages he might have caused anyway. Joe was like that. He would purchase car insurance for the sole purpose of getting the tag and then let it cancel for nonpayment the following month. As it was with other things, I couldn't do anything about it except pray he didn't kill anyone.

After a couple of weeks, the nursing home finally took notice of the lovely white car that never moved. Maybe they figured out who it belonged to by the tag? They determined Joe was too self-sufficient for their nursing home. He had gotten a couple of the residents high, and he had wheels. They determined he was well enough to live somewhere else.

I ended up having to transfer Joe to another nursing home - with his car. I had to acquaint myself with the new nursing home, new staff and new rules. But I would still seek the Lord every day. I couldn't do this without Him.

One day my phone rang at work. Our being happy and everything going pretty smoothly came to a screeching halt!

In a gruff, yet panicked voice, I heard, "Net, I need cigs! Net, I need them today! I am out of cigs Net."

Hmm. What do I hear right now? Was that a bird chirping outside my window? Was someone calling me from the other side of the office? Surely someone was asking me if I wanted figs. Perhaps I heard a plane buzz by? Surely I didn't hear him say he needed cigs. Naaa.

Again I heard, "Net, I need cigs!" The intensity moved up a bit.

I sat there patiently searching for something to say, and the only words that came to mind were these, "Joe, remember what you said when I told you not to buy the car?"

Silence.

"Joe you said, "I'll cross that bridge when I get to it. Guess what bro? We're standing at the bridge. I hate to say I told you so, but I guess I just did."

The truth was staring him in the face. The awful, yet realistic truth. The phantom bridge was now before Joe.

His voice was getting a bit more excited; I pictured him pacing, "Net, I need cigs! I'm out Net!"

"Joe I understand you're out of cigarettes, but what am I supposed to do? I'm at work right now, and I'm two and a half hours away. I can't drive down there today to bring you cigarettes."

Almost immediately and a little sterner, "Net, you don't understand!"

"Joe you don't understand! I can't bring you cigarettes today!"

"But Net, I'm out."

"Joe I get that, but you need to find half butts and smoke those." And with that, I hung up.

Talk about frustrated and a bit surprised that he called to ask me for cigarettes.

It wasn't that I didn't want him to have cigarettes. After all, what's one more nicotine stick going to do to his health at this point? I knew they brought him some comfort, a comfort I never understood. For him, it was something to do during the day. He could go outside and spend a few minutes with other residents, talk, or stare at the sky. I'm sure a lot of deep thinking occurred as he puffed away. For him, it was more than just an addiction to nicotine. It was bigger than that. Still, I couldn't help but remember what I implored of him a few weeks earlier. *You don't need a car brother. You live in a nursing home.*

Who buys a car while living in a nursing home? Most nursing home residents are not thinking about buying cars. Some are going through the emotions of having to give up their driving privileges and relinquishing their freedoms.

I never knew anyone to purchase a car for

themselves while living in a nursing home. A motorized wheelchair, yes. A real car, with insurance, and specialized tag? No. But then again, this was Joe Duby, and he did whatever he wanted – he always did what he wanted despite sound advice.

We were standing at the bridge - now what?

My office phone rang fourteen times over the next several hours. Each time it was Joe asking me for cigarettes. At or around call number ten, he was begging me to bring him cigarettes. His demands now turned into begging and pleading. By call fifteen to my cell phone, now at home, he was begging and pleading for cigarettes in every message left on my phone. They were pathetic pleas for help.

By the eighteenth call, I abruptly answered my phone and lost my temper. I couldn't take it anymore.

"WHAT...DO...YOU...WANT...JOE? WHAT DO YOU WANT?" I yelled into the phone.

I continued to yell, "If you call me one more time and ask me for cigarettes, I'm going to disown you for good and let you stay there!! Do you understand what I'm saying? You will not get any cigarettes! DO YOU UNDERSTAND ME? DO YOU?"

Exasperated, I waited for a reply.

I waited for him to start yelling at me. After all, in past arguments we yelled at each other. I waited for him to tell me again I didn't understand his plight. I didn't understand the urge. He was right, I didn't understand the urge, and I still don't.

Our relationship in the past had been more

about yelling at each other than speaking kindly to one another. We irritated each other because I was always looking for Joe to get with the program and to make a change. I wanted so desperately for him to do something better with his life instead of making the life-altering choices he continued to make, which to me were purposely sabotaging himself.

Silence.

He didn't yell at me. Instead, he quietly and humbly pleaded with me for cigarettes. Joe apologized for calling me so many times over cigarettes. He knew he had pushed me over the edge. He knew he'd better smooth things over with me quickly if he was to have any chance at getting what he wanted.

I had lost my temper with him. And I hated that.

I had been very patient with him all these months. I had been very empathetic to his situation. I understood he was hurting. He was right about me not understanding what it felt like to need the smoke, to jones for it, to crave the nicotine. But no matter what, he knew I was right. I hated telling him I was right. I hated telling him I told you so. *But bro, I told you so.* The bridge looks so far away, especially when you have what you want.

As God would have it, always in control, I still had friends who lived in West Palm Beach. They lived a few miles from the nursing home. The fastest way to resolve this was to ask one of my friends to buy a pack, or even a carton if they were willing, and take them over to the nursing home the next day.

The next morning I put out an urgent request on Facebook hoping some of my friends down in West Palm Beach would see the post.

Facebook post dated July 14, 2009:

Anyone down in WPB want to take a dying man a few packs of no menthol cheap cigarettes? Joe called me 18 times yesterday to tell me he is out of cigs. Woodlake Nursing & Rehab off Jog Road, Room #203. Otherwise, you could call him and tell him that his sister sent you over.

To my amazement, I got a response back from the one person farthest from my mind. It was an old boyfriend from many years ago. Get this – his name was Ray. Of all people to respond to my request, an old boyfriend of years before named Ray responded to my plea for help. My father's name was Ray. My father also smoked cigarettes all his life. I smile now because I think about how my father and Joe parted ways and here was an old boyfriend named Ray answering the call to take Joe cigarettes. I believe God has a sense of humor and He weaves the littlest details in and out of our lives. I didn't recognize this back then, but I smile about it now.

Ray and I dated for a while, and it just didn't work out. There were no hard feelings on either side. Thankfully. He wasn't feeling it for me and did the honorable thing and broke it off.

He saw my request on Facebook and contacted me right away through Facebook Messenger. He was happy to help a desperate, dying man who happened to be the brother of his ex-girlfriend. What are the chances? I told him a pack would do for now until I could get a carton shipped down to him. But he was willing to buy Joe a carton. Ray was willing to go to the nursing home, Room #203 and bring a poor guy smokes so his sister could get some relief. He didn't want any money in return. He gave so willingly. I was pleasantly surprised, and it was a real blessing. Joe was a happy guy again. My phone quit blowing up for a while.

Facebook post dated July 15, 2009:

God sends angels in the most trying of times to remind you that He is in control and hears us. Bro is much happier now that he can satisfy that nicotine craving. I am much happier now.

A normal day at the nursing home for Joe was getting breakfast in the morning, then taking his meds. Then he walked around and paced the halls. When he got tired, he'd sleep for awhile. Then it was back outside for more smoking. He'd wander around till lunch; take more meds, smoke another, walk around, pace the halls, sleep, eat dinner, take more meds, smoke, and finally go to sleep for the night.

The next day he got up and did it all over again.

Once in a while, there would be the occasional stroll to the corner convenience store to get some beer. Yes, Joe would wander to the convenience store to get beer. And Joe being Joe, sensitive and a giving person, he would bring some beer back to the nursing home to share with some of his friends. He and a few of the residents would sit out back and secretly drink the beers together. They even had the occasion to smoke some marijuana together which he got from a friend. You might be wondering if the nursing home ever had a problem with the little private parties. They did, and my phone rang.

Nursing homes are responsible for all patients, and when another patient brings in alcohol and drugs and freely shares them with other patients who are on various medications, it calls for eviction, at least it did in this case. When your brother has upset the nursing home director with his antics by failing to follow the rules yet again, they look to evict pretty quickly. And evict they did. Oh, we had a little time, but we were on the way out.

Finding another place for him to reside wasn't easy. How do you explain to the potential new nursing home that your brother needs a room in their facility because he is being evicted? They all know each other. You hope they don't ask about his previous residency and why he won't be staying there any longer.

Oh, let's see, because he brought drugs and alcohol onto the grounds and was good at sharing. Yep... that's it. Oh and by the way, because he owns a car that stays parked in your lot. Yep....

God was good because we were able to place him in the new nursing home pretty quickly. The same nursing home he called me from for the cigarettes. After his move, Joe knew he would have to behave. He knew the partying had to stop. He knew he couldn't come to my house in Orlando. He knew he didn't have a whole lot of options. He also knew he was fighting the biggest battle of his life. And he needed those people and what they could supply.

We got him settled in the new nursing home, and things seemed to settle down as he continued to battle cancer. At this point, AIDS had taken the back seat.

The daily phone calls continued, two to five times daily to discuss the same things, occasionally talk about different things and other times to cry over his current situation.

There were days he lost all hope, and it was all I could do to encourage him to push through the pain. But I knew what I was asking was very difficult.

I wasn't in his shoes, and I couldn't relate. The pain continued to intensify despite the medications, and it played a role in how he was feeling. But what else can you say in those moments? Your brother is dying and you know it. Knowing he was suffering was heartbreaking, especially when I knew there was nothing else I could do to fix it. All I could do was support him as best I could, be a compassionate, listening ear and hopefully show him the love of Jesus in each interaction.

It was in those moments I remembered his laugh. It was so genuine and reminded me of happier times. There had been little flickers of light among the darkness that surrounded him. God was present, and I knew it.

In one of the many phone conversations we enjoyed, Joe said in a somber voice, "Net, I beat AIDS all my life, and now cancer is going to take me out. I figured out how to fight AIDS, but I can't figure out how to fight cancer. It's going to kill me

Net, it's going to kill me."

There were days he just wanted to give up and not go on anymore. There were days he just wanted to scream. There were days he just wanted to admit he messed up. I let him say whatever he wanted. I let him feel whatever he wanted.

My goal was to always give him a safe place to vent, a safe place to cry, and a safe place to ask questions. I wanted to be the safe place he could land while he fought through each day, however many days he had left.

I had no misconceptions about where this was headed and sadly neither did Joe. What Joe hadn't realized in all of this was that God had been providing everything he needed all along the way. He was aware of his situation and the pain he was going through, and He never stopped loving Joe despite all he had done.

The days can be long when going through this process. I was praying for Joe daily and talking to God about how to progress and move forward, knowing I had to fully rely on God each day. It would take everything in me to get through this.

"Trust in the Lord with all your heart, and lean not on your own understanding, in all thy ways acknowledge him, and he will make your paths straight." Proverbs 3:5-6

CHAPTER FOURTEEN

Costly Decisions

The day finally came when Joe admitted he made a mistake and his sister was right. I wrote this one down.

"Net, about the car."

"What about it Joe?"

"Net, I've been thinking. You were right about the car. I should have never bought the car Net. I'm going to sell it to the junkyard. It has caused me a lot of problems."

"What? Sell it to the junkyard? They won't give you more than few hundred bucks. You paid $1,500 for the car. You can sell it for more than a few hundred bucks, Joe."

"Net, it's not worth it. The junkyard already said they would come pick it up and give me $400 for it."

"Joe, surely someone would pay more than $400 for that car."

"Net, they are coming tomorrow. It was a mistake to buy it. I can't drive anymore."

Ding, ding, ding!

The next day the car was gone. The junkyard came and towed it away, tag and all. They paid him $200, not $400. We now had enough money for cigs.

Joe continued to struggle more each day. I think one of the most frustrating things about his current condition was the colostomy bag. Realizing it would never be undone was another blow to his hopes and dreams of beating this thing. He would never go back to being like everyone else. By now cancer had done too much damage and couldn't be controlled with medication.

The bag supplies were poorly made. Back then when Joe was on Medicaid, the supplies appeared to be of a cheaper quality, and were not as good as the more expensive ones. The materials felt thinner and weren't as sturdy. Too often, because of Joe's medicinal state, he struggled to get the rings to line up properly on the bag that attached to the piece of skinfold. Joe had a hard time getting the bags to connect properly to the skin fold, which caused leakage, which in turn caused soiled clothing, namely shirts. There were times Joe didn't even realize he had messed himself. It was hard to watch a grown man messing himself on his shirt. There were days he was so out of it; he didn't realize what was happening. Those were the days when I realized this was all too real.

I remember a time, shortly before Joe sold the car, going down to West Palm Beach to visit him while he did a brief stint in the hospital. He had taken ill while living in the nursing home and needed more care. That's when I finally met his doctor face to face who had been managing his case for a while. Prior to now, we had always communicated over the phone. I was so glad to be able to finally meet him. He advised me Joe's condition was steadily progressing. He wasn't sure how much longer he had on this earth.

When Joe was able, we walked down to the visiting area and sat down to talk. While we were sitting there chatting about nothing, watching people walk around, I looked over and noticed he had just soiled the front of his shirt. He didn't feel it. He didn't smell it. He was oblivious to the dampness. How could one not notice such an unpleasant occurrence? The medications kept him in a state of calm, but they also clouded his ability to recognize the little things going on around him or on him.

"Joe, um... you...uh...went to the bathroom on your shirt bud." I pointed to the soiled spot.

He looked down and said, "Oh crap. I'll be back."

I thought to myself, *"Crap is right. Literally."*

He stood up and started walking back to his hospital room. By now the disease had progressed so much and the meds had been increased to tolerable, yet manageable levels. He walked like a little old man. He shuffled his feet at a snail's pace. I sat there and watched him shuffle all the way to the elevator and go out of sight.

As I sat there, I wondered how many times this had happened. *Did he notice it happening or did someone always point it out to him? Did he finally smell the stench of feces on his clothes? How many people steered clear of him because he soiled himself?*

Admittedly, I didn't want to touch him without gloves. Memories of my initial treatment of Joe when I first found out he contracted HIV came flooding back to my mind.

Here we were again, facing the true reality of the situation. He was just as contagious today as he was back then, even more so because he was now considered full blown. The reality was that he still had a deadly infection and the infection could spread through bodily fluids. To me, feces was a bodily fluid, right or wrong. The facts hadn't changed over the years. There still wasn't a cure, and I still had to be careful around him. But now I was more educated and was more comfortable being around him.

I wondered who would clean his shirt. Don't get me wrong; I wasn't offering. *Would he just throw it in the corner? Would he throw it in the bio-hazard bag or the normal trash can? How would they handle the biohazard?*

The colostomy bag was a 24/7 deal, so logic says this wasn't a one-time thing. Sometimes it's easier not to think about those little details. Sometimes it's best to move on and push it out of your mind. But for the man or woman stuck with the bag, it doesn't go away that easily. They can't run from it. It's permanently attached to their left front side a little above the waistline. It's embarrassing, bothersome, inconvenient, inhumane, painful, costly, dirty, disgusting, and shameful – it's anything but glamorous. It goes against our natural ability to empty our stomachs the way we have always emptied our stomachs since birth. Food goes in one hole and comes out another. That's what we learned. On the flip side, it has given the patient an alternative method to empty the waste so they can continue to function as normally as possible.

For Joe, however, his dignity was compromised. He felt weak and useless. What would his contribution be to society now? His life was defined by doctor appointments, medicine regimens, a painful combination of two wicked diseases, neither having the compassion to put their aggression aside for the good of the other. They battled each other for control of the body as it broke down more each day. AIDS had resided in his body for many years. The cancer had moved in and complicated matters. As a medical professional, which disease do you attack first, or more or less? Which disease do you try and control? As a patient, which one do you want to discard first? Neither are easy avenues or easy answers.

For twenty minutes, a myriad of questions and thoughts rolled through my mind as I saw other patients and loved ones walk the hospital floor. The flurry of activity was almost silent compared to the thoughts running through my mind. I hadn't been in this place before. I was on a journey, of which the end was pretty clear, but the path to get there was anything but easy and transparent. I would have to continue to trust God and seek Him daily. He knew what was coming and He knew I was weak.

"But He said to me, "My grace is sufficient for you, for my power is made perfect in your weakness. Therefore, I will boast all the more gladly about my weaknesses, so that Christ's power may rest on me." 2 Corinthians 12:9

About twenty minutes later Joe reappeared, shuffling back to his seat. Frankly, I was impressed he remembered where I was sitting. He was all cleaned up, wearing a clean shirt and giving me a reassuring look that everything was ok.

Joe was a strong man, and yet he had softened in his mannerisms over the last few years. As time drew closer, Joe always tried to make me feel comfortable. He took great care in making sure he was as upbeat as possible around me, so I didn't get upset. He cared for how I felt, and he knew it was hard for me to be in this situation and to see him this way.

It was a brotherly love for his sister, a sister he had regrettingly spent many years separated from as a result of his own choices. A sister he had gone head to head with over the phone. A sister who showed him compassion and let him make his own decisions. A sister he had wrestled to the ground more than once. A sister he had pestered and begged. A sister who had shunned him in the beginning stages of his disease for her own well-being. I believe he came to understand my position. There is the off chance he simply forgot those earlier days. Joe appreciated that I didn't try and control his final months on earth. I just let him live. I hadn't been happy about the car, but it was his life and his money. He had nothing else.

As he made his way closer to me, I couldn't help but think of what a great doctor he would have been. I pictured him walking into a patient's room, wearing the white coat, the chart in hand with a gentle smile on his face, understanding and compassionate. I pictured him standing beside their bed listening to the patient explain how they felt and him offering reassurance they would be fine in a few days.

But here we were sitting in a hospital for a different reason, a hospital which had he made a different choice, he could have practiced medicine. He could have been on the other side of these diseases now ravaging his body. He could have been the one consoling the families of sick loved ones. I could have been back at my office going about my day. Our phone calls could have been more about the latest and greatest in medicine or what the family was up to. I wouldn't have been there to watch my baby brother struggle on the wrong side of AIDS, and on the wrong side of cancer. But those days of wishing Joe had made a different decision, sadly, were gone. Only in my dreams for him would they reside now. *Dr. Duby, please report to Room 203. Dr. Duby, please report to Room 203.*

We visited for a while longer, watching people pass. We stared out the window to the garden and watched the flowers sway back and forth in the sea breeze. The hospital wasn't far from the beach, and the ocean air always seems to make its way inland.

Silence occupied more space than I wanted, but by then I had no words left. It became more about spending quality time with my brother. We didn't have to talk. Spending time watching flowers sway in the breeze was a blessing I will always cherish. I think it was supposed to be that way. I think we were just supposed to enjoy each other's company without saying a word. That would be the last real visit we would enjoy together in a nice set-ting. It wasn't a cold room with boring walls, no personality, or the sounds of beeping and endless television noise. There was no unpleasant odor of Lysol spray or dirty mop water. It was pleasant, and I enjoyed it. I believe Joe enjoyed it too.

When his boney butt could take no more from sitting on the hard seat, he rose to his feet, and we hugged and said our goodbyes. I had to get back home to my daughter. It was a two and a half hour drive northward to home. As I walked away, I turned and stopped for a moment and watched him as he shuffled back to the elevator. He waved one last time, smiled, and then he was gone behind the elevator door.

My phone started to ring less and less as each day passed.

Facebook post dated August 7, 2009:

Update on the bro: Down to 125lbs and goes Monday for 2 pints of blood. He's trying to make it to his 40th birthday, September 17. Please continue to be in prayer that he stays pain-free as he goes through all this. Thanks in advance for the prayers for my family and me.

There's a song that speaks to me so powerfully. Hillary Scott sings the song with such beauty and grace, and it's a well-known song titled, "Thy Will." The song summarizes the countless times I struggled with the very thoughts of being confused and wondering if I heard the Lord correctly. Each time I questioned myself, I remembered it wasn't about my will, but the Lord's will. His will be done, not mine.

As the song says, there are days I don't understand despite hearing the Lord loud and clear. It hurts going through this and watching a loved one struggle with a serious illness, and there's nothing much you can do except support them.

I continue to remind myself daily that the Lord is good and His plans for me are good. I know He sees me and He hears me. His ways are for me and He has goodness in store for me, so I keep moving forward. I believe He has goodness in store despite the pain and the fears.

CHAPTER FIFTEEN

Steak, Eggs & Quiet Time

In Mid-August of 2009, I started the fall term of college. My pastor of a few years prior had suggested I go to college to get an Associate degree in Divinity. We had ministered together along with some dear friends of mine. The pastor saw something in me that no one else saw. I remember him telling me that if people were to take me seriously, I needed some education. Ministry wasn't always pretty and it still isn't today. There are days ministry gets ugly, and he felt me having some formal education would help me grow in my faith so I took his advice.

I was baptized in 2006 as an adult. It felt more satisfying being able to decide as an adult. Being baptized as a baby didn't allow me to choose, but now I could make the decision myself, and it felt great reconfirming my decision to follow Jesus.

I was now in the third year of college. At this pace, I would graduate in another couple years with my Associate's degree in Divinity. I realize an Associates should only take a couple of years, but when you're a single mom with one income and a child to raise, taking two courses a semester without using student loans makes getting your Associates seems like getting a Bachelors, minus the benefit of a Bachelors.

Taking online courses made it so easy and worked great with my hectic schedule. To stay on track, I took two more classes for the fall. I knew it was something I had to do despite the distractions of my recovery from surgery and what was going on with Joe. School represented some normalcy I hadn't seen in a while, and I was glad to get back to the discipline. In the back of mind, the words the Lord spoke to me months earlier; *"September for Joe"* kept rolling around. September would be here before I knew it, then what? What would September hold for me? For Joe? For our family?

One of the classes I was required to take was a Bible journaling class. There were several things you were required to journal each day in your quiet time with the Lord. I had never seriously journaled before. Journaling is a great way for you to record your thoughts and prayers to God, preferably each day. We had to select a text from the Bible, write down our prayers, record our insights, reactions, and any thoughts we might have in our quiet time with God.

The teacher suggested we do our quiet time first thing in the morning.

Morning quiet times are best in my opinion and a great way to start your day. I have found that waiting till bedtime doesn't work as well and isn't very effective when all you can focus on is the back of your eyelids as the Bible, and your journal slide down the side of your body to the sheets. Hours later you wake up and realize you missed your quiet time with God and your side hurts from laying on your books.

Getting up first thing in the morning meant getting up earlier, before the rest of the house. I was already having a difficult time sleeping with everything going on. Some would call this a sacrifice to get up even earlier despite the lack of sleep. Sacrifice wasn't the word I would choose. It was more of a commitment. I was committing to get up early and spend purposeful time with God. Before this class, it should have been something I was already doing. I admit I hadn't been doing quiet time quite like this. I had been spending daily time with God, but it wasn't as specific as the course required.

So on August 24, 2009, I woke up early and started my purposeful quiet time with God. At first, the routine of it was a little awkward. I was used to having my style of quiet time with God for years. This quiet time required purposeful action steps on my part and looking past the normal routine of talking with God and going about my day. It required me to search myself and the Scriptures, to pull out nuggets of truth, insights, reactions, and prayers. I must admit, starting this way was a little difficult, but as each day passed, it got easier.

I started looking forward to getting up early each day to spend quality time with God. I wouldn't say the times prior weren't quality and quantity, but this was different. Walking through these difficult days with Joe, it was as if I had a coach walking along side me, encouraging me, teaching me, and leading me each day. It was as if we sat down each morning and strategized about the day's events and how they would be handled rather than me scrambling at every turn. Having God's presence each day to discuss some of the most difficult aspects of Joe's situation made going through it so much easier. I was so thankful for God's presence and so thankful I knew Him as my Heavenly Father. Oh, where would I be if I hadn't known the Lord? I'll tell you where I'd be. I would have been trying to handle it in my strength, which wasn't much strength at all considering the situation. I was experiencing a new kind of peace, a peace I so desperately needed as I rode the waves daily, waves which could overtake me at any moment.

August 24, 2009 - This morning I started my DDT (Daily Devotional Time). I thought about where to start my reading, and I decided to start in the book of Hebrews. Hebrews has always impressed me, although not sure why. Today's prayers covered a multitude of requests and concerns. I want to experience the growth I know will come from this experience, It's a new discipline for me. I am feeling anxious and bored all at the same time. I'm missing some interaction with people. Having been down after surgery for three weeks, I got used to all the attention. Now it's back to the norm for me and everyone else. Prayer for all my friend's kids going back to school. Thank you God, for sending your Son. My heart goes out to my friend who lost his wife. She was a friend of mine too. Must be so hard to believe, such a shock. I pray God comforts him. I pray she knew Jesus as her Lord and Savior. I'm just not 100% sure. Comfort all who loved her Lord.

I received another update on Joe's condition from the hospice nurse. We try and touch base every couple days on his condition. He is progressing a little bit further each day, but the progression is in the wrong direction. The hospice nurse has been very patient with me as I navigate my way through this. I certainly have a new appreciation for all those who have traveled this road before. It isn't easy watching your loved one move closer and closer to death. I believe this is one of the many life lessons God wants to teach me.

I didn't hear much from Joe over the weekend. As a matter of fact, I hadn't heard much from him at all over the last couple of weeks since seeing him in person.

I remember the day, a few short weeks prior. I decided to take another trip down to West Palm Beach and visit him. I hadn't seen him since having my surgery. My daughter went along for the ride this time.

I wanted to see him and get a sense of his current status and how he was doing. I wanted to see the physical changes, his weight loss, his difficulty in getting around, and his inability to focus.

When we arrived, Joe was meandering in the hall. There he was standing among a few wheelchair bound adults, some hunched over asleep with drool rags to catch the saliva that slowly dripped from their open mouths. Others were sitting upright in their chair mumbling to themselves, and still, a few were frantically watching nurses pass back and forth before them.

If you have never been in a nursing home, it's an experience you won't soon forget.

The front entrance is always welcoming, and you may meet a resident or two hanging around. But as you make your way down the long hall, you are usually greeted with several adults sitting in wheelchairs. Some are pulling themselves along with their feet on the floor.

Others are sitting there asleep, and some hunched over in what looks like a terribly uncomfortable position. Sometimes you will meet someone who calls you over, wanting to talk, but all they can do is repeat the same questions again and again.

One time I had an older gentleman call me over to him. When I got close to him, he grabbed my hand and held it tightly. He didn't want to let go. He muttered words I couldn't comprehend and I politely shook my head in agreement. I hoped I didn't agree to something bad.

I intended to treat them all with dignity.

I imagined them young like me, vibrant and able to work and move and raise children. I imagined their excitement when grandchildren came over or when momma cooked food for Thanksgiving. I imagined them dressed up in their Sunday best. I imagined those people who were once in my shoes.

They had been independent and vacationed. They remembered those days as they watched me walk by to my brother's room. For some, the memories were long gone. They were a shell of their former self. For some the memories never left.

It's a very lonely existence for some of the residents in a nursing home. They don't get many visitors. It's sad because some have been, as the term goes, "dumped" there. They either had no family, or they had been abandoned by family or friends. Among the various elderly sitting around in the hall that day, there stood Joe, hand on his chin, playing with the few chin hairs adorning his frail face. There was no conversation. He was standing there looking off into a prism of light. It was all a blur.

Sometimes I wonder what Joe thought about living in a nursing home. *Did he fully comprehend the reason he was there? Did he realize this was most likely the last stop? How much of the way he lived his life ran through his mind on a daily basis, concreting itself in a hole called regret? How many hours had he spent reconciling with God. How many hours had he spent talking to God about the last twenty years?*

I walked up to him very slowly, not wanting to startle him or the other residents. They all wished I was there to see them, but as I passed them one by one, they realized it was not them I was there to see. It doesn't matter who you are when you walk into a nursing home. The residents are happy to see someone who isn't drooling, sleeping or dropping their food. They welcome the company and the conversation even if they don't remember anything you say five minutes later. They still want to be treated with respect. They long for someone to pay a little attention. They long for love and affection. They know this is most likely the last stop. They long for their spouse who died last year. They long for their children who are too busy to visit them. They long for their independence again.

Joe noticed I was standing in front of him now and he smiled a little bit. I could tell he had his morning regimen of medicine and that was ok. I asked him how he was doing and he nodded gently up and down. His hand still rested on his chin as he picked at his stubble beard, eyes lost in a glance. It was his way of relaxing.

The day nurse saw me as she was filling medications for the other patients.

"Joe, wait here, I'll be right back."

He watched me as I walked away.

"Good morning," I said to the day nurse.

"Good morning. How can I help you?" the nurse asked.

"I am Joe's sister. I came down from Orlando to see him."

"Oh yes, yes. You are Jeanette, right?"

"Yes."

"Have you seen your brother this morning?"

"Yes, he's standing over there. It looks like he had his morning meds already."

"Yes, a few hours ago. Joe isn't due for the next round till after lunch."

"Oh ok, good. Listen, I was wondering about something. Do you think it would be possible to take Joe out for an hour or two today? I'd like to take him out to lunch."

"Um....well... I suppose so. He seems to be good today. If you bring him back by uh, let's say 1 o'clock, and then we can give him his afternoon meds. Would that be enough time for you?"

"Yes, yes, that would be plenty I think. I don't want to keep Joe out long. Besides, I don't know that I could handle him all afternoon. I'm a little nervous about what he would do if I kept him out any longer. So, 1 o'clock would be the latest. Besides, I'm thinking IHOP. He loves eggs and pancakes."

"Great. Ok, just make sure you check Joe out at the front desk when you leave."

"Ok. Thanks."

The nurse warned me to be careful and watchful as his walking was not very steady. I have to admit the walking wasn't my biggest concern – it was the colostomy bag. What if he has another accident? I wanted to take some spare clothes with us but ultimately decided against it. After all, we'd only be gone for about an hour. An hour was pretty much the extent of my nursing ability. I didn't know how he'd manage out in public.

After we finished helping him get ready, getting his shoes on, and his favorite ball cap, I went and pulled the car up to the front entrance. Joe came shuffling out to the car, grabbed the door and held on. I was already standing there, door wide open, ready to receive him. He backed his way into the car seat very slowly, very senior adult like as if he was a hundred years old. Thoughts raced back to the time he wrestled me to the ground to prevent me from getting into his car. It was a different picture now.

We drove east toward the beach. The nearest IHOP was about a mile from the Intracoastal Waterway.

Joe loved steak and eggs. It was one of his favorite meals. He loved to cook in his younger days, often cooking wonderful food like steak and seafood. The guy loved seafood. I could care less about seafood and would go out of my way to avoid anything even remotely fishy.

IHOP had a decent steak and eggs breakfast I thought he would enjoy. I have to admit, having dentures didn't make chewing steak easy, and he would have to consider that now. But could he fully grasp the dilemma of chewing steak while under the influence of the morning regimen? I guess we'd see.

The waitress approached our table, and she could tell by looking at him something wasn't right with this guy. He looked old and frail. His face was drawn and thin. His facial features were starting to sink in, and she could tell he was on something.

She didn't know his story, but I would guess she imagined all kinds of scenarios other than medical illness. You never know what you'll see in an IHOP restaurant from day to day. This day may have been different from other days, then again maybe not. Today a healthy looking female with a young girl was dining with a very sickly looking man who looked much older than her.

"What can I get you dear?" the waitress asked.

Joe stared off into the distance watching the cars drive back and forth.

"Joe, the waitress wants to know what you want to eat. Do you want eggs?"

As he fumbled with the menu, he answered,

"Yes - Yes - two eggs, um - over easy – and - steak. I want steak. Potatoes and toast."

Joe had to have toast with his runny eggs. He loved dipping the toast into the runny yokes. I, on the other hand, find it disgusting. I can't stomach runny yoke. But to each his own.

"Ma'am, for you?"

"I'll have two eggs scrambled, hash browns, bacon and rye toast please. My daughter will have the pancakes."

She finished taking our orders and walked to the kitchen out of sight.

We sat in silence for a good bit as he tried to focus on his surroundings. The nursing home had given him his medications, and he was somewhat zoned out. I was ok with it. I felt more confident that Joe wouldn't try and make a run for it. At the same time though, it was like managing a little old man.

As we sat at the table, we watched his every move. His eyes were trying to focus, but they looked like he was in a fog trying to see clearly. His mouth hung open slightly, lips very dry and cracked. Joe always struggled with thrush in his mouth. Thrush made it very difficult to eat and drink. It was just inconvenient, painful, and embarrassing. For the first time in years, we were sitting down to eat a meal together. There weren't a lot of words said. We just enjoyed our time together.

"Eggs and steak for you sir," she said, as she placed his food in front of him.

"Ma'am, your eggs and bacon. Sweetie, here's

your pancakes. Can I get you anything else to eat? Hun, would you like more coffee?"

"Yes," as Joe stared down at his plate.

She topped off his coffee cup which didn't take much.

I learned that day when someone is on medication like Joe; eating can be a very challenging task. He was struggling to eat. The fork full of food wasn't reaching the proper destination. He was trying to dip his toast in the runny eggs and get it to his mouth, but he wasn't very successful there either.

"Joe…hey, um, wipe your face. You have food on your chin."

Slowly, the napkin made its way to his chin, wiping ever so gently, barely touching.

He ate a few more bites and then gave up. Joe was finished. He was full already. He played with the steak on his plate, the fork moving it around in no particular pattern. It was like watching a snail move across concrete. He never enjoyed his favorite meal as the food sat there and got cold.

He wasn't the same Joe who'd dive into the plate of food and polish it off within minutes. His favorite meal didn't satisfy him anymore. The sad reality was obvious in his appetite too. The diseases now claimed his love for his favorite foods.

As we finished our meal, he sat there pretty quiet. He moved his spoon in the coffee cup a bit.

Occasionally he would mouth a few words which I couldn't understand. I just nodded in agreement.

We sat in the cold booth staring at each other.

I was looking at a young man who had drastically changed from the man always on the run. His face was tattered; gray hair had moved in overtaking his beautiful red hair. Joe always had red hair. I used to call him carrot top. He never lost his carrot top red hair when he became an adult until now. It was slowing turning gray. My red hair faded naturally.

It was weird as I watched him look at me because I was very aware of my surroundings, but I wasn't too convinced he was. I imagined he could only see me through fogged glasses that probably showed six of me instead of one. The ability to focus on his surroundings and me at the same time were difficult at best.

Medicine does that to some people. One day you're with your loved one at IHOP, remembering all the times you laughed and joked and the next you're staring at each other, searching for words. We didn't have many moments together as adults, but as kids, there were plenty of times we played together and fought. And as you sit across each other now in silence, you wonder if they still remember any of those times. It wasn't likely today.

After a while, I motioned to the waitress for our check. She gave me my change, and we got ready to leave. As he did when he walked in, he shuffled his way back to the car. Coffee hadn't made any difference in his steps. He did well in the restaurant. We made it through lunch without any mishaps or accidents.

That was our last meal together. It was the last time I enjoyed time with my brother outside a medical facility. It was the last time I got to treat him to his favorite meal. Thoughts swirled in my head at the rapid progression of his condition. Enjoying his favorite food was over for him. It was a new harsh reality.

We headed west, not bothering to drive over to the beach even though we were close. It was getting close to one o'clock, and I didn't want Joe to be late.

We drove in silence, radio playing softly in the background, neither saying a word. My daughter stared out the back seat window.

When we arrived back at the nursing home, we helped get him settled back in his room. I advised the nurse on duty he had returned and brought her up to speed on what he had eaten. I went back to his room, hugged him gingerly, and said goodbye and left. When I walked out the door, tears streamed down my face. I wasn't sure I would ever see him again.

The trip back to Orlando was long as a thousand thoughts raced through my mind. And there were no good answers to any of them. Music played in the background as my daughter slept in the rear seat. But the only thing I could hear was road noise.

CHAPTER SIXTEEN

The Water Is Getting Deeper

August 25, 2009 1:20 pm– Missed the DDT in the morning. I forgot to set my alarm clock which is a rarity for me. Instead, I used my lunch hour as my quiet time and went to a little park tucked nicely behind a small neighborhood to study God's Word and pray. I thought about lots of different things and reflected on what life was like before I was on fire for God. I often think and wonder where people are in their walks and prayer life. I'm sure some would say there's room for improvement as do I. I'm still struggling to find an accountability partner locally and spent time going through the list. I asked God to bring someone to light. He is faithful. I need to trust.

Work was always busy, and these days I wasn't complaining. After all, keeping busy for me was a necessity when walking this difficult road. I wondered throughout the day what Joe was doing. *Was he shuffling through the halls? Was he lying in bed staring at a television? The ceiling? Out the window? Was he behaving himself?*

August 26, 2009 1:00 pm- I prayed yesterday for God to show me a direction for my accountability partner. I had put the prayer request out there to a few people in my inner circle. Two got back to me with the same response – ask someone from your class. It wasn't quite the response I was hoping for, but I understood their reasoning behind it. Now I just need to know who. This morning in my prayer time, I offered up many thanks for all God has done in and through my life. I also prayed for my Sunday school class and sent out an email to all of them regarding the lesson for the upcoming weekend. I was prompted to include others as well who don't currently attend Sunday school at this time. I prayed for them as well. This morning in my reading of Hebrews 2-4 ending with Chapter 4; 14-16, it says we do have a great high priest who sympathizes with our weaknesses, has been tempted in every way and yet was without sin. We can approach the throne of grace with confidence so that we can receive mercy and find grace to help us in our time of need. How reassuring is that for me and can be for others who are struggling. God is good all the time. I had a good visit with my best friend yesterday evening and her family. May God cure her of sickness and make her well again.

August 27, 2009 – Spent time this morning in Hebrews again. The verse that spoke most to me was Jesus, our high priest. He is our intercessor, bringing prayers to our heavenly Father. To picture Him on His knees pleading for me, I'm not worthy of love like that. Praised God for sending a Son such as that, for sacrificing for the sake of His people. Tomorrow is a funeral of a friend, who meant a lot to so many people. If I speak, I pray God will give me the words, so I can bring glory to Him and not myself and maybe someone will accept Christ tomorrow at her service.

August 29, 2009 7:00 am – I've been up since six talking to God about everything that happened yesterday. My friend's funeral brought out so many people I haven't seen or spoken to in years. There were two sides, men who had made choices to fight each other, and standing with them were those who chose their side. It's a long story, and maybe someday I'll tell it, but for now, I'm glad I determined not to choose either side, instead choosing to extend love to all. I watched people cross over and comfort each other. After all, we were all just pawns and victims in a bigger battle of what appeared to be greed and vengeance between three partners. God help each of those men rid themselves of the bitterness they feel toward each other. Lord, this morning in Hebrews 9:14, it says, "How much more then, will the blood of Christ, who through the eternal Spirit offered himself unblemished to God, cleanse over consciences from acts that lead to death, so that we may serve the living God!" How appropriate for yesterday. Lord, there are so many people who are hurting, so many people lost. Help me to be nonjudgmental as to where they are in their relationship with you. I lift up my brothers and sisters to you, those that chase you and those running the other way. Father God, I love you with an everlasting love, and I am so grateful you love me.

Facebook post dated August 30, 2009:

I wouldn't mind having a Flintstone car so all the water coming into my car from the A/C near the firewall could just run out onto the ground instead of settling under my feet only to stink up the car and create mildew. I also wouldn't mind if the thermostat housing didn't leak radiator fluid all over my garage floor. These two things would be nice right now. Challenges, challenges, but I will prevail. Might be some big bucks, but I will prevail.

College for me continued, and I found the strength and the time to complete the assignments and reading. But now I would have to implement a new way to do my devotional time with God. The teacher asked us to get more specific. And he didn't want us using a journal with pre-printed Bible verses. He asked us to set up our journals to include the following elements:

General Reflection

Needs

Insight

Reaction

Memory Verse

Prayer Requests

Praises

Are you kidding me was my first reaction, admittedly not a pleasant one.

Get more specific in my devo time?

I already started recording all my thoughts in a journal with pre-printed Bible passages. Why was it a problem? It was working well for me. What would I gain from the new format besides having to write more?

Begrudgingly, I started using a Mead college-ruled notebook for my journaling. Surely God had hidden something special inside this new method of journaling He wanted me to find. He wanted me to go deeper in my devotional time. I had barely scratched the surface, but it was time to go deeper. It was time to evaluate the Scriptures and my time with God more deeply. So with pencil and my new Mead notebook in hand, I began.

August 31, 2009 6:05 am

General reflection

Today starts a new way of journaling in a new book. I had been journaling for the past week in a book that had pre-printed Bible passages on it and had been doing my own format. Now I have to add all these elements, and I'm not sure how that will go. Hoping God will speak to me in some way today, as I enjoy it.

Text for today – Hebrews 9

Needs – Repair on car that is cheap and easy; me to grow as a Sunday school teacher

Insight – Show me my weaknesses so that I can strengthen them

Reaction - That I may be obedient

Memory verse – John 14:21

Facebook post dated August 31, 2009:

I just can't say what's on my mind right now. There isn't enough room. I just don't understand why some things have to be the way they are. I thought water in the car and a leaking radiator was bad enough this weekend. Today was even worse. Please pray for me as I am just overwhelmed.

September 1, 2009 5:30am

How awesome is your name O Lord in all the earth and heaven! I'm not worthy of your love, but you love me anyway!

General Reflection

Been up since 4:30, on my knees weeping and confessing to God all my fears, my frustrations, my grief over my brother and mother, my job, my broken car, and the people in my Sunday school class. Confessing all my sins and weaknesses and praying for wisdom to get through this very difficult time when I feel so overwhelmed by it all. I haven't been on my knees for prayer in a long time. I picked up the survival book from class only to flip to the page that has eight verses, every one addressing my very prayers and petitions this morning.

Psalm 119:11; Romans 12:4-5; Galatians 5:16, 22; Philippians 1:6; 1 Corinthians 2:14; 2 Timothy 3:16; Philippians 4:6; Matthew 28:18-20

All of these REASSURANCES FOR ME TO

KEEP MOVING FORWARD. Reminders that God is in control and knows what's going on and that I am to remain faithful and keep going, keep doing what He wants, what He has started, that He is there and will be there. The Lord has taken such great care of my daughter and me all these years, day after day, providing for both of us faithfully. I am so grateful. I know I must persevere.

Text I'm in – Hebrews 10

I expressed my needs to God this morning. I told God I couldn't live and do this life without Him. I don't know how people do it without Christ as their rock. I need Christ as my base. Hebrews 10 gave me such a reminder as well this morning in verses 35-36. **Do not throw away your confidence, persevere and do what God wants for its coming. Do not shrink back or you will be destroyed.**

I can keep going. I can do all things through Christ who strengthens me. Thank you, Jesus, thank you. This morning was filled with God's reassurances to my petitions this morning. He gave me the strength to keep going.

My memory verse as well this morning: Psalm 1:2-3 "But his delight is in the law of the Lord, and on his law, he meditates day and night. He is like a tree planted by streams of water, which yields its fruit in season and whose leaf does not wither. Whatever he does prospers."

Psalm 51:16-17 – "You do not delight in sacrifice, or I would bring it. You do not take pleasure in burnt offerings. The sacrifices of God are a broken spirit; a broken and contrite heart, O God you will not despise."

"He is jealous for me
Loves like a hurricane
I am a tree
Bending beneath the weight of His wind
and mercy
When all of a sudden
I am unaware of these
Afflictions eclipsed by glory
And I realize just how beautiful you are and
How great your affections are for me

And Oh, How He loves us so

Oh, How He loves us

How He loves us so."

"How He Loves" (originally by John Mark McMillan)

Facebook post dated September 1, 2009:

God is GREAT! He met me this morning and stayed with me all day long. What a God I serve!!!! Prayer is a very powerful tool you all, keep it up. It isn't all over yet, but boy I feel strengthened for another day! I just love you guys!!!

"We are His portion and

He is our prize

Drawn to redemption by the grace in His eyes,

If grace is an ocean we're all sinking

So heaven meets earth like an unforeseen kiss

And my heart turns violently inside of my chest,

I don't have time to maintain these regrets

When I think about the way

He loves us so

Oh, How He loves us

How He loves us so."

"How He Loves" (Originally by John Mark McMillan)

September 2, 2009 6:00 am – Faith, Faith, and more Faith

O Lord, I just keep going over yesterday in my mind and my heart. The ways you moved at my job and how you provided regarding my broken car. These things have been weighing on mind among everything else. I was so blown away by you yesterday. You made yourself known to me, you showed yourself, and I felt your presence all day long. You answered so many of my prayers yesterday. You worked out so many things that had been weighing heavy on my mind. I'm just so amazed and humbled, thankful Lord, that you love me, forgave me, made yourself known. O God, words just aren't enough for you, they just aren't. Then this morning I open the text, and it's all about faith. Lord, if I didn't have any faith yesterday morning, I surely have it today after yesterday's events. Lord, I long for more days like that. I long to have my faith strengthened in you.

Text - Hebrews 11 – By faith

Lord continue to work in my life, strengthen my

faith and the faith of those I love. I saw you Lord, and it was glorious and surreal. I want to shout it from the rooftops and tell everyone. Praise your Holy name. Praise you for all your attributes. So thankful you are a loving, compassionate God, slow to anger, quick to love. Thank you for all the faith of just people who helped us get where we are today. Thank you for their sacrifice and their faith. Thank you, God, for creation as the text points out yet again. Lord God I confess to you again my sins of which you already know. Help me to be a better child of God, a better mother, daughter, worker, friend, teacher, person, student, sister. Father God I'm a sinner, and I ask again for your cleansing blood and power to wash over me anew. I can't do this life without you Lord, and I feel sorry for those who don't know that faith or knowledge. Blessed assurance is mine.

Memory verse – Psalm 1:2-3; Psalm 51:16-17

September 3, 2009 5:30am

I awoke this morning to the dog wanting out which ended up being my alarm clock to get me up and meet with the Lord. This morning I felt moved to pray for three specific requests (people). Lord God, the sin, guilt, bitterness, and pain that entangles each one of them, entraps them and forbids them from being free, from being able to live a life that would glorify you, Lord. The hurts and their pride keep them from you. I've prayed Lord you would release them from the bondage of sin so they can experience true joy in you, my Savior.

The text I'm in this morning is Hebrews 11 and how appropriate for it to address your discipline and our sins that keep us from you.

Needs – Watch over my finances, continue to provide, be a better parent, teacher, student; my sinful desires that hinder your wisdom

Insights – I recognize that I am weak in several areas

Reaction – My desire to improve and grow

Prayer – You are our Father, who loves and disciplines us for which I am glad. Your creations are magnificent. You are Holy. You are Holy, Hallelujah to you. I can't live without you. I recognize my sin in me and long to correct it. At first, I was hesitant to go through this process, but almost immediately I am so surprised and moved by its effect and presence in my life, unlike anything I have ever known. It can only have come from you, Lord. Forgive me Lord for past feelings of resentment toward members who are older and in charge.

Memory verse - Psalm 1:2-3; Psalm 51:16-17 with which I'm struggling so

Thank you, Lord, for our time this morning. It means so much to me you love me for me, and I rejoice that you will complete your work in me some day. Amen.

Facebook post dated September 3, 2009:

I got a call from Hospice today. Joe's weight is now down to 115 lbs, and he isn't getting up out of bed as often. It would appear we are starting to see a turn. Please continue to pray for our family, especially our mother. I thank you all for the prayers and support. God bless you.

September 4, 2009, 4:50 am – Need strength

Yesterday I received a call from the hospice nurse on my brother's condition. He now weighs 115 pounds. He isn't up and walking around as much. She told me that I should get down there as soon as I was able. I sent word to my other brother that I would be going down Sunday after church. As I sit here this morning, he is the only person that comes to mind for prayer beside myself. I haven't been in a situation like this with a family member in twenty years. The relationship with my mother is strained at best right now, so that adds another element. I just keep praying God you would take him in his sleep quietly, so I don't have to face all the emotion and watch her break down. Only God knows. I keep thinking back to when we first found out back in May and I kept hearing a still small voice tell me September was the month. Well, here we are, and he is fading, and his 40th birthday is only 13 days away. Only God knows when He will pull him from this earth. If he does pass away this month, I will be so honored and blessed, even more, to know and confirm that you sent your Holy Spirit to speak to me and give me that message and to confirm for me even more what I already knew and felt all along. You are real; you are in control. You do make yourself present, and you do love us, your children with an everlasting love. As the text in Hebrews Chapter 13, verse 5 and 6 says to me this morning – "Never will I leave you or forsake you."

O God what a promise for me this morning.

Text I'm in – Hebrews 13 – Final chapter of Hebrews

Needs – Strength, compassion, abilities to keep it together

Insight - I know I am strong. However, I am weak and still need you

Reaction – I have read in your Word this morning about your love, and how you will never leave me, you will never forsake me. Hebrews 13:6 says, "So we say with confidence, "the Lord is my helper. I will not be afraid. What can man do to me?" How appropriate for this whole thing. Verse 21 says, "Equip you with everything good for doing his will and may he work in us what is pleasing to him, through Jesus Christ, to whom be glory forever and ever. Amen."

Prayer – May you strengthen all of us for the task ahead. O God, I will continue to praise your Holy name.

Memory verse still - Psalm 1:2-3; Psalm 51:16-17

Facebook post dated September 4, 2009:

Today, Joe didn't know where he was at all, and I could barely hold a conversation with him over the phone. He just kept saying yeah – yeah – yeah – yeah -totally lost. Quite sad considering that odd little laugh he has wasn't there at all today. Hospice says he is still taking food by mouth, but not much. He got my note today and ripped it open, so that was encouraging. I am seeing him Sunday. Don't know what I'll find.

September 5, 2009 – Perseverance
My God, my God, how I have seen and heard

from you all week, even this morning. In so many things this week, you have made yourself known and answered prayers for me. You have been working on this stuff with mom and Joe. When I think back to three months ago, you were working then and had continued. You have helped heal some relationships, test others and make known some that needed some real work. All along you have been with me, teaching me how to handle this, and what to do. I have never been in this position. I have always watched from afar. Your Word to me this morning just goes right along with this past week, these past months. James 1:2, "Consider it pure joy, my brothers, whenever you face trials of many kinds because you know that the testing of your faith develops perseverance. Perseverance must finish its work so that you may be mature and complete, not lacking anything. James 1:12, "Blessed is the man who perseveres under trial because when he has stood the test, he will receive the crown of life that God has promised to those who love him." This situation with Joe takes perseverance to deal with his sickness, but more so to deal with a mother who is falling apart. Tomorrow will be difficult at best seeing Joey and his deterioration and seeing my mother in her emotional state, of which I'm not as tender-hearted as I should be.

The text I'm in – James 1 – Just fascinating that it continues to speak to me about these difficult times I'm going through right now.

Needs – Wisdom, be more sympathetic, stronger

Insight – God is still here with me making His presence known

Reaction – I couldn't be more honored and

pleased that God is here and cares for me, a sinner every day of my life. God's grace abounds in and around my life.

Thank you God for your grace, mercy, peace, forgiveness, and sending your Son to save us. Lord, please don't leave me alone. Please help me to be a better person and servant of yours.

Memory verse – Psalm 1:2-3; Psalm 51:16-17

O God, I stumble on these, help me to retain them to memory.

Facebook post dated September 6, 2009:

Have seen my brother Joe. Skin and bones, very different from June. Not keeping a thing down, fluid or food. Can hold some conversations, but doesn't seem to be as aware as he has been. Mother very upset over his condition. Not at all what she expected to see. Supposed to meet with hospice and nursing home staff Tuesday to all get on the same page. Holiday weekend, no one working. Thanks for prayers.

On the advice of the hospice nurse, we all gathered in West Palm Beach to see Joe in the nursing home Labor Day weekend. We knew the news wasn't good. When hospice calls and suggests you might want to come down, you know in your heart, the time is getting closer. The hospice folks are wonderful, caring people who are so compassionate and kind to the sick and dying. They treat them with dignity, and they know the signs of progression and active dying.

Joe was cared for by the traveling hospice unit in Palm Beach County. They service various nursing homes. It's when you go to an actual hospice facility that they care for your needs twenty-four seven until you pass away or go home. Most people don't come out of hospice alive.

When we arrived at the nursing home and walked into Joe's room, the sight was unbelievable. Joe lay on his bed, head slightly elevated, staring at the television on the wall - vomit covered the floor near his bed. He had missed the trash can multiple times. The smell was horrendous.

We knew something was terribly wrong. Why were Joe's surroundings so disgusting? Why hadn't anyone been in to see this and clean it up? When did he eat last? When did he have something to drink? What in the world is going on here?

No one was looking after him. He uttered softly he had been sick a few days. Granted it was Labor Day weekend, but surely the staff from the nursing home would still make their rounds. At the very least the traveling hospice nurse should have been in some time over the weekend. I had just spoken to her over the phone a few days before coming down. Where is my brother's care? What's happening to my brother? Questions. We had a bunch of questions.

We couldn't stay in the room with him. The room was so gross. It was also dangerous to be in there, wet floor, germs galore. There's no other way to say it except to say - it was horrible, and we were very upset! I thought to myself - *if we hadn't come down when we did, would he have made it through the holiday weekend? When was someone going to see him?*

The staff was very apologetic, but it wasn't going to answer the questions we had or dismiss what we had seen. They sent a maid to his room to clean it up. She wiped everything down and mopped the floors. We stood out in the hall and waited.

While we waited, we did the only thing we could do at the moment. We pitched a fit and asked to speak to the director of the nursing home. We wanted answers. We needed answers. Since I was technically Joe's health surrogate, I asked to speak to the nursing home supervisor. I also asked to speak to the hospice nurse on duty. Neither of them were there because it was a holiday weekend.

By the grace of God, we did get a very nice woman who managed the place on weekends, including holiday weekends. She felt horrible for what happened and offered to help. They got everything cleaned up, checked Joe out, cleaned him up and helped him get comfortable.

Then another thought occurred to me - *Did Joe wonder why we were all there at the same time to see him? Did he realize he was dying? Did he grasp the concept that he was losing the fight?*

He had been engaged in a very long battle and more and more, the end of the battle was coming to an end. He had put up a good fight, but he was noticeably losing ground.

They scheduled our meeting for Tuesday morning. We would meet with both parties and get to the bottom of this fiasco.

Facebook post dated September 7, 2009:

I saw Joe today. He weighed again this morning at 111 lbs. And he was wearing clothes and shoes. So you can figure from there what he is now. He is with it today, alert, and still telling stories of old. Went to Walmart and bought him small sweatpants. Pray for tomorrow as mom and I meet with the staff from the nursing home. She has a list started.

The nursing home determined he couldn't stay there anymore. His condition had worsened, and he needed constant care. Joe needed more care than the nursing home could give him. *Um hello, you weren't giving him any care, but ok. We get it.*

We contacted the hospice nurse, and she arranged for Joe to be transported to the hospice facility located roughly twenty minutes away. Transport eventually arrived, wheeled him out on a stretcher, and drove him across town.

Facebook post dated September 7, 2009:

Joe has been transferred to Gerstenburg Hospice facility to be monitored 24 hours a day, to be given all his meds by IV, and hopefully get his vomiting under control. He has not stopped that all day. Every sip comes right back up. He is dehydrated and weak, but he is aware. They say this is a short term visit and then back to the nursing home. We'll see what happens.

The hospice facility was beautiful and comfortable. What can you say about a hospice facility? When we arrived, it felt like a small, fancy hotel.

Carpeted floors offset tile in the rooms, beautiful pictures lined the walls, and vases full of flowers adorned the tables. The seating areas had a couch and love seat for family gatherings and a big screen television. Joe's room was very nice and clean. It was probably the nicest room Joe ever occupied.

They wheeled him into his room, transferred him to the hospice bed and checked all his vitals and got an initial report on him.

When they finished, I remember Joe finding the strength to make his way to the patio area outside to smoke a cigarette. I believe it was the last one he ever smoked. As he puffed on his cigarette, did he look around and take notice where he was? Did he comprehend he was now in a hospice facility or did he think we transferred him to a nicer nursing home? What thoughts were going through his mind, if any, as he watched the wind carry away the gray smoke before his face?

He only smoked half of the cigarette and put it out. Smoking half the cigarette and saving the rest for later had become the newest habit. It was a great way to conserve his limited supply. Joe shuffled back inside and made his way to his room.

Minutes turn to hours as you sit there, looking around, looking at each other, watching the nursing staff and in many cases just sitting in your loved one's room watching every breath. You find yourself watching their every move. You listen for every sound they make. Oh, the first twenty-four hours seem like an eternity. Everything and everyone are new, and you assume you won't be staying for long. Don't get to know the others well because they won't be around for long. Don't get too close with other families because they'll be grieving the loss of their loved ones, leaving, and never returning to see how you're doing.

You find yourself pacing, checking out the other rooms, and occasionally talking with someone else who's there for their loved one. You find yourself looking into the other rooms to see who's lying in bed. Are they older? Are there any Joe's age? How much time do they have left? Do they have any family with them? What's their story? How did they get there?

Sadly, some hospice patients don't have any family with them as they live out their final days. Alone, their final moment comes and goes. Not a tear shed, not a song sung, not even a whisper – nothing but silence. The only person overseeing them is the nurse on duty. What goes through the nurse's mind as they care for those who die alone?

I saw several rooms occupied when we first arrived. By the time we left several days later, I had seen at least six rooms change occupants. I witnessed one woman all alone in her room. She was in her final moments on this earth, and the hospice nurse came in and held the phone up to her ear so her family member on the other end of the phone line could say one last goodbye. As the person on the end of the phone said their goodbyes, the nurse put the phone to her mouth and advised the family member their loved one had just passed. She extended her condolences and then I heard her say, "Will you be calling the funeral home to come get them or should I?"

I watched as the nurse put the phone down. She

tenderly did a few things to the deceased woman and exited the room, shutting the big, heavy white door behind her.

I got familiar with the routine pretty quickly. When the doors shut, it meant the transport was on their way to get the body. It's such a cold feeling as you watch the door close. I can say, however, I never once saw transport take someone out. It was as if they came in the through the back even though there was no back way. One moment they were there, the next moment they were gone.

Tuesday morning came, and we anxiously waited to hear from the nursing home supervisor. We arrived at the nursing home for our meeting with the director as well as the hospice representative of the traveling hospice unit. By now Joe was comfortable in the hospice facility and being looked after consistently.

We didn't have to wait long before they called us into the meeting. The staff led us to the big conference room at the end of the hall. We made our way around a big table with several chairs and sat down. The room was a bit tense; no one knew the direction the meeting would take. The goal was to get answers to our questions. We weren't interested in hearing excuses. We wanted to understand what had happened. Why had Joe appeared to have been left untreated for days?

The nursing home supervisor asked me to explain to the others at the table what we found when we arrived a few days earlier. We told them everything - Joe's condition, the vomit all over the floor and what appeared to be a lack of care. Both women were at a loss as to what happened. They couldn't believe the scene we described. Surely something was amiss. As the conversations continued, it became more and more apparent to us there had been a huge disconnect between the two entities. That's when we realized communication between the two entities was severely lacking, and my brother had suffered because of their failure to communicate with each other.

Both parties thought the other was in charge of Joe's case and treatment. Since they both thought that was the case, neither was caring for my brother. It was so upsetting, and we asked how long this had been going on. Neither had an answer to the question. When did the plan change? As far as I knew, it hadn't, and that was the confusing part.

My next statement to both sides was, "If this is happening to my brother, how many more people in this nursing home are experiencing the same lack of treatment? How many other people are you all confused about? How many are not receiving adequate care right now, today, if any at all? One, five, ten, twenty? Do you even know? The situation needs your immediate attention now!"

You could have heard a pin drop.

"I suggest you all figure it out quickly. The lack of care is completely unacceptable."

The room was still quiet. No one moved paper or pen.

No one could tell us how long this had been going on. The rep from hospice could only tell us what hospice had records of, which was about as much as I already knew from talking with the hospice nurse over the phone a few days before we arrived. But she never mentioned it appeared Joe wasn't being cared for by the nursing home staff when she was there.

It had to be a more recent development because I had just been there not too long before that when I took him to IHOP. Did I miss something the last time I was there? I didn't think I had because Joe had been out in the hallway with the others. The lack of care appeared to be more so in the last few weeks when things starting falling apart and communication started breaking down between the two entities.

If for no other reason to be there that particular weekend, we may have helped someone else who hadn't been receiving any care because of the confusion.

When a family member is in a nursing home, it is vitally important you stay in contact with them and their nurse, stay connected and be sure your family member is receiving the proper care at all times. It's important that you randomly check in on them, perhaps do a surprise visit to be sure they aren't lying there in a pool of vomit or feces. My brother was so sick, he wasn't able to clean up after himself. I felt bad for Joe's roommate. He didn't know any better either. He didn't know enough to say something to someone about the condition of his room or roommate. When I think about it now, I didn't see the guy there.

Facebook post dated September 8, 2009:

Back home from a long three days. Feel better

though knowing Joe is now in a very nice hospice facility. Hospice doctor says he needs to evaluate him for the next few days to determine which way this is going to go. Joe has nine more days till he turns 40. All he wants to do is turn 40. That's the goal.

Facebook post dated September 9, 2009:

Well, today was a good day for Joe. He has his color back, kept down apple sauce and Gatorade. Still couldn't get a real IV in his arms or hands. As far as the doctor can tell, he doesn't think he has a blockage in the intestine. We'll see what tomorrow brings. Thanks for all the prayers, I feel them for sure. Eight more days till he turns 40.

Facebook post dated September 9, 2009:

Yeah, Joe just called me. It's 10:30pm. He says, "Net, I'm hungry as heck. Where's mom? I want food." I said, "Well that's a good thing, but call the nurse, that's why they are there. Mom's asleep, she will see you tomorrow." He hung up.

Facebook post dated September 10, 2009:

Just got a call from mom. It appears yesterday was a rally day for Joe. Today he's been out of it, moaning from pain, back to vomiting and not eating. Dr. has increased the meds and cautioned this could be it. Breathing is changing slightly. Please pray for my mother who is there, give her strength God to see this through.

Facebook post dated September 10, 2009:

Thanks. I knew I could count on you all to pray for us. I remembered the last time I saw Joe. We were in the hospice room alone the other day, and he took my hand, kissed it gently and said goodbye. Then he smiled at me. I'm glad I got to share these last several months with him. I'm just sorry he spent so much of it alone and that I couldn't do more for him than I did. May he go to Jesus peacefully and may Jesus take his hand ever so gently the way Joe took mine the other day. I'll be happy when his suffering is over. O God, please forgive him, I pray on his behalf. I look to you Lord for the comfort only you can provide.

September 10, 2009 9:30pm

Been five days since I journaled. Have had plenty of conversations and prayers with and to God, especially over Joe. Went down to see him this past Sunday and spent two whole days trying to spend some quality time with him and tend to his needs in hospice. God made some special people caretakers and such, something I could not fully do. Despite the challenges of the nursing home with Joe's care, I walked away knowing he had made friends there as well. They didn't get to say goodbye to him either, as he was whisked away on the transport gurney. I saw God working through and around us the whole weekend. Mom finally forgave my ex-sister-in-law after ten years. For the first time in ten years, all of us except Joe had dinner together. We all pulled together for Joe's sake. It has been a rough road to get to this place, but it would appear we made it. The hospice doctor who took his case

*has been great to mom and the rest of the family.
After several days of Joe struggling, he finally had
his rally day yesterday and enjoyed some liquids, light
foods, and conversation with mom. He was acting
more like himself. However, today it all changed,
and he's beginning to lose the battle. O God, I
just keep praying for peace. I just keep praying
for forgiveness on his behalf, as most of his life
he was tormented with evil, suicidal thoughts, and
poor choices. It's so sad that he was never able to get
on the right track and become the doctor he was so
capable of being.*

*Joe was such an intelligent man. I know I'm
writing in the past tense now, but the guy I knew
is already gone. All that lay there now is a shell of
what remains waiting to go home. O God, please
end the suffering for him and my mother. God, I
thank you for my life, and I thank you for Joe and
who he was to me.*

*Text for tonight was James 2 – Favoritism,
Forbidden and faith and deeds*

*For the first time since starting this journaling,
the text didn't jump out at me. I always remember
Joe saying how proud he was of me and how well
he thought of Nicole and the job I've done raising
her. He's always told me that for as long as I can
remember. I'm so glad I spent the last several
months trying to keep our relationship upbeat,
real and loving. I tried to show him Jesus in me. I
tried my best to do as best I could for him. I'm just
sorry there were times I was impatient with him.
I'm just sorry he was scared and alone, no one to be
with him and provide comfort all those lonely years.
He fought so hard, and he beat AIDS of 20 years,*

but the cancer is what will beat him in the end. A dear friend of mine sent me a verse tonight –

Psalm 55:22, "Cast your cares on the Lord, and he will sustain you; he will never let the righteous fall."

I was reminded again of when I said goodbye to Joe Tuesday when we were alone in the room. He grabbed my hand and kissed it ever so gently and gave me a smile. I knew that would be the last real communication between us. Lord grab his hand I pray and kiss it gently.

Oh please, God give me the strength and wisdom to get through the next several days and whatever they bring. Please forgive me my thoughts, words, and actions that have been unpleasing to you. Amen.

September 11, 2009 – 6:00am

On my knees this morning, in prayer over Joe again. My God, my God, please forgive him and accept him into your kingdom. I know he believes. Lord, please continue to give my family strength to get through all this. I confessed to the Lord my uncleanliness with my mouth, my heart, and my mind. I want to be a better servant of the Most High God. There is only one God. That's all there's ever been throughout time and all there will ever be despite the many people who worship other gods today and back then.

The text I read after confessing my sins and praising God was James 3. And just like God on so many occasions before, He gave me some insight into taming my tongue. The other verse He gave me this morning regarding my confessions was verse 2. We all stumble in many ways. It gives me comfort to know I'm not the only one who stumbles and not the only one who can't tame the tongue.

Needs – Wisdom and strength to get through all of this. Help with my finances – an area I am most weak and worried over

Insight – Acknowledged my fears over my finances and Joe's conditions.

Reaction – Why am I worried? God has always taken care of me. Why would I think that would change?

Confessions – My sin

Praise for all the answered prayers I've seen in the past few weeks that have been so clear. Also for reflecting back to the end of June, the first part of July and being told September would be the month Joe's condition and well-being would change. God spoke so clearly to me about it, but I'm afraid no one will believe me. But I know the truth and what I heard. I believe even more.

Memory verse – I'm finally getting the two verses in Psalms down. These were very hard for me with everything going on. I'm not surprised. Thank you, Lord, for giving me another day to get it right.

Facebook post dated September 11, 2009:

Update on Joe: Hospice doctor was in today. Seeing steady decline, gave Joe about 7 to 10 days tops. As we all know, he was given two months to live back in May and here we are. I'm trusting in God as He knows best and when. We'll just take this thing one day at a time.

Facebook post dated September 12, 2009:

Please pray for me. I am going to retrieve Joe's stuff from the nursing home today, and then I'm going to spend some time with him. Also, pray as my mother has asked me to put something together for his service when the time comes. Seeking direction from the Lord on what to say that will bring the most comfort to all, honor God, and will have made Joe happy. Thanks for the prayers.

I arrived at the nursing home, intending to clean his room out and gather the rest of his personal belongings. Everything happened so quickly the other day; we didn't think about grabbing the rest of his stuff. When I got to his room, many of his things were already gone. It appeared other residents had helped themselves. One of the things remaining, however– his new Bible my cousin had given him. I grabbed it and the few pictures on the cork board. Among the few things also remaining was an envelope with a small card inside which read,

"Dear Joey. Hi! You don't know me, but I am a friend of Jeanette's. I have been praying for you for over a year now. I asked God to shine His light in your life and reach down to hold you in His hands while you have been sick. I asked Him to forgive you for the choices you have made that don't honor Him. He says that when I pray on your behalf, He listens and works in your life for His Glory. I hope you will spend your final days on this earth knowing He made you, He loves you, and if you have truly asked Him into your life, you will live with Him forever in a beautiful place called Heaven. There are no drugs, no addictions, no hurts, no pain, no

sadness, no grief, no one else bossing you around, and no problems there. Only one God to worship, food and luxuries that you have never had and love like you have never felt! Won't it be beautiful then! Much love to you, Michele."

Reading the card brought tears to my eyes. It reminded me that I hadn't been praying alone. I had a bunch of people specifically praying for Joe, and it was such a blessing.

I finished going through all the drawers and the small closet, packed up a couple of clothing items and slowly walked out of Room #203.

There would be no more visits to the nursing home. There would be no more walking the halls and smoking outside. There would be no more accidents or medicines to take.

As I was walking out, a few of the workers who knew Joe stopped me and asked how he was doing. I shook my head, and they knew it wasn't good. They expressed their condolences and were saddened by the news of his decline. He had made friends while he lived there and they thought well of him.

Facebook post dated September 12, 2009:

Got here to the hospice unit and am spending time with Joe. He looks worse than this past Tuesday if that's possible. He is in and out quite a bit. I did manage to get him to smile at me several times and drink some Pepsi. It's those little moments I'm thankful. Appreciate the thoughts and prayers of you all as we go through this. I read to him from Psalms today, and he nodded off. He's peaceful and I'm glad.

Later that day, Joe's friend came by hospice to see Joe. He had been a friend of his for a long time and had put up with a lot. He and Joe ran in the same circles together.

After his visit, I walked him out to his car to thank him and say goodbye. We made small talk for a while. I thanked him for all he had done for my brother. He was a life saver so many times when it came to Joe, and I wanted him to know how much we as a family appreciated all he had done. He was glad to do it and was sad at the same time, knowing this would be the final act for his dear friend.

One question kept stirring in me as I stood there with him – did he know Jesus?

So I asked him if he believed in God.

"Believe in God?" he replied.

"Yes, do you believe in God?"

He shook his head and replied in a flipped fashion, "Your God doesn't love me. Remember, I'm gay. Your God doesn't love gay people."

"What?" Of course, He does," I hastily replied.

"Not according to Romans 1 he doesn't. Remember all gays and lesbians are damned. He doesn't love us, Jeanette. He doesn't love me. How can I believe in a god who doesn't love me?"

It was an uncomfortable silence. Sadly, I didn't have an adequate response at that moment.

A few seconds went by for what seemed like years, and he hugged me and said he would see me again in a few days provided nothing new happened to Joe. I thanked him again for stopping by as he got into his car. He drove away, and we never talked about God again.

As a Christian, how would I reconcile that God didn't love gay people? I didn't believe it then, and I don't believe it now. God loved us so much He sent His Son to die on the cross for me, for you, for all humanity. He didn't put an exception clause in John 3:16.

Homosexuality is a sin like so many other things. I have done so many things in my life I wasn't proud of, sinful things, and yet I could feel God's love for me so powerfully during these last several years, more than I ever had before. I believe it is because I was seeking Him and wanting to grow closer to Him. I had repented of my sins. I had turned away from the old me, and I was being transformed into a new me, into a new creation, more like Christ than ever before. God was transforming me from the inside out, and it was good.

"Therefore if anyone is in Christ, he is a new creation. The old has passed away; behold, the new has come." 2 Corinthians 5:17

"Do not conform to the pattern of this world, but be transformed by the renewing of your mind. Then you will be able to test and approve what God's will is – his good, pleasing and perfect will." Romans 12:2

As a Christian, I am also called to love God and love my neighbor as myself.

> "Jesus replied, "Love the Lord your God with all your heart and with all your soul and with all your mind. This is the first and greatest commandment. And the second is like it; "Love your neighbor as yourself."
> Matthew 22:37-39

God loves you and me. He is the perfect example of how to love people.

Am I completely sin free today? No. Will I ever be while living on this earth? No. When I recognize I messed up, I repent right then. I don't want to wait nor do I need to wait. I have the freedom to bring it to God right then as I pray to Jesus to forgive me of my sins. He is the only way to the Father. When I repent and ask for forgiveness, I am saying to God I will make every effort to not repeat the same sin again.

I continue to strive to live for God while He continues to transform me each and every day. Transformation, I believe doesn't happen overnight. God continues to teach me how to love Him and people every day. I believed God would continue to sharpen me and teach me through the rest of this process with Joe.

CHAPTER SEVENTEEN

He Made It!

Have you ever experienced hemorrhoids? Have you ever experienced the uncomfortable and painful feeling inflamed hemorrhoids can bring?

I learned a few years ago from a dear friend suffering from hemorrhoids; actually, her doctor told me as I quizzed him, that we all have three internal hemorrhoids. That was shocking information to me. I didn't know anything about hemorrhoids or how painful they can be, but let me tell you something; I sure do now.

At the beginning of the week, I had made the trip down to hospice to be with Joe. The end was drawing near. I started feeling sore, but it wasn't a pain I recognized. It also hurt to go to the bathroom. Boy did it hurt!

While spending time at the hospice facility, I had several occasions to go to the bathroom. Due to this new, unusual pain, I was experiencing, I purposefully searched for the furthest bathroom I could find. I found a bathroom on the opposite end of the building. It was somewhat secluded, mainly comprised of offices and storage rooms. I would sit on the toilet in there for at least an hour each time I had to go to the bathroom. I was in so much pain from the hemorrhoids. It turns out they decided to flare up the very week I determined to stay down in West Palm Beach till this was all over. Never in all my life have I had a hemorrhoid flare up. Why of all weeks did they decide to flare up? I just couldn't understand it at first. I had so much to do. I was in and out of Joe's room multiple times each day and they wouldn't improve. I spent the next several days suffering from these blasted hemorrhoids. I spent several hours in the bathroom in excruciating pain - pain no one knew.

My mom and stepdad were there with Joe every day too, and I couldn't let them know, or they'd be asking me about my bottom every hour.

Hemorrhoid flare-ups are embarrassing, to say the least, and very painful, especially when you are trying to do your business. I had to go and buy hemorrhoid cream. I didn't even know where to look for it in the pharmacy. I just knew I needed something to quench what felt like a burning fire.

Here I am, spending my time at the hospice facility with my brother who's in the final days of his life, and I'm held up in my secret bathroom having to self-treat my hemorrhoids. It was awful.

I couldn't believe I was experiencing this. The nights I didn't stay over with Joe, I'd go back to my friend's house to clean up and sleep. I'm sure they wondered why I spent so much time in their bathroom. I had been soaking in a nice soothing, hot bath to help alleviate the pain.

Sadly, nothing was working. Hot baths didn't

work. Hemorrhoid cream didn't work and standing on my feet all day didn't help either. I was in pain, but I couldn't show it to anyone, especially Joe.

What do you say, "My hemorrhoids are flaring up this week." Not me, that was too embarrassing. Besides how insignificant were they compared to Joe's current battle to stay alive?

As I lay there in bed one night, relaxing after a hot soothing bath, all I could think about was the pain I was experiencing. Suddenly a thought occurred to me.

For the past several days, I have been dealing with pain in my bottom from those blasted hemorrhoids. My brother has been dealing with pain in his bottom for many months. Not days. Months.

My eyes welled up with tears as I suddenly discovered a new appreciation for the pain he had been experiencing all these years with no real relief.

Why was I complaining?

I had the better end of the suffering. I knew how I felt, and he must have felt a hundred times worse, and there wasn't anything he could do about it. Of all weeks to get a flare up, the first ever in my life, this was the week chosen for me. I came to appreciate just what my little brother had lived with all this time. If he could go day to day with the constant pain in his bottom from cancer, then I could live with these painful, annoying hemorrhoids for a little while longer.

The hemorrhoid cream did give me some relief, but it didn't get rid of them completely. Let's just say the temperature on that fire had cooled off a bit, but it hadn't gone completely cold. Each day while at the hospice unit, I suffered terribly and no one was the wiser.

There were days my folks would ask me where I'd been for the past hour to which I replied, "Out walking, just getting some fresh air."

They never knew any different. The truth was, I had been sitting on a toilet for the past hour trying to go the bathroom pain-free. Oh, it was horrible.

Facebook post dated September 13, 2009:

Spending the night with Joe tonight so mom can rest. He is peaceful right now, but it's daylight. Heaven only knows what awaits me in the wee hours. That's ok; it's only one night. I can do it. He's worth it. Every now and again, I get a couple of words from him, and today those words were "I love you too," so I'll take that and be blessed.

There they were those three little words, "I love you." Only this time, I wouldn't cringe at the sound of them because I had made every effort to tell Joe I loved him and to hug him whenever I saw him. Jennifer's lesson of so long ago had enabled me to extend love to my brother in a way I hadn't done before. It was because of love, God's love for us, I could get through.

I found myself singing to Joe, *"Yes, Jesus loves me. Yes, Jesus loves me, Yes Jesus loves me, for the Bible tells me so."*

Night time gets a little eerie in a hospice

facility. Everyone is so quiet at night. You can hear a pin drop. I didn't turn on the television in his room, and there was no music. I could barely hear him breathing. It was just Joe and I. The room was cold and dark.

My newest friend from church worked the night shift at the hospital. She worked in ICU, so I spent a lot of time texting her in the middle of the night-while she was monitoring patients.

Ironic isn't it? My new friend from church was the very person who would help guide me in regards to the medical stuff. God knew I needed someone to talk to. She was perfect for this specific time, especially since Joe quit talking. He wasn't say anything anymore. I got tired of listening to myself talk. For all I know, he did too. He probably welcomed the break.

He just stared at the ceiling.

The nurses fixed my pull out bed, and I lay down, hoping to fall asleep quickly, but I had so much on my mind, I texted my friend instead. We went back and forth for a while until I nodded off.

About 12:30 in the morning, I was awakened very abruptly by a loud sound. It scared me to death. Those probably aren't the right words to describe my fear. After all, I was at the hospice facility where death is prominent.

Joe had somehow managed to reach over and slap the handrail to my pull out bed. He smacked it so hard, it woke me up. I jumped up expecting to see a nurse or someone else standing over my bed, but it was just Joe and me in the room. I looked at him, my eyes still trying to focus and he said, "Hey."

Hey. Hey? I rubbed my sleepy eyes and looked at him surprised he had done that. He hadn't moved all day or said a word.

I moved closer to his bedside and got in his line of sight and whispered, "Hey yourself. What's up? Do you need something?"

Silence gripped the room again as he continued to stare at the ceiling. He said nothing.

Confused, I said, "Joe did you want to talk about something?"

Nothing.

I sat back down on my bed, pondering what to say next. Joe woke me up for a reason, and since he wasn't saying what the reason was, I assumed he just wanted company. So I did the only thing I knew to do – talk.

"I remember when we were little Joe, you were so cute. Your red hair and freckles melted everyone's heart. You had that cute little face, and your smile was so contagious. I also remember our little dog, Schwartz. Oh, do you remember Schwartz, our Dachshund? Remember the time Schwartz bit your little butt? Oh, man did you cry as you lay across mom's lap, it was so funny. We laughed as the dog ran around the room, barking with excitement. Oh and how about all the times you used to run around the dining room table trying to get away from me because you did something that made me so mad? Oh, I hated those nights. Mom and dad used to go out, and they left me to watch you boys. You two always misbehaved. You did it on purpose. It used to make me so mad when you guys ran around the table. You were both a bunch of chickens. But I knew you would stop eventually, and I would get you then.

Joe, I remember the drum set the two of you got for Christmas when you were little. It was so noisy, and neither of you knew how to play. You all were so young. You just banged on those drums. The noise was awful, and neither of you ever got good at them. Our uncle thought it was the funniest present ever. Of course, he didn't have to listen to them. I don't know what happened to those drums, but someday I need to repay the favor.

Or how about the time dad drove the two of you to juvie hall and dropped you off on the front steps on a Sunday morning and they were closed? I was so happy you two were gone. Do you remember that? You guys wouldn't clean your room the way they asked you to, so dad threw you two in the car and dropped you off on the front steps of juvie hall. Of course, he went back and picked you up after a while. You guys came home crying and cleaned your room pretty fast. I was so disappointed you were back. I thought I finally had the house to myself. No more walking through my room to get to yours. Do you remember that? I hated the way the house and our rooms were set up."

The early morning minutes ticked by slowly.

"Oh, how about the time you locked your keys in your car at your graduation? That was hilarious! Remember the local newspaper took a picture of you trying to fish the lock open? I was so happy you graduated high school man.

Joe, do you remember all the times we used to play "kill the man with the ball" in the front yard of our house on 179th Street? We ran through three front yards to play ball. We loved all the open space. Then there was the time I beat you up in our front yard, and mom came outside and beat me up with the belt and made me pee myself in front of all my friends as you lay in the grass crying. Remember her taking me inside to beat me more because she thought I was trying to kill you?"

No words. No expressions. No smiles or nods. Joe just stared at the ceiling as I rambled on through the wee hours of the morning. I cried a few times recalling the memories.

Facebook post dated September 14, 2009:

I spent the night with Joe. He did well, but the little turd scared me though when he slapped the rail on my bed and said "Hey." Woke me up, so we lay there looking at the ceiling, me babbling, him nodding off. We are starting to see those signs of things changing colors that aren't pretty. Don't think we're talking about much longer. Thanks for all the prayers, I DO APPRECIATE THEM.

Facebook post dated September 14, 2009:

Mom stayed with Joe tonight. I have a feeling it's going to be a long day tomorrow, so I came home to rest. He is quickly going downhill. Joe has changed so much in the last 12 hours. It's very hard to watch, especially when he doesn't close his eyes to sleep at all. So sad to watch a vibrant person deteriorate so much.

Facebook post dated September 15, 2009:

Well, today started off different than any other day. We watched two from Joe's wing be wheeled out on a stretcher to their final resting place. The nurses asked for prayer as they are very busy today. Joe is still with us, resting, but it won't be long now. God is teaching me something in all this no doubt.

Facebook post dated September 15, 2009:

All three of us are spending the night with Joe. That doesn't mean we know anything is going to happen. It's been quite the roller coaster ride thus far. He's wide awake right now, staring at the ceiling. I'm beginning to think he might have us all fooled.

Facebook post dated September 16, 2009:

Came back to where I've been staying to get some much-needed sleep, refreshed and ready for tonight. Only a few more hours and Joe turns the BIG 40. I don't know of anyone who has celebrated that milestone in this manner do you? God is all around, and I just need to sit back and continue to watch Him work.

It was my turn to stay overnight with him again. Besides, I wanted to. Despite the complexity of the situation and the imminent outcome, I wanted to be there to see him turn 40. I had given this day a lot of thought. There were times I didn't think he would make it. He had progressed downhill so quickly; it was looking less likely he would make it to the day. I determined that in the morning, I would go to the store and get the prettiest bouquet of flowers I could find to celebrate his big day. We were going to celebrate his birthday! It was only a few hours away.

I spent the next several hours walking the halls of the hospice unit. I didn't want to risk falling asleep and missing the big event. I wanted to wish Joe a happy birthday as soon as the clock struck midnight. So I walked the halls of the facility, praying over each room as I walked by quietly. I prayed for the families of the loved ones in the room. I prayed for the nursing staff and the doctors.

As I walked by the nurse's station, I stopped and said hello to one of the night nurses. It had been a very busy day, and she was working on paperwork. We got to talking, and she asked me a few questions and I the same. Come to find out, she had experienced the same thing with her parents in a hospice facility and was so moved by the compassion and care they received; she decided to return in a nursing capacity to give back what she received. It was a pretty cool story. I mentioned to her it was getting close to the time and so we said goodnight. She wished us well.

Facebook post dated September 17, 2009:

It's September 17 at 12:05 am, and Joe made it! I went to his room and woke him up to tell him Happy Birthday! You made it to the big 40 brother! Bittersweet and our God is great. Every once in a while I forget in those difficult times and then I have moments like these that bring you right back to what matters.

After my mini celebration at midnight and wishing Joe a happy birthday, I finally hit the sack. I didn't know what the next 24 hours would bring, but I knew I needed to rest.

I woke up early around 5:30 am. I celebrated Joe still being here this morning for his very special day. He was now 40 years old. He made it! I was tired, but feeling thankful.

The nurses came in early to check Joe and perform their morning rituals.

The room smelled nasty. The stench of death is a smell you don't soon forget. It's a very powerful and unique smell. One thing I learned from all of this is fresh, unbrewed coffee grinds is a wonderful way to combat the stench of bodily decay and excreting fluids.

The odor filled the room, and I couldn't wait to step outside and breathe in some fresh air. The air is pungent when you first wake up in those surroundings. You want to leave the room immediately, but you struggle with a little guilt knowing your loved one is laying there dying, and the only thing you can think of is how bad your loved one is stinking up the room.

The nurses came in and pulled his diaper off, rolled him on his side and cleaned him up. They were very gentle, not wanting to cause him anymore discomfort.

They put a new diaper on him and rolled him back over and made him comfortable.

To help with the nasty odor, they put several coffee filters full of fresh coffee grinds around the room. They placed one in each corner and one directly under Joe's bed. It helped a great deal so I could stay in the room with him.

At 6:30 am, I left and headed to the local grocery store. I was in somewhat of a hurry because I didn't want to leave him alone for long. What if he died while I was gone? I'd feel bad if he died alone.

The grocery store was just opening, and I ran to the florist section of the store. In a colorful vase, sitting on a shelf, I saw beautiful red roses. Normally, I'm too cheap to buy roses for someone, but this was a once in a lifetime purchase. It was my brothers 40th birthday, and we were going to celebrate with the prettiest red roses and a birthday balloon. After all, I knew it would be his last birthday. I knew there was no coming back from this - not this time. Joe managed to escape death so many times before. But this time it was closing in on him at breakneck speed, and there was no escape. Joe wasn't walking out of this facility alive.

The florist was so sweet and understanding when I told her the nature of the occasion. It was very early in the morning, so I was surprised she was even there. She took great care in trimming the thorns from the stems. She put them in a beautiful vase with a pretty ribbon tied in a bow.

I raced back to the hospice facility, roses in hand, hoping Joe was still holding on. He had to. It was his 40th birthday. The celebration was just beginning. His only wish since finding out he had cancer was to make it to his 40th birthday. It's all he wanted, and it was his motivation each day. The guy was determined not to give up, and with God's help, he never did. He fought through each day. He pushed through the pain every day. He may have made it difficult for himself many times, but he always made it through.

He wanted to turn 40, and God had heard his plea and answered his prayer. He was now 40 years old and had lived with HIV/AIDS for twenty years. However, cancer would claim another victim.

I still think about what Joe said to me on one of the last nights he could communicate – "Net, I lived with AIDS my whole life and beat it. And now cancer is going to kill me." He said it with such disgust and anger.

I understood why he felt that way. For years we had watched his health decline, constantly watching his T-cell count, never imagining he would ever get colorectal cancer that would move up his lower body and ultimately be the cause of his death. It's those times in life you shake your head and wonder how it could be. There are times I wonder if he knew it was a possibility and he never said anything.

Lifestyle choices have such a way of turning on you. The choices we make today can have a lasting impact. They can affect our future. They can affect our lives today and every day for the rest of our lives. Joe's one decision to believe another young man when he said "The world doesn't know anything about HIV/AIDS," ultimately cost him his life when he chose to have sex with this man.

One has to wonder what the young man was thinking as he lay there dying from a disease he had laughed off and discounted earlier. One has to wonder how many men he shared his opinions with and how many of them contracted the disease and died shortly thereafter. One has to wonder if he felt any remorse for his recklessness while he was alive.

God knew what was to come. God knew what He was going to teach me. He used Joe's situation to teach me a lot of lessons I didn't know I would learn, valuable lessons I still draw on today.

I remember one other night as Joe lay there still able to speak. He looked at me with tear filled eyes and whispered, "Net, if I could make a different choice, I'd go back to that day over twenty years ago, and I would have never listened to him or believed him when he said AIDS was no big deal. Oh, how my life would have been so different Net, so different." Tears streamed down our cheeks as he spoke those words.

I nodded and said, "I know Joe, I know."

There's a song called, "Dear Younger Me" by the band, Mercy Me. It describes a conversation one has with their self about the younger years. The lyrics start with the singer addressing himself as "Dear Younger Me." It talks about life lessons and the painful memories that still run around inside our heads. The song talks about the choices we make and how they remain. If we knew then what we know now, things may have been different.

The song continues with letting the younger version know they are loved and they have been redeemed by Jesus when He died on the cross for their sins. The younger version of us has been set apart with a new heart and we are free. Every moment, every heartache, and every valley brings us closer to who we are meant to be in Jesus.

But there was nothing I could do about Joe's situation now. It was too late, and we both knew it. Joe couldn't undo the past. He couldn't undo the mistakes. I couldn't fix it for him. I had access to numerous resources, but nothing would fix this now. The air in the room stood still.

Regret hits you in the face sometimes when you aren't looking. Sometimes regret comes knocking as you lay in bed in a cold, sterile room not your own. It isn't home. The familiar scents, the old photos, the dusty tables aren't there.

Regret comes running to the forefront of your mind again. It reminds you of all the dumb decisions you ever made when you thought you knew better than everyone else. It laughs at you as you lay there silently wasting away. Regret knows no boundaries, and it claims its victims every single day. It was claiming another one today.

Later in the morning, my folks showed up to see Joe and wish him a happy birthday. We all knew we were in for a long day, but none of us knew how the day would end. We were just taking it hour by hour as they came, and we were grateful for them. We knew the inevitable was coming, but it was ultimately up to God as He already pre-determined the time. I believed that with all my heart, especially after hearing back in June, "September would be the month for Joe."

Mom and dad came in and wished him happy birthday with a kiss to the forehead. They tried to be as cheery as possible, but I knew the pain of losing a child would devastate her. Dad, my step dad, had only been a part of our immediate family for a few years, so he hadn't experienced everything we had experienced over the years with Joe and his lifestyle and crazy, life threatening choices. He hadn't lived with the years of him running away, living homeless on the streets or stealing from loved ones and friends. He hadn't experienced the same pain we had, but it didn't make him any less compassionate in his interactions with Joe. He was still very kind and very patient with him. Admittedly, he had been more patient with Joe than my father had ever been.

My father had a temper, and his patience with my two brothers diminished and was almost non-existent most times.

For years, I also struggled with an anger issue, but I finally came to the realization it doesn't benefit anyone, not me, not my child, not those I love or anyone else. As I grew in my relationship with Jesus Christ, my anger issues thankfully started to fade away.

Oh sure everyone gets mad or upset now and again when the right buttons get pushed, and my buttons still get pushed from time to time especially by certain people. However, I realized I was going down the wrong road and I had already seen the movie. I knew the ending and it wasn't good.

Get rid of all bitterness, rage, and anger, brawling and slander along with every form of malice."
Ephesians 4:31

Dad has been dead for many years, and it's still a struggle for some of the family. It's been difficult for them to forgive my dad for all the outbursts of anger inflicted on them when I was a child. Ironically, many of those outbursts were Joe's fault.

Joe was crafty. He was a schemer, and he had a knack for making it look like my other brother did it. My other brother took the fall many times for Joe. Joe rarely confessed his deceptions to our dad. He let his brother take the fall and the beatings.

Painful memories can control you long after the perpetrator is gone. Forgiveness is a path to freedom from the control of those painful memories. They do not have to dictate your future. There is freedom in Christ, but you must choose to forgive. You must choose to let the hurtful feelings go so you can experience the freedom from the pain. Not everyone is willing to do that, instead holding onto them as if they are permanently attached. When we choose to hold onto the pain, we choose to be locked up in bondage to the pain. We say to God we don't trust Him with our painful feelings. We don't trust Him to take it for us. We choose to live in shackles instead of living freely.

"Be kind and compassionate to one another, forgiving each other, just as in Christ, God forgave you."
Ephesians 4:32

CHAPTER EIGHTEEN

Happy Birthday

Joe's birthday roses were absolutely beautiful. The light in the room hit the rose petals just right. The room desperately needed color. The gray and earthy colors didn't bring much to the depressing surroundings. The red roses brightened up the room perfectly.

I set them on the table in front of Joe, in his line of sight. There was no movement, no glance, and no turning from side to side. It was a fixed, awkward gaze directly at the flowers. He spoke no words. His face was expressionless. I believe he saw the flowers. I also believe he heard all the staff, family and friends gathered in the room that morning to lovingly sing, "Happy birthday to you. Happy birthday to you. Happy birthday dear Joey, happy birthday to you."

Everyone stared for a moment or two, their faces looking down and sympathetic. Some smiled with small tears running down their faces. Others with their head tilted sideways, gazed at him lovingly.

We breathlessly waited a few moments to see if

Joe would acknowledge our beautiful rendition of happy birthday. Perhaps he would whisper thanks. But nothing. There were no words.

One by one, the staff left the room and returned to their duties. We took our seats after a somewhat awkward moment of staring. It was the first time in a long time we were together to celebrate Joe's birthday and sing. Only it wasn't the ideal birthday party. There was no cake, candles, or gifts. All he received was a vase full of beautiful red roses from the grocery store and a slightly off-key rendition of an old familiar birthday tune.

After a while, I left the room and went to the bathroom. My bottom was still killing me, but I couldn't let on about the pain.

I completed my bathroom routine and headed to the cafeteria. The hospice facility had a decent place to eat. They cooked food to order if you wanted something specific, but most of the time, they prepared it in advance for the day. The workers and visitors could eat there pretty reasonably. It's a very convenient way to eat three meals a day when you are staying on sight. It can get pretty costly going out for fast food three times a day, not to mention it can be super unhealthy. Some people didn't want to leave, so having food available was a wonderful benefit for the families.

I grabbed my tray and made my way through the food line. Nothing looked good today. Besides, how could I eat when my brother lay there dying? How could I eat when going to the bathroom was excruciating? Ugh...food, but I knew I needed my strength for whatever was to come. I made my way through the line and found an empty table. I didn't feel like talking to anyone. I hoped other families would sit elsewhere. Honestly, it isn't the kind of place you sit around hoping you get to know each other better because the place is more solemn. Everyone is there for the same reason, and we all know it.

A short time later, my stepdad walked into the cafeteria, grabbed a tray and a plate of food and came and sat down at my table. We ate together and talked about a few things, mainly Joe and mom. He was concerned about her and how she would handle everything. We didn't know what would happen. We were just taking it one day at a time.

Joe was her baby boy. He was the youngest of her three children. And he was the favored one of her three kids. We all knew it. Joe could do no wrong. Even when he cursed her and wished her dead over the years because he didn't get what he wanted from her, she took him back every single time.

Luke 15:11-32 speaks about the prodigal son. The footnote in my Bible says:

"The younger son, like many, rebellious and immature, wanted to be free and live his life as he pleased, and he had to hit rock bottom before he came to his senses. It often takes great sorrow and tragedy to cause people to look to the only One (God) who can help them. The father watched and waited. He was dealing with a human being with a will of his own, but he was ready to greet his son if he returned. In the same way, God's love is constant and patient and welcoming. He will search for us and give us an opportunity to respond, but he will not force us to come to Him. Like the father in the story, God patiently waits for us to come to our

senses. Are you trying to live your life your way, selfishly pushing aside any responsibility or commitment that gets in your way? Stop and look before you hit bottom. You will save yourself and your family much grief."

Over the years, Joe was free to live as he wanted and he did whatever he wanted despite the many words of advice, encouragement, rebuke and the like. And when he went off on one of his tangents, it wasn't too long before he called wanting something, and all was well once again till next time.

Dad finished his food first, then politely excused himself, and headed back to the room to be with mom. I sat there taking my time. I was in no hurry because it had been a long night, and I was so tired. I hadn't gotten much sleep. I think I checked Joe's breathing at least ten times over the course of several hours during the night. Once 12:01 am arrived, and I wished him a happy birthday, I anticipated the end. I'd quietly get up at out of bed, turn on my little flashlight and shine it towards the wall. It gave off just enough reflection; I could see his chest going up and down ever so slightly. I'd lie back down and try to fall asleep again. The few times I managed to fall asleep, I'd wake up and shine my flashlight wondering if I had missed it. I hadn't missed it yet.

As I sat there quietly staring off into the distance, another familiar face came into view. It was Chaplain Nino. He had come into the cafeteria to grab lunch for himself. He moved through the line with his tray, paid the cashier and made his way to the soft drink counter. I watched to see if he was going to sit with anyone. His eyes caught mine and he made his way over to my table.

"Mind if I join you?"

"Not at all. Please have a seat."

"How are you?" he gently asked.

"As good as can be expected I suppose. You know how this ends. It's not easy."

"I can't imagine. It was very nice of everyone to sing happy birthday to your brother earlier."

"Yes....yes it was. It was pretty special seeing all the staff and you come in just for that. It was very sweet. Chaplain Nino, I have a question to ask you."

He nodded as if to say go ahead and ask.

"You know I've been curious about one specific thing regarding Joe. I just have to know, and I don't want you just to tell me what you think I want to hear."

"Go on."

"About his salvation and going to heaven - do you think he's ready now?" I nervously asked.

With genuine concern for my feelings, he replied, "Jeanette, your brother is ready. I have had many talks with him about his faith, his life, his sins, him asking for forgiveness for his sins over the last few months. We had some good conversations, and I believe your brother is ready to see Jesus."

I paused briefly and exhaled slightly. I had unknowingly been holding my breath as the chaplain spoke.

"You know his salvation has been my biggest concern since finding out he had cancer. I wanted to be sure he knew Jesus Christ and had accepted Him as his Lord and Savior. I don't know if you remember when I first called you some months back. Where he was going when he left this earth was my biggest concern."

He replied, "Yes I remember. I think Joe is going to be ok. I think he's ready."

"Good," I said, "Good."

"One other thing if you don't mind."

"Sure, what is it?"

"Do you think he was capable of anymore sin in these last few weeks, I mean since your last visit?"

"No. I can't imagine the state he is in having sinned in any way. It may have even been well before that, but I'm not sure. Why do you ask?"

"I was just wondering about it, just curious as to what you thought about someone in such a state being capable of any further sin."

"I don't see how they could," he replied.

"Ok, thanks."

"No problem."

Chaplain Nino finished his plate and excused himself. He wished my family and me the best and told me he would check in on Joe later. He had other patients to see. He had a tough job. He dealt with the families of loved ones, and he saw death and dying every day. God had given him the special ability to handle all the emotions families experience when their loved ones are dying. Most importantly, God put on his heart to have those difficult conversations with the dying. He gave him the ability to ask the hard questions like, Do you know Jesus? Do you have the reassurance of where you will spend eternity? Have you asked for forgiveness of your sins? Do you have any questions about heaven or hell?

Chaplains are very special gifts from God. And I know for me, Chaplain Nino was a wonderful addition to the team of people God provided to help me genuinely care for Joe. He didn't judge Joe in any way. He simply made him feel comfortable enough to open up to him and asked him the hard questions we so often are afraid to ask ourselves and others.

Many people are looking for someone to comfort them in their last days. I believe they are looking for kinder souls, folks who aren't standing there with a mallet in their hand waiting to pronounce judgment for all they have done to them or in their lives. I believe they want quieter, gentler moments where they can relax.

I've seen death many times now, and one thing always rings true to me – if the dying person believes in Jesus Christ as their Lord and Savior and is saved, the countenance on their face is usually very peaceful looking in the end.

If they haven't put their faith in Jesus Christ as their Lord and Savior, the end of their life looks and feels very stressful and unsettling. They aren't sure what life will be like when their heart stops beating.

I have seen it both ways. There's a peaceful countenance on the faces of believers. There's restlessness on the faces of unbelievers. The difference between the two is very noticeable.

I would say the same is true for the family members going through the process with them. If the family member believes in Jesus Christ and the dying person does not, it brings a particular grief no one else can comprehend. The thought of their loved ones spending eternity eternally separated from God is very painful. We want our loved ones to be with us in heaven. We want them to spend eternity with Jesus Christ.

Listen loved ones, if you haven't asked Jesus Christ into your heart yet as you are reading this book, then I would encourage you to stop right now and consider the following:

1. God loves you and created you to know Him personally.

God's Love: John 3:16 says, "For God so loved the world that He gave His only begotten Son, that whoever believes in Him should not perish, but have eternal life."

God's Plan: "Now this is eternal life: that they may know you, the only true God, and Jesus Christ, whom you have sent." John 17:3

What prevents us from knowing God personally?

2. Man is sinful

"For all have sinned and fall short of the glory of God." Romans 3:23

"For the wages of sin is death." (Spiritual separation from God) Romans 6:23

The third principle explains the only way to bridge this gulf.

3. Jesus Christ is God's only provision for man's sin. Through Him alone, we can know God personally and experience God's love.

He died in our place. "But God demonstrates His own love toward us, in that while we were yet sinners, Christ died for us." Romans 5:8

He rose from the dead. "Christ died for our sins...He was buried...He was raised on the third day, according to the Scriptures...He appeared to Peter, then to the twelve. After that He appeared to more than five hundred..." 1 Corinthians 15:3-6

He is the Only Way to God

"Jesus said to him, "I am the way, and the truth, and the life; no one comes to the Father but through me." John 14:6

It is not enough just to know these truths...

4. We must individually receive Jesus Christ as Savior and Lord; then we can know God personally and experience His love.

We must receive Jesus Christ. "But as many, as receive Him, to them he gave the right to become children of God, even to those who believe in His name." John 1:12

We receive Christ through faith. "For by grace you have been saved through faith; and that not of yourselves. It is the gift of God; not a result of works that no one should boast." Ephesians 2:8-9

When we receive Christ, we experience a new birth. "Now there was a Pharisee, a man named Nicodemus who was a member of the Jewish ruling council. He came to Jesus at night and said, "Rabbi, we know that you are a teacher who has come from God. For no one could perform the signs you are doing if God were not with him." Jesus replied, "Very truly I tell you, no one can see the kingdom of God unless they are born again." "How can someone be born when they are old?" Nicodemus asked. "Surely they cannot enter a second time into their mother's womb to be born!" Jesus answered, "Very truly I tell you, no one can enter the kingdom of God unless they are born of water and the Spirit. Flesh gives birth to flesh, but the Spirit gives birth to spirit. You should not be surprised at my saying, 'You must be born again.' The wind blows wherever it pleases. You hear its sound, but you cannot tell where it comes from or where it is going. So it is with everyone born of the Spirit." John 3:1-8

We receive Christ by personal invitation

"Behold, I stand at the door and knock; if anyone hears my voice and opens the door, I will come into him." Revelation 3:20

Receiving Christ involves turning to God from self (repentance) and trusting Christ to come into our lives to forgive our sins and to make us the kind of people he wants us to be. Just to agree intellectually that Jesus Christ is the Son of God and that He died on the cross for our sins is not enough. Nor is it enough to have an emotional experience. We receive Jesus Christ by faith, as an act of the will.

How can you receive Christ?

God knows your heart and is not concerned with your words as He is with the attitude of your heart. The following is a suggested prayer:

"Lord Jesus, I want to know you personally. Thank you for dying on the cross for my sins. I open the door of my life and receive you as my Savior and Lord. Thank you for forgiving my sins and giving me eternal life. Take control of the throne of my life. Make me the kind of person you want me to be."

Does this prayer express the desire of your heart? If it does, pray this prayer right now and Christ will come into your life; as He promised.

Do not depend on feelings - The promise of God's Word, the Bible – not our feelings – is our authority. The Christian lives by faith (trust) in the trustworthiness of God Himself and His Word. We are to place our faith (trust) in God and His trustworthiness and the promise of His Word.

Now that you have entered into a personal relationship with Christ, many things happened, including the following:

Christ came into your life (Revelations 3:20 and Colossians 1:27)

Your sins were forgiven (Colossians 1:14)

You became a child of God (John 1:12)

You received eternal life (John 5:24)

You began the great adventure for which God created you (John 10:10; 2 Corinthians 5:17; 1 Thessalonians 5:18)

Can you think of anything more wonderful that could happen to you than entering into a personal relationship with Jesus Christ? Would you like to thank God in prayer right now for what He has done for you? You can do that right now.

Pray right now....

I believe many want someone to guide them to the one who can forgive them of their sins. I believe death brings out an uncertainty for a time. Did I do all I could? Did I live the best life I could? Did I do my best with all I was given? Did I make a difference? Did I pay back that twenty bucks I owed?

I believed what Chaplain Nino said as we sat at the dining table together. I believed Joe was ready to go. I had been praying about this for years. I was perfectly fine with it not being me he confessed his deep dark secrets to. I accepted the fact it was a complete stranger he confided in about his life decisions. It didn't need to be me. When we come to that kind of acceptance, the pressure is off us and we can partake in the rest of the process knowing someone else is handling the salvation aspect of it.

It's not that I didn't want to. It's that Joe felt more comfortable telling a stranger he never met his deep dark secrets, fears, and concerns. I think sometimes we get wrapped up in wanting to handle it all. We want to know it all, and we fail to see that our loving Lord has provided and equipped certain people to handle that for us. Would our family members be forthright and honest in those moments knowing how much we want that for them? Would they tell us the absolute truth if they didn't believe in Jesus, knowing we did in the interest of not wanting to hurt our feelings, lie, or spare us the awful news? I believe some would if we pushed them.

Strangers don't know the family history. They don't know what the dying person has done. They can imagine it hasn't been easy for someone like Joe, for example. Chaplain Nino knew he was an AIDS patient dying from cancer. He imagined Joe had made some life-altering decisions somewhere along the way. But he wasn't there to judge Joe or tell him what a bad person he was. His main concern was spiritual. "Joe, do you know Jesus? Have you asked for forgiveness of your sins? Have you confessed that Jesus is the Christ, the Messiah? Do you have the assurance of where you'll spend eternity?" He wasn't there to give him a pass or fail. He was there to be the hands and feet of Jesus Christ.

My mind goes back to the time my cousin and her husband drove up from the Miami area to see my brother while he was still in the nursing home. They hadn't seen each other in many years. She heard about his diagnosis and his impending fate and the most important thing to her was whether Joe believed in Jesus Christ or not. She was going to share the gospel with him if he didn't. We spoke, and I told her I had asked a chaplain to visit Joe often and he had assured me they had those discussions. She was happy about it and asked if Joe had a Bible.

"I haven't seen one in Joe's room so I would say

no, he doesn't have a Bible."

"We would like to bring him a Bible when we come to visit. I would like to read to him from it," she replied.

"I love the idea! Please by all means do. I think Joe would like it very much."

When I saw Joe in the nursing home Labor Day weekend, there sat the Bible. She had brought him a beautiful red Bible (his hair was red), and on the inside cover, he had already signed his name, Joseph A Duby. I still have the Bible with the pictures of our family we hung on the walls of his room. While writing this book, I pulled the Bible out to look at it again and found a piece of green cardstock I had written a note on to Joe dated September 1, 2009:

"Hey brother, hope your day is going ok, better than the day before. I remember when I used to chase you two around the dining room table when mom and dad were out. You guys were such chickens to run around it and run from me. Remember our dog Schwartz bit you on the butt? That was hilarious. Remember locking your keys in your car on graduation day? You dummy. Of course, who can forget the way you two kept your room – quite messy - everything crammed under your beds. Had to walk through my room to get to yours which I hated. Remember when I kneed you in the back in the front yard, and mom beat me till I peed and she beat me again with the belt? Now that I think about it, you were quite the trouble maker then too. Ha-ha. Just thought I'd let you know that I still remember those things. I still remember when dad used to fart and mom would yell at him to check himself as he probably crapped

his pants. Oh, I remember that so well. Remember all the noise coming out of the downstairs bathroom at 1008 10th Way? Haha, fun times. Love ya, Sis xoxo."

As I reread this, I am taken aback by how much it bothered me the two of them ran around the dining room table. Geez, it must have gotten under my skin as I kept bringing it up again and again!

Knowing my cousin and her faith and love for Jesus Christ, I was pretty excited for their visit. It would be a long drive for them back and forth from Miami, so this was no small thing. I was so thankful some family members came to see Joe. I appreciated them taking time out of their week despite Joe's health and circumstances. I knew she and her husband prayed for him and that gave me such comfort.

After Chaplain Nino left the table, I spent some time alone, watching other families stroll in and out. I knew the pain some were experiencing, and I could relate to the waiting. I wondered how they were coping. When you are going through the process, so many thoughts run through your mind. Some are random at best, and others stay around for a while. You can't plan much in advance when you are going through something like this because it's all dependent on God's timing. It's in those moments you just wish God would send you a private message or post it on a sign somewhere – TODAY WILL BE THE DAY. But then again, I do recall how God spoke to me back in June and told me September, so I guess I already got my private message, I just didn't know what day in September.

My job now was to wait, stay faithful, prayerful and be ready for the end. Tired of sitting and still hurting from the hemorrhoids, I got up and made my way back to the room.

It wasn't long before Joe's good friend showed up again.

"Hi. It's so good to see you," said mom as she stood to greet him.

He wrapped his arms around mom and they hugged for a bit.

"How's he doing today?" he asked.

"Ok, I guess. We sang happy birthday to him earlier, together with several of the employees. It was very sweet. He has been looking at the flowers all day today," I replied. I didn't want to tell him he hadn't stared at anything else since before the flowers arrived, but what benefit would it be for him? He was already hurting. He knew where this was going. I think it was pretty courageous of him to come and see Joe in that condition. Not everyone can handle the sights and smells.

We all stood in silence and stared at Joe. No one said anything. We just looked at him lying there.

His friend made his way around the foot of his bed and sat down by Joe at his bedside. He grabbed his hand and held it in his. No words were spoken. Joe's hands hadn't moved for a while. His stare stayed fixed on the flowers. He was holding the hand of a dear friend, knowing when he left it would be the last time he would see him alive. As he sat there, he looked into his eyes. Still no words were said. We all eventually sat down and tried to pretend we weren't intruding on a special moment between two friends. Small talk seemed so insignificant. The television was still off, the drapes drawn, and the smell of fading coffee grinds attempted to overcome the lingering odor.

After a while, he brought Joe's hand up to his lips and kissed it gently and then set it back down. He gently stroked the top of his hand a few times and then tenderly pulled away. Sitting there quietly, he took in the last moments. He captured Joe's face one last time in his memory.

After a few minutes, he rose to his feet and stood there a bit gazing down at my brother. When he was done saying his goodbyes to Joe, he came over to us and said goodbye, hugging each one of us, and then he left. I knew he was heartbroken. He had put up with Joe and seen him at his worst in the past year, and now that would be coming to an end. I knew Joe impacted his life.

For the next few hours, several people came in and out of Joe's room to check on him, say hello, and visit with us. Who else came in that day is a blur to me. There were a few times I left the room to give my mom some privacy with Joe and the other visitors. Sitting down wasn't comfortable, and my feet were killing me standing all the time. So I walked around the facility, taking an inventory of who was still there.

When I think of the week I spent at the hospice facility with him, I believe Joe had a peaceful look through the dying process. His running from trouble, battling HIV/AIDS all his adult life, fighting suicidal thoughts, struggling with self-destructive actions, scraping by each month financially, and ultimately battling cancer and losing, would soon come to an end. The demons that chased him daily would soon be no more. He would finally be at peace.

That afternoon after everyone left, I sat on his bedside and looked into his eyes and held his hand. Like the moment earlier with his friend, his hand did not respond as you would expect. There was no reciprocal grasp from him. I stared into those baby blue eyes of his looking for any signs of what was to come. We were getting closer, but how much closer, only God knew. His eyes weren't quite as clear as the weeks before. His coloring had noticeably changed. He couldn't focus on me or turn his head. He didn't move a muscle. He lay there in silence staring at the roses.

At or around 6:00 pm that evening, I was sitting at his bedside, gently rubbing Joe's chest, my hand resting on his heart. All of a sudden, his heart jumped quite significantly that I could feel it.

Wow, what was that? I was surprised by what just happened.

I noticed he started getting a little agitated. I whispered to him softly, "Hey bro, its ok. Settle down Joe. It's alright."

I started rubbing his chest lightly again trying to calm him down and reassuring him everything was ok. I wasn't sure what was happening or why, but I could tell his heart was beating a bit faster. Mom was standing by his bedside, and she also noticed something was different.

After a few minutes, he calmed down and seemed less agitated. I watched his eyes for any signs of movement, but they remained steady. His body seemed to relax, and he was still breathing the same. It was just mom and me in the room. Dad had gone back to Vero Beach earlier in the day to get some sleep and grab dinner with his sisters.

After a few minutes, Joe seemed to settle down. I felt pretty comfortable with his current status, so I decided to go back to the house and get a quick bath and soak in the tub. My hemorrhoids were still bothering me something fierce, and I needed to get a little relief and treat them before going into the long night. I didn't know what the night held, but I knew I needed to be there. After what just happened, there was no telling what the night would bring.

"Remember not the sins of my youth and my rebellious ways; according to your love remember me, for you are good, O Lord." Psalm 25:7

CHAPTER NINETEEN

He Slipped Away

Traffic seemed to drag so slowly. The car ride back to my friend's house seemed like an eternity. I couldn't concentrate on anything else except the road and Joe. Maybe he would be here for another few days. He hadn't started laboring in his breathing like some other people I have watched enter their final rest. But I knew we were close. He quit communicating, eating and moving. His stare was locked in.

As I was making my way through traffic, my cell phone rang with an unfamiliar number, however, a very familiar area code of 561. I knew there weren't too many people who would be calling me from that area code. I saved everyone I knew in my contacts.

"Hello."

All I could hear was a very emotional woman sobbing on the other end of the phone saying, "Net, it's mom. He's gone! Net, he's gone! Joe's gone!"

"What? I was just there! I just left fifteen minutes ago! I'm on my way back!"

Traffic didn't matter anymore. I swung the car around and raced back to the hospice facility. Alone in my car, words began to fly from my mouth in rapid fire as tears streamed down my face, *"Joe you knew I wanted to be there when you passed. You knew I stayed there on purpose all that time so our mom wouldn't be alone when you died. I didn't want her to be alone with you when you died. Why did you wait until I left?"*

I don't remember red lights or speed limit signs. All I could think was my mother was alone with my baby brother. Her baby boy was gone. His suffering was over. His demons left the building. He wouldn't be tormented anymore, and she would forever have a gaping hole in her heart no one could fill but God alone.

"Blessed are those who mourn, for they will be comforted." Matthew 5:4

I couldn't believe he was gone. I had kept vigilance for several days. I had cared for him and overseen everything for him for the past three months. It all came down to this. It was his 40th birthday, and he made it past the time he was born, and then he was gone.

I managed to make it back to the facility in one piece and ran to Joe's room where I had left him just twenty-five minutes before. When I walked in, I found my mother sobbing and Joe lying there just as peaceful as when I last saw him alive. He was wearing his favorite ball cap again. Mom had placed it on his head. His eyes had finally closed. Joe looked so peaceful.

The disease that viciously ravaged his body twenty plus years ago was no longer in control of anything. Cancer that took up residence in his body was no longer battling for control. The desperation, the depression, the struggle to live, to fight, to scream out in frustration – all gone. The peace I had prayed for Joe so many years finally rested on his face. The days, the nights, the weeks, the months – the years of worrying about Joe were now over for our family. We knew where he was now. We didn't wonder anymore.

Mom had already called my step dad to let him know, and he was already on his way back to the facility from Vero. As we waited for him to arrive, we started calling family and friends alike to share the sad news. Most people couldn't believe we had just celebrated his 40th birthday earlier that morning and were grieving his death that same evening.

As I stood there staring at his lifeless body, all I could think about was what God had told me months before – "Get your surgery done now. Joe will be September."

God didn't tell me it would be on his 40th birthday.

Joe had finally gotten his wish – to make it to his 40th birthday. I think back to all the times he told me what he wished for, "Net, I just want to make it to 40. I just want to see my 40th birthday."

He never spoke any words about living past that day. Funny, sometimes I wonder if he knew all along.

The nurse came back in to check on us and asked if we had made the call to the funeral home. We had and advised of our location. A half hour seemed like an eternity waiting for them to arrive. As we waited for the representative, we cleaned up all our belongings, packed all the stuff we had gathered over the last few weeks. We wanted to be ready to leave as soon as the crematory rep arrived.

My stepdad soon arrived, entered and embraced my mother as she cried. I knew it was heartbreaking for her and him. The two of them stood there and looked at Joe, who was so peaceful now. After what seemed like forever, he started carrying her stuff out to the car.

It wasn't too long, and the man from the crematory place arrived. He was so gentle and very sympathetic and patient with mom. I remember him being a very tall man with big broad shoulders. He had to have been at least 6 foot 3 inches high. He had come by himself to pick up Joe. We could tell he had a caring heart and we had no doubt he would take great care of Joe.

As he waited in the hallway with the gurney, we took a few more minutes to kiss Joe on the forehead and say our final goodbyes.

Leaving the room was a very difficult thing to do, but we left Joe in the man's care. We took the vase full of roses along with another flower arrangement that had arrived days earlier and dropped them at the nurse's station. It was a long, slow walk back to our vehicles. We were leaving someone we loved behind. Joe was gone, but would live forever in our hearts.

For several days I had watched families leave the facility without their loved ones. I had watched the turnover day after day. I had seen the nurses take such great care of every patient who came into their facility. I had seen the doctors consult families, read charts, and spend their time caring for the dying. I had come to understand why some family members go back to work for hospice after losing a loved one there.

The door to his room would finally close.

Facebook post dated September 17, 2009:

To all who prayed for us, Joe went to be with the Lord tonight at 6:25 pm on his birthday, how appropriate. He and mom were alone. I had just left 15 minutes prior, so it was just the two of them together in the end as it was at the beginning of his life 40 years ago today. Thank you for all the support. Please continue to pray for our family.

Facebook post dated September 18, 2009:

Thank you! Words can't express my gratitude for all who have prayed for me and my brother, a guy whom most had never met. Just goes to show God's love has no boundaries. He is finally at peace. The service will be Tuesday, September 22 at 2:00 pm at Riverside Memorial in Jupiter. Pray for me as I am officiating. To God be the Glory.

CHAPTER TWENTY

Fifty-Six Good Things

September 19, 2009 – Joe is finally at peace

I haven't journaled in eight days. I returned from West Palm Beach yesterday after having spent a week down there at the hospice facility. For six days off and on, I watched Joe lay there and die slowly. I reflect back to those days, and I realize God was teaching me something through all this – what families and loved ones go through watching their loved ones pass and all the emotions, exhaustion, decisions, fears, and tiredness that go with the dying process. I had never fully grasped it when I would pop in on the sick during my hospital visits until now. I now understand their pain. It's an exhausting time, mentally, physically, and emotionally. It just drains every bit of you. Your mind is an empty space running on emotion. The thoughts, fears, and doubts begin to battle each other, and you find yourself questioning decisions you made about their care.

All through this process with Joe since September a year ago, I have tried to be compassionate. I've tried to be understanding, merciful, and loving to him so that in some way he would recognize Christ in me. I wanted him to experience what I knew to be true – God is faithful, loving, kind, truthful, merciful, slow to anger, quick to forgive, magnificent and awestruck. God reigns on high.

Through this process, I look back and I can see that God was working all through this horrible situation, but none as prevalent as in the last several weeks and months. I have no doubts God took a horrible, painful disease in my brother and brought many good things out of it. For all those and the role I got to play, I am eternally grateful.

**Here's a list of the wonderful things God did during this traumatic situation:

1. Brought Joe and me back together

2. I was able to witness to him

3. Allowed me to play the role of health surrogate which helped me learn what mom went through with my dad

4. Allowed mom to take a break from it all

5. Mom went to counseling to deal with all the pain in her life

6. I was able to set boundaries with them

7. Brought my other brother back into my life

8. My other brother and his ex-wife are talking again, together with the kids

9. My brother being a father to his kids again

10. Mom and my ex-sister-in-law apologizing to each other after ten years

11. All of us, except Joe enjoying dinner together for the first time in ten years

12. Meeting Joe's case worker of eighteen years who turned out to be a very loving and compassionate, straight, black man who genuinely saw Joe like a son

13. Meeting Joe's friend, who I got a chance to speak to about his relationship with God. He also has been there for Joe several times.

14. The wonderful staff at hospice who were kind and compassionate

15. My friends, church family, and family members praying for us diligently for the past year

16. The meeting we had at the nursing home that opened their eyes to patient neglect

17. All the kind things said about Joe and the kind things he did. I didn't know so many people thought well of Joe and liked him – it was comforting to me.

18. Mom witnessing my tenderness and compassion with Joe and him relating to me in return

19. Me getting to witness to my friend who still lived in West Palm Beach and being able to attend church with her while I was in town

20. Another local lifelong friend and I got to spend time together talking about all that God has done in our lives. When we first met, we had no interest in what God could do. All that has changed for both of us, and we didn't realize it till we met up again

21. Having the chance to pray for the other sick and dying which led to other opportunities to bring comfort to someone there at the hospice facility

22. God giving me the strength and abilities to get through all this

23. Work was so supportive during these difficult times

24. My ladies Bible study praying for me and supporting me

25. Allowing a new friendship to grow through all this with my new medical friend and being able to testify to her through all this to help us both grow

26. Having the medical friend in my life at this specific time and being able to draw on her medical advice regarding Joe and my health issues. Being able to talk to her in the middle of the night was such a blessing to me.

27. God spoke to me back in June when I was trying to decide on doing my surgery. He spoke to me and told me to do it now because September would be the month for Joe. O God – you spoke to me, your child whom you feel is worthy.

28. Joe's wish came true. He made it to his 40th birthday even past the time he was born. Who else could ordain?

29. The witnessing of love we showed the staff at hospice by keeping vigil at Joe's bedside

30. The film crew who came in and filmed Joe receiving final communion so they could show the film in Japan. The Word of God will be

shown in Japan through Joe's illness. A hospice facility will open in Japan.

31. The single rose that stayed alive in a vase at work and was being watched by my office for two plus weeks and what it spoke to some unbelievers and doubters; the new growth

32. Sending my friend Ray to help get cigs

33. Being able to mend some fences with my mother

34. Allowing Joe and mom to be together in the end

35. The strengthening of my mother, having her go through this and being there for Joe, and getting the quality time with him before he died.

36. The staff and friends he made at the various nursing homes

37. The compassionate weekend manager who happened to be working Labor Day weekend and all she helped us resolve

38. Keeping all of us healthy to get through it

39. The care my daughter received from my friends during this time

40. The honor I received being chosen to officiate and the lessons it will bring from his funeral service

41. The forum, Facebook, which allowed me to share what God has been doing. The dignity I was able to show Joe

42. Allowing me to get to West Palm Beach and back several times in my old car and providing me with a free place to stay

43. Small ways this has brought the family back together

44. Joe confirmed his belief in Jesus to Chaplain Nino. Me being able to witness to him, read to him, and sing to him about Jesus in those final days. We got some real tender moments together

45. Tender moments with Joe in those last six days of his life; him holding my hand and kissing it, telling each other we loved each other, and us staring at each other in loving sibling ways; me reminiscing with him about when we were little and how he was a pain in my butt. Moments that will always remain in my heart

46. God spared me the pain of watching Joe's final moments

47. Being able to celebrate his 40th birthday. The first birthday I recall spending with him in over ten years, if not twenty. Watching all the love poured out to him on that day by numerous people.

48. Having been able to wake him up at 12:01 am that morning and be the first person to wish him a happy birthday and tell him he made it.

49. Having met and talked with Chaplain Nino and him comforting me about Joe's situation and his assurance's Joe was ready to go spiritually speaking

50. The cremation guy who came to get Joe was very compassionate to my mother and me

51. For my stepdad who was with us and who took care of my mom and loves her

52. For all who have reached out to me in love during these times. I'm so grateful for them

53. For my wonderful, loving daughter whose smile yesterday when she saw me was worth it all. I'm so blessed to have her for a daughter

54. Getting a chance to apologize to some folks for my past mistakes

55. Joe received a Bible and loved it. Him seeing his cousin and her husband

56. God has worked all those things for my good through a dying young man

To God be the glory forever and ever. Amen.

<u>56 Good things – 1 Bad thing</u>

"And we know that in all things God works for the good of those who love him, who have been called according to his purpose." Romans 8:28

"I will praise you, O Lord my God, with all my heart, and I will glorify your name forever." Psalm 86:12

CHAPTER TWENTY-ONE

Grow in Grace

Mom had asked me to officiate Joe's funeral. I must admit I was a bit surprised by her request, but honored none the less. I also knew Joe didn't have a church home or a minister he saw regularly, and since I was currently studying for my Divinity degree, I would work just fine. I had never officiated a funeral before. I have spoken at plenty of funeral services and saw plenty of people in their final hour, but officiating someone's funeral from beginning to end was a new experience. The question remained – what would I say?

Joe's life was anything but glamorous. It was quite the opposite. Most of our family hadn't spoken to Joe or seen him in many years. We didn't know a lot of Joe's friends and the ones we did know, we had already touched base. We weren't expecting a huge crowd of people. The service would be quaint and personable. But what to say that would honor Joe the best? Prayer - I needed to seek the Lord on this one. He led me here; I was confident He wouldn't leave me here. At least I pretended I was confident.

"Show me your ways, O Lord, teach me your paths;
guide me in your truth and teach me, for you are God my
Savior, and my hope is in you all day long." Psalm 25:4

So I did the only thing I knew to do after praying - I contacted my pastor. I asked him for some advice. He was relatively new to our church, so he didn't know me well, and he certainly didn't know my brother. He thought it best to refer me to my old pastor (not as in age-old, but as in previous) who had been called to pastor another church just north of West Palm Beach. It's just like God to lead me to the same county my brother had resided. They had been living there for a few years. The funeral service would be in the area, so I could stop by his office and speak to him about officiating Joe's funeral and get some ideas.

I contacted my old pastor and brought him up to date. We talked for a bit, and he gave me a few suggestions and told me to pray about them over the next 24 hours. He knew I didn't have much time. He wanted me to seek the Lord based on the couple suggestions he gave me. He told me whatever I decided, God would honor it. He told me I needed to have confidence in myself, that I could do this, and I would not be alone. His encouraging words gave me strength.

Joe's life was such a roller coaster. How do you bring the intensity of his life and the irresponsibility of his decisions in line with dignifying him and treating him kindly? How do you share a message of hope with family and friends using Joe's story and the Word of God? How do you accurately convey all that had happened in the last twenty plus years?

Should I share what happened? Should I just keep it to Scripture? Should I give a little bio on Joe's life? I had so many questions about the format. I took pastor's advice and I sought the Lord.

"Commit your way to the Lord; trust in Him, and he will do this; He will make your righteousness shine like the dawn, the justice of your cause like the noon-day sun." Psalm 37:5

Before I hung up the phone, I asked my old pastor if when I finished writing out the sermon, he would review it for me. He said he'd be happy to help.

However, when I finished and contacted him, he passed and told me he was confident it would be just fine, and he didn't need to review it. He knew my heart, and he knew how I felt about Joe. He also knew I was currently in school, having just studied this exact subject not too long before this happened, so he felt pretty secure in letting me ride the bike with no training wheels on the first attempt. I on the other hand, still wanted those training wheels.

Most people play some music before speaking at a funeral service or as some call it, a celebration of life. So I went through all my CD's and came across some Josh Groban CD's (I'm a big fan of his). After looking at the titles and listening to a few songs, I chose "Ave Maria." It is a beautiful song, and the sound of it reminded me so much of Joe.

I love Josh Groban's rendition of the song. Honestly, anything Josh sings is simply beautiful even if he sings them in another language. The guy has a gift from God, and he uses it quite beautifully.

As I sit here, thoughts run through my mind of how God prepared me for this very day. I had just completed a college course on funerals, weddings, and other ceremonies a pastor may partake or participate. I suddenly remembered I still had the textbook from the class, so I referred to it, making sure I covered every element needed to make this a smooth and meaningful ceremony. I didn't want to embarrass myself or my family. I certainly didn't want to embarrass Joe in any way.

I drafted an outline of the service and created a color flyer which included a wonderful picture of Joe. Good pictures of Joe were hard to come by if I'm honest. I didn't have very many photos of Joe. It had been years, and the last photos I had of him were when he was in the hospital getting ready for surgery and a couple of photos of him in the nursing home. We just didn't have those kind of Kodak moments captured in pictures. Photos are a rarity when you are living from place to place, especially when you are homeless. There would be many years without a picture of Joe. Cell phones didn't capture the memories back then.

Everything was ready to go. Rehearse, rehearse, and rehearse some more. There's nothing quite like writing up a sermon and not reviewing what you wrote. I needed it to flow smoothly and appear as if I had done this before. I wanted it to be perfect. I wanted the message to honor Joe, but more importantly, I wanted what I put together to bring glory to God.

"May the words of my mouth and the meditation of my heart be pleasing in your sight, O Lord, my rock and my Redeemer." Psalm 19:14

Facebook post dated September 21, 2009:

Tomorrow is the big day, Joe's memorial service. Those who plan on attending, dress comfortable as the chapel they call it, is outdoors, so a tad bit warm you might say. May God get all the glory for tomorrow and may the words of my mouth, and the meditation of my heart be acceptable to you Lord, my rock, and my redeemer.

The day finally arrived. The moment you realize all eyes are on you and it's not the kind of moment where everyone is happy. It was a very sad occasion for my family. Part of me, if I'm to be honest, was glad he wasn't suffering anymore. I was glad his long battle with the disease had ended. The disease robbed him in numerous ways for so many years.

For so many years, he ran. For so many years, he shed tears. For so many years, he felt ostracized from some family, friends, and society, granted some would say he brought all of it on himself. I can understand the thought process behind some of those feelings, but I also think of God's grace and the mistakes I have made and how he still loves me regardless.

Joe made mistakes, some pretty big mistakes, and like all of us who make mistakes or irresponsible choices, he suffered the consequences of those mistakes. It didn't mean God loved him less and you and me more. God still longed to have a relationship with Joe, the same way He does with you and me.

The cemetery was small and located in a small town on the outskirts of Palm Beach County, not far from the ocean. As you drive into the cemetery, the roads are lined with shade trees, tombstones, and marble benches on each side. At the roundabout, you take a left. As you make your way around, to the right are three small open courtyard buildings. Each has an inner courtyard where the deceased are placed inside marble niches. The walls surrounding us were made of marble with names and dates etched into the faces. I always like reading the dates and the various names. What were they like? Did they die a natural death or was it from some horrible disease? How old were they? Were they missed?

Joe's ashes would be placed inside a niche on the outside of the building. For now, his urn was with us, sitting on a table in front of everyone inside the courtyard area. Everything the disease did to him was now contained in a little vessel, no longer able to hurt him or anyone else.

Inside the courtyard of the mausoleum were roughly twenty chairs and a small podium. Two small marble benches sat to the rear of the courtyard. Random flowers both fake and dead filled the various vases attached to the marble slabs. Someone attached a balloon to their loved one's vase. It was a birthday balloon, but it was losing air and drifting toward the ground.

I thought it pretty appropriate there was a birthday balloon in the very courtyard we were sitting. I had purchased a birthday balloon for Joe, and by now it too would also be losing air.

The area was somewhat dark and cold. The opening of the courtyard faced south, so you didn't get the full effect of the afternoon sun.

One by one, family and friends arrived and took their seats. Sadly, some chairs sat empty. We knew most of our family couldn't be there because they lived in other states and the service was in the middle of the week, making it difficult for them to attend. But we felt their prayers and were thankful for them.

Here's the Order of Service:

- Thank everyone for coming - 3 minutes

- Play "Ave Maria" Song – 4 minutes

- Opening Words of Scripture – Psalm 23 – 2 minutes

- Prayer - "May the words of my mouth and the meditation of my heart be pleasing in your sight O Lord, my Rock, and my Redeemer."

- Reading of the obituary – 3 minutes

- Sermon

- Play Josh Groban's song – "Don't Give Up" – 4 minutes

- Prayer – 2 minutes

- Open for comments, stories about Joe – 10 minutes

- Benediction Prayer – 2 minutes

- Move to final resting place for committal words and prayer

It was now time to start the service and to say I was nervous was an understatement. This would be the very first funeral I would officiate. I guess one could say it was a blessing my first one was my kin. If I messed up, grace would abound by my own family.

"Good afternoon. Thank you for coming today to help celebrate the life of Joseph Anthony Duby, born September 17, 1969, and entered into rest on September 17, 2009. Joe lived in West Palm Beach. Please enjoy a song I believe Joe would have loved, "Ave Maria.""

After starting the CD player, I took my seat in between my brother and mother. Mom whispered over to me that "Ave Maria" was her mother's favorite song. I had no idea. I guess a little piece of grandma had made it into the service.

The music was simply beautiful. The acoustics in the little courtyard were perfect. The notes filled the marble space. As I sat there listening to the music, my mind went back to the days when we laughed and cried. The music reminded me of my grandma, especially when mom told me it had been her favorite song.

I pictured all of us swimming in my grandma's pool. For lunch, she always made us bologna and cheese sandwiches. The boys always put mayonnaise on their sandwiches. I hated mayonnaise and still dislike it to this day. I always put mustard on my bologna sandwich. We also stacked Lays potato chips in between the meat and bread. Grandpa always ate spam or some other gross stuff called liverwurst. It was the worst alright. We sat around their dining room table at every meal.

Jalacy windows from floor to ceiling allowed us to peer outside into the big backyard with the fenced in pool and our families on either side. To the left of grandma's house, lived grandma's son and his wife who had a big backyard with a swing set. To the right, my aunt, my grandma's sister, had an equally big back yard with a huge tree great for climbing and swinging from its branches. I also remember the towering palm trees in the rear of her yard whose trunks reminded me of crawling up a slide. The angle allowed you to climb as high as you could until the tree went vertical. I loved going to grandma's house because we had so many options for playtime and plenty of space. We seemed to spend a lot of weekends at their house.

I couldn't help but think of Joe as it played. He loved classical music among other genres of music, although I never imagined him liking country music. Somehow country music didn't seem to fit the bars he frequented in South Miami. I pictured him smiling. I imagined him saying, *"Nice choice Net, nice choice."*

When the music finished, I stood up and made my way back to the little podium. There beside me on a small table was Joe's urn. All eyes were on me now. They didn't know what to expect. I had planned it all by myself according to the outline in my textbook and with the Lord's help.

Opening with prayer, knowing full well I needed the Lord, I wanted the Lord's presence for the next twenty minutes. I knew the message I was about to deliver might be the first time some of the folks had heard the gospel account. Maybe there were a few on the fence about God. The opportunity was now. It was too late to change anything. I needed to walk in obedience to what I felt the Lord had led me to say.

CHAPTER TWENTY-TWO

Time to Share

"Joseph Anthony Duby, age 40 of West Palm Beach, Florida passed away September 17, 2009, following an extended illness and cancer. Joe was born on September 17, 1969, in North Miami, Florida. He was the son of the late Raymond Duby, Sr. Joe is preceded in death by his grandparents, cousin, and half-brother. He graduated in 1987 from North Shore Community High School located in West Palm Beach. He is survived by his mother and stepfather, sister, brother, half-sister and her family, two half-brothers and two step brothers. He is also survived by two nieces, one nephew, and other step-nieces and step-nephews and their families, aunts, uncles, cousins, and all their families.

Joe's Last Four Wishes

1. He wished to have his family and friends know that he loved them.

2. He wished to be forgiven for all the times he had hurt his family, friends, and others.

3. He wished to have his family, friends, and others know that he forgave them for the times they may have hurt him in his life.

4. He wished for his family and friends to think about what he was like before he became ill some 20 years ago. He asked that they remember him this way after his death.

Joe's greatest love was detailing cars, but his real dream was medicine, although he never got a chance to fulfill that dream. He worked for Motorcars of Delray Beach for many years. He could take a dirty car and bring it back to life inside and out. Till the day he died, he always talked about his job and the people he worked with at Motorcars. He never forgot you. Over the years, Joe volunteered with people who were also impacted by HIV/AIDS. One such program was the 2nd Annual Benefit auction to support NMAPLA, in May 1993 in Albuquerque, New Mexico. Joe also spoke at various other engagements on HIV/AIDS. The family wishes to thank his friends and various organizations (Mom & Pop Clark) over the years for supporting Joe. We would especially like to thank JC Ewald from CAP (Comprehensive AIDS Program) who was by his side for 18 plus years. JC, you went above and beyond the call of duty as Joe's case worker to be sure he had what he needed. You supported him even in the most trying of times. Joe had such admiration and love for all of you that helped him over the last 20 years. As you go forward to help others, think of the difference you made in his life.

Cremation (Edgley, WPB) and his final resting place will be at Riverside Memorial Park in Tequesta, Florida.

Instead of flowers, please send a gift in Joe's memory to the following:

The Lord's Place, 2808 North Australian Avenue, West Palm Beach, FL 33407

Comprehensive AIDS Program, 2300 S. Congress Avenue, West Palm Beach, FL 33406

My text today comes from John 6, a familiar story in the New Testament recorded by all four gospel writers - Matthew, Mark, Luke, and John. It's the story of Jesus feeding the 5000 with five loaves and two fish.

John 6:1-15 wherein it says,

"After this Jesus went away to the other side of the Sea of Galilee, which is the Sea of Tiberias. 2 And a large crowd was following him because they saw the signs that he was doing on the sick. 3 Jesus went up on the mountain, and there he sat down with his disciples. 4 Now the Passover, the feast of the Jews, was at hand. 5 Lifting up his eyes, then, and seeing that a large crowd was coming toward him, Jesus said to Philip, "Where are we to buy bread, so that these people may eat?" 6 He said this to test him, for he himself knew what he would do. 7 Philip answered him, "Two hundred denarii worth of bread would not be enough for each of them to get a little." 8 One of his disciples, Andrew, Simon Peter's brother, said to him, 9 "There is a boy here who has five barley loaves and two fish, but what are they for so many?" 10 Jesus said, "Have the people sit down." Now there was much grass in

the place. So the men sat down, about five thousand in number. 11 Jesus then took the loaves, and when he had given thanks, he distributed them to those who were seated. So also the fish, as much as they wanted. 12 And when they had eaten their fill, he told his disciples, "Gather up the leftover fragments, that nothing may be lost." 13 So they gathered them up and filled twelve baskets with fragments from the five barley loaves left by those who had eaten. 14 When the people saw the sign that he had done, they said, "This is indeed the Prophet who is to come into the world!"15 Perceiving then that they were about to come and take him by force to make him king, Jesus withdrew again to the mountain by himself. (ESV)

The first point I'd like us to see in this story is that Jesus saw the people and he had compassion on them. He was pleased with their attendance. He didn't look at them and say "Oh come on, I have been talking all day and I'm tired. Please leave me alone." No, instead he was pleased and compassionate. He showed concern for their welfare. Society today may look at a lowly person, someone who is different than them and not be pleased to see them or have to deal with them. We may not have compassion in our hearts for them. But in the text here, Jesus is setting the example of how to treat others that are not the same as us or may not be in the same place we are in life. How many times do we see guys standing on street corners and we automatically assume they are drunks, low life's, or lost? Do we ever look at them with compassion in our eyes? Do we ever reach out to them?

Joe spent many years on the streets, wandering from place to place, living from shelter to shelter, and always looking for someone to show him compassion or something that would make the pain of his decisions go away.

He was wandering around like a lost sheep without a shepherd. When sheep don't have a shepherd to guide them, they run around in circles. There's confusion, they get lost from the pack, and they wander off. They wander out into the open pasture all by themselves, and in some cases, are maimed or killed. They never feel accepted or part of the pack. They never feel that bond or the love which comes from being part of the pack.

Joe, like a sheep, struggled most of his adult life to gain acceptance, to find love, and to feel like he was part of the pack. However, many times he looked for it in the wrong places.

We do that as well. We look for love in the wrong places. We look for it in the wrong ways, and we look for love from the wrong people. Instead, our focus should be on the shepherd who is Jesus Christ. Jesus Christ in this story showed compassion for the people even though they didn't believe in Him yet. They saw something that attracted them to Him, and they wanted to know and see more.

Next I want you to see that Philip who was one of the first disciples of Jesus, shows his lack of faith in regards to how they are going to feed the masses. Philip had been with Jesus from day one. He saw the miracle Jesus performed turning the water into wine, and all the other miracles He had performed, and yet here he questions how they are going to feed the people. It will take almost eight months wages.

There are times in our lives when we find ourselves in situations that we don't know what to do. And instead of seeking out the answers from heaven, from our Heavenly Father, we seek to fix the problems ourselves. We say, "Oh I can do that...I can fix it...I have all the answers. I'm going to do it my way." But the Bible says our thoughts are not His thoughts, our ways are not His ways. Thank God they aren't.

That is one of the things I learned through this whole process with Joe in the last two weeks of his life. My thoughts and ways are not Gods thoughts or ways. I wanted Joe to pass in his sleep. I wanted to be there when he passed so my mother wasn't alone when he drew his final breath. I didn't want him to make it to his birthday for the simple fact that I didn't want to see him suffer anymore. I wanted his pain to be over.

You see, God's ways were not my ways. God had a plan. He already had it all figured out, and He was still working through and in this situation. It's when we don't seek out God's provision for our lives that we end up frustrated. We make bad choices and bad decisions that end up causing pain and discomfort. I'll share a story with you.

Back in May Joe was living in Darcy Hall nursing home. We just found out how bad the cancer was and that Joe had been given until the end of June. He was staying in this nursing home at Medicare's expense for the first 100 days.

Joe being Joe decided to buy a car while he stayed there. He called me up and told me he bought a car. This car was in mint condition, ran great, and the a/c was ice cold.

Do you know the old saying, "Beauty is in the eye of the beholder?" I don't need to say any more about the condition of this car.

My first thought is *"Who buys a car in a nursing home?"* I asked him about the tag, insurance, and registration. He told me he already took care of that stuff. Not only did he register the car, but hey if you are going to drive one last car it better have a special license plate on the back. So he spent the extra money and got a special tag made up, "DUBYDOO."

He got into two fender benders with this car. Thank God he didn't hurt anyone.

The nursing home decided Joe was too self-sufficient and could take care of himself, so they kicked him out of the nursing home. His free ride on the Medicare system was over.

It wasn't long after that Joe ended up in Wood-lake and his condition was such that he wasn't able to drive anymore. Thank God for small favors. Now he had to pay for where he lived. He had an empty bank account, and the nursing home was taking his entire check each month, all but $35. So I asked Joe, "How are you going to pay for all this, the monthly insurance, your cell phone, and your cigarette habit?"

He responded, "I'll cross that bridge when I get to it."

I had a feeling we were going to get to that bridge pretty quickly. And we did. Joe was a smoker. The one thing Joe had left was smoking cigarettes all day long. Now he is calling and asking me for cigs, and I'm thinking to myself, *you wouldn't be asking me if you had not bought the car.*

We have arrived at that bridge I mentioned earlier, and he is looking for me to pay the tolls. He was now trying to make his bad decision my problem.

I gently suggested to him several times to sell the car. With great hesitancy, he finally did. Afterward, he would say to me, "The car caused me so many problems with my mother and you. I have spent the last few months trying to justify to you what a stupid decision it was to buy the car."

I didn't want to say to him, "Well I could have told you that."

He took the long way around problems, instead of cutting straight through the middle.

You see, that's what we do with God. We think we can fix things ourselves. We think we have all the answers. We find out that we can't, and we get to a place where we finally admit we were wrong and God's way was right. In God's mercy and grace, He forgives us and still loves us despite ourselves. And He calls us to Him and tells us that He still loves us and asks us to seek Him first.

And what Philip and Andrew should have done or said was, "Jesus we know you can do it. We have seen what you have done concerning others. We have seen the miracles you have performed."

But like Philip and Andrew, we let our pride and our ability to be self-sufficient get in the way for our own good. We allow doubt in God to run ahead of our belief in God and His ability.

Lastly, I want you to see that Jesus didn't want anything to go to waste. He instructed the disciples to gather the pieces that were left over. They filled twelve baskets - note the number twelve for the number of disciples. Coincidence? I don't think so.

Jesus took great care of the remaining pieces. He let nothing to go to waste. How much time do we waste? How many things do we waste? How much food and water do we waste?

God has given us provisions, but we often think nothing of wasting what we have been given. We waste a lot of time and energy chasing after the wrong things because we think there is some fulfillment that we can't get from anywhere else.

The people saw this great miracle take place right in front of them. Jesus didn't hide it from them. Instead He was real and genuine in front of them. Then the people started to say, "Surely this is the prophet that has come into the world."

Miracles that Jesus performed demonstrated that He was the Messiah promised. Many were convinced He was the prophet who should come into the world, and yet they did not receive Him because He didn't match their expectations. They were looking for someone to come in and take over, to lead them politically and rescue them from their enemies. But that wasn't Jesus' purpose in coming.

It is possible for a man to acknowledge that Christ is that guy, and yet turn a deaf ear to His calling. "I know Christ is out there, I believe He exists, but you know what, I just don't have time. I don't have time to read His Word much less pray to Him. I'm just too busy with my plans."

Often we do things the way we want to do them, and we spend a lot of time running around and staying busy. As a result, we never fully develop a relationship with Christ that will take care of and handle most everything we worry about and fear.

I believe Joe figured out toward the end of his life that Christ is where love resided. He finally figured out after years of running in the other direction that Christ was where it was at all along. The love and acceptance he so longed for were with Jesus Christ all along, and he wasted a lot of years figuring that out.

The great thing about God is that as often as we go in the other direction and seek to do things our way, God is standing right there in our midst. God never moves and never wavers, as He waits for us to come to Him - with all our cares, concerns and fears. But most importantly to come to Him with our faith and our love. We waste so much time running away from God.

I believe when Joe finally figured it out, he found God's open arms waiting for him to tell him how much He loved him and had loved him his entire life.

All Joe wanted was for someone to understand him.

He wanted someone to love him through it, and in it, and in spite of who he was, or the discomfort and the fears.

Isn't that what we all want?

We want someone to walk with us through it, and in it, and in spite of our fears, our pains, and our discomforts despite who we are and what we have done. We're just like Joe.

Guess what? Jesus gives us that! He is with us through it, and in it, and in spite of who we are or what we have done. He is with us in the pain, discomfort, and fear. Jesus knows us and knows pain, discomfort, and fear. After all, He made the ultimate sacrifice by dying on the cross for all humanity, a suffering He didn't have to endure, but because He loves us, He made that sacrifice so all could be saved.

It wasn't so much that Joe's life was bad and full of bad things because we all have bad things in our lives - we all have sinned. No sin is worse than another the Bible says. A sin is a sin. Joe's were just a little more flamboyant perhaps than others we know. But he was no more complex than you or I. He had no fewer ambitions or desires. He made mistakes. We make mistakes. He wanted things to be easy. We want things to be easy. He was afraid people wouldn't accept him for who he was. We are afraid people won't accept us for who we are.

But ask yourself this, "Did God love him any less than He loves you?"

No, because God loves you the same.

So, when I look at Joe's life, what does God want us to learn from it?

The only thing you may know about Joe is what you heard today. You may have known him since he was born forty years ago and you may have known him more intimately during the last twenty years. What does God want you to take away from this? God put this guy on the earth for a reason, and He wants us to value him. How can we do that?

If you are here today and you don't know this

Jesus I spoke about, please see me after the service, and I will be happy to tell you about Him.

If you know Jesus, but you are saying to yourself, "I don't think I have a close relationship with Him," you can have that starting today.

Or perhaps you feel that your sin is too big for Jesus, and that He won't forgive you. Our God is bigger than all that and longs to draw you closer to Him. He wants a personal relationship with you, and He is capable of forgiving all your sins if you would only ask.

I take great comfort in knowing that despite all Joe's sins and failures, and all my sins and my failures, God forgave Joe and He forgives me and loves us anyway. I rejoice in the fact that Joe finally got it.

Don't waste time. Run to the Father; He's waiting for you.

Words of Assurance

John 5:24 – "I tell you the truth, those who listen to my message and believe in God who sent me have eternal life. They will never be condemned for their sins, but they have already passed from death to life."

Romans 8:16-17 – "The Spirit himself testifies with our spirit that we are God's children. Now if we are God's children, then we are heirs – heirs of God and co-heirs with Christ, if indeed we share in his sufferings in order that we may also share in his glory."

When I finished my sermon, everyone stood up and we made our way over to the side of the building where we would commit Joe's ashes to their final resting place. Everyone gathered around.

Words of Committal

In that God has ordained that the soul of our beloved brother be returned to Him, we commit his earthly body to the ground. Earth to earth, ashes to ashes, dust to dust, looking forward to the resurrection when we shall be united with him.

Let's pray - Prayer of Comfort:

Heavenly Father, you are the source of all comfort. Your Word says, "Praise be to God and Father of our Lord Jesus Christ, the Father of compassion and the God of all comfort, who comforts us in all our troubles so that we can comfort those in any trouble with the comfort we ourselves have received from God." Father God you love us that much, you care about your children. O Father God we rest in the promises you have given us, and we look forward to the day when you will return. Amen.

Benediction:

As we leave here today, let us ponder the things we have heard and the Scriptures we have read. May we look into our hearts and see what needs to be cleaned out. Take note of those things that we would like to change and start today. May your relationship with Christ grow, may it take root in your life. As Philippians 4:19 says *"and my God will meet all your needs according to his glorious riches in Christ Jesus.*" I pray that God will continue to bless and guide you daily. On behalf of our family, we would like to thank each of you personally for coming today. We would also like to thank you for the love you extended to Joe and our family during this difficult time. Thank you.

CHAPTER TWENTY-THREE

Reflection is a Good Thing

Facebook post dated September 23, 2009:

Joe's service went well. God is amazing! He carried me right through it. To God be ALL the glory for how well it went. Now back home and drying out the inside of my car. Time to work on getting that fixed, the sprinkler system fixed and some much-needed sleep. I'm thinking the fixes are going to be easier than the sleep.

September 25, 2009, I got through it – I persevered

This morning I spent my devotion time praising God for the past year of my life and all that I went through regarding Joe's illness and life and all that came from it. God was with me throughout this journey and He showed me His love, grace, and mercy. I can look back and recognize it now so clearly. The funeral service went well for my first time officiating. I truly believe even in that, God worked in and through me to put it all together between the music, the verses of Scripture, sermon and the help He gave me, and the support of the people that love and care for me. I was able to show members of my family where my passion lies and in whom I believe. I was able to plant some seeds of hope which I pray will take root someday. Glory to God!

The text this morning came from James 5, and it's so fitting yet again because it ends in verse 20 "Remember this: Whoever turns a sinner from the error of his way will save him from death and cover a multitude of sins." The other two subtitles were "Patience in Suffering" and "Prayer of Faith." Ha-ha – God you are so good!

Needs – Healing for my health, need restoration from pure exhaustion, need strengthening, need to get back on track

Insight- I have learned so much from this whole experience

Reaction – Take what I have learned and use it for the greater good

Prayer requests – Restore my health, my energy, my mind. Midterm exam next week, catch up on class work, car problems, work, children's church, fall festival planning

Praises– Your mighty hand Lord, in and through, and all around, in all things. Your presence in my life, your grace, mercy and love abounds - my cup overflows.

Confessions – My sinful nature, thoughts and words that aren't glorifying you

Memory verse – I have to get back on track with those and learn the new ones assigned during the last two weeks

October 1, 2009, 7:30 am – New month living for God

This morning, once again it was hard to get up, not feeling 100% yet, not feeling energetic for another day. In my prayer time, thankful to God for giving me another day. Talked to God about all the people I know hurting, suffering, and all about the provisions I recognize in my life. I just asked for renewed strength, continued support, and wisdom to get through. I'm concerned about school and two midterms coming up. I just can't seem to retain much of anything. Everything feels shallow in my brain. I know my mind is occupied with lots of things and people, other than God. I need to focus on Him and what His word says. I also want to feel better. I never caught up on my sleep from when I was down in West Palm Beach with Joe. Yesterday I came into work, and the rosebud had finally fallen, the green stem slowly turning to brown.

Text this morning was from 1 Peter, Chapter 4, which I enjoyed as a lot of it tied to the book, "Pursuit of Holiness" that I am currently reading for class. The verses also deal with sin problems. The verses that touched me the most, verses 1 through 6.

Need – To be able to catch up on school, especially the memorization of the four verses. I am having the hardest time recalling and memorizing them. Need for clarity.

Insight – Seeing a lot of verses and reading on sin lately

Reaction to the insight – Asking to be searched and I can't help but to look around at others and be saddened by it. Judging isn't the right thing to do either.

Thank you, Lord, for the provisions in my life

Confess- I don't always put God first

October 2, 2009, 7:40 am – Be self-controlled and alert

This morning's prayer time was all about God's grace. I just sat there in awe of His grace in my life and the lives of others. I remembered where I came from and what I used to be. I remember that Jesus came to save me from my sins 2000 plus years ago and how He gave me a new life. My life changed, many years ago now, in 2004, after the painful breakup with my boyfriend. That's when I started to see what was happening and when I saw that God had been there all along, even back 22 years ago when I wasn't even thinking about God and His plans for me. His grace and mercy abound. I love how other people are experiencing things that I have experienced and are in the same place where they are wondering why people don't see it or get it. I love that! Just confirms for me that I am not crazy because someone else is experiencing God as well, moving and showing Himself to them. It's wonderful to see and hear. May they continue to follow and walk in His path and plan for them. The great thing about God is He takes us in our brokenness and uses us for His glory. We think we're no good and not useful broken. The enemy would have us believe the lie.

The text this morning was 1 Peter, Chapter 5, and in that was a great reminder in verse 8 and, "The enemy prowls around looking for someone to devour. Resist him and stand firm in your faith." Believe it; it does work!

Needs – Of course, to continue to resist the enemy and stand firm in the faith. Continued wisdom needed to do just this.

Insight – We are in such a war zone spiritually. As I told my friend the other night - when you set out to serve in the way she is, prepare yourself for the battle, because it's coming your way.

Reaction – But here's the great thing about that – I know my Lord stands with me in the battle and I already know who WINS THE FIGHT, WHO WINS THIS WAR. WE DO!! JESUS CHRIST WINS THE BATTLE!! HE WINS THE WAR!!

What a victory and promise we have in Jesus Christ! This helps me keep moving forward my friend.

"There's victory in Jesus, my Savior forever. He sought me and bought me with His redeeming blood."

"My brothers, if anyone among you wanders from the truth and someone brings him back, let him know that whoever brings back a sinner from his wandering will save his soul from death and will cover a multitude of sins." James 5:19-20

"Come to me all who are heavy laden, and I will give you rest. Take my yoke upon you, and learn from me, for I am gentle and lowly in heart, and you will find rest for your souls. For my yoke is easy, and my burden is light." Matthew 11:28-30

My life hasn't always been easy. These days

whose is? But if there is one thing I learned – if we are to reach people with the gospel of Christ, we need to act more like Christ and less like our old selves before Christ came into our hearts. If we want to win people for the Lord, we need to quit acting like we never met the Lord. It is then that the people who are hurting and lost in this broken world will recognize something in us, that same something they want themselves.

There's a popular song by a Christian artist named Toby Mac that speaks about God's love. God's love broke through the darkness of my life as well as my brother's life and brought us back to Him.

Personally speaking, I was lost in my own doing. There were times I felt hopeless. I ran in the other direction, but God's love broke through and pursued me. He pierced my heart and mind and showed Himself to me. God loved me enough to pursue me. And He would get me, heart and soul. I serve the Lord today with a grateful heart. My heart is on fire to see lives changed for the gospel and for people to come to know the gracious God I met on the streets so many years ago. I've got good news to share – real good news!

God loved Joe enough to pursue him too. Joe tried everything to undo himself and yet, God continued to pursue him, because of love, God's love.

You might be saying right now, "But you don't know what I've done."

You're right, I don't, but God does, and my answer is still the same. It's never too late to seek the Lord.

The enemy, the devil would have you believe it's too late for you because of everything you have done. I've been in that place before, and I can tell you from personal experience that is so far from the truth. I am not proud of some of the things I did, but God took a broken woman and transformed her into His masterpiece and is using her to bring Himself glory. It's called grace.

I know God can do the same for you if you would allow Him to do so. If you allowed Him to chip away all the ugliness so you, the beautiful diamond shines through, you too can experience the joy that comes when you are walking in right relationship with Him.

My brother's story is a perfect example of the magnificent work God can do in someone's life and the amount of grace God extends to each of us. I watched from the front row seat, and I can tell you it was fantastic!

Oh, how He loves me! Oh, how He loves you! God is in the business of pursuing us, and He's pursuing you because He loves you! Oh, how He loves you!

So, what will you do with what you have read? Will you keep it a secret or share it with a friend? Will you let stubborn pride stand in the way of a lasting and meaningful relationship with Jesus, the Savior of the world?

Are you blinded to the arrow heading for your heart?

Allow love to break through.

At this point, what do you have to lose? The better

question is – What do you have to gain? Everything.

Everything!

So, where will you spend eternity and who will you spend it with?

Things I Learned

When everything calmed down in my life, and things had returned to normal, I decided to get a physical. I had been so tired and worn down from the past year between the surgery and everything with Joe. I wanted to be sure I was healthy. But more importantly, having walked side by side with Joe as he dealt with colo-rectal cancer, I wanted to get a colonoscopy done. Cancer had now made its presence known in my sibling, despite the avenue it came.

I was 43 at the time. I knew the recommended age for getting a colonoscopy was usually 50 or older, but I didn't care. I was going to ask until someone agreed to do the test.

I went to the doctor for my check up and I explained what I had just experienced over the past year.

He agreed with my reasoning and validated my concerns. I had the colonoscopy done, and to my surprise, they found a polyp. Had I waited another seven years, closer to the recommended age for this kind of test, I could very well have been facing my own cancer battle.

Several years ago, my mom was diagnosed with stage 3C colon cancer. She had a softball size tumor removed from her colon and went through chemotherapy and lived.

I tell you all this so you can decide for yourself. If you have a family member who has been diagnosed with colon or colorectal cancer, please consider getting a colonoscopy even if you haven't reached the recommended age. When it runs in the family, most are not opposed to doing the test. Because they found a polyp in me, I had to get a colonoscopy every three years until the tests came back clear. I am happy to say I am now on the five year plan.

Do yourself a favor and pay attention to your body. Don't do what my brother did – because he was embarrassed and thought he could handle it himself; he allowed a deadly disease to ravage his body and ultimately kill him.

Again the Lord would lead me in this, and I was so grateful I had followed His leading.

Allow me to share something else that is super cool. When I first started writing this book, I simply wrote the rough draft in a very rough form. I wrote down everything I could think of that I wanted to share. I just started writing, no rhyme or reason, just writing. As the weeks progressed, I would sense the Lord reminding me of some things I had forgotten, and so I wrote those down and included them in the rough draft.

I finally came to the place of going back to the very beginning and rereading and editing every single line. As I edited every single page, I began to insert chapter breaks along the way.

I don't know if you caught this or not, but when you read Chapter 17, you would have read about Joe's birthday which was September 17. That was not dumb luck or pre-planned on my part. I believe it was completely orchestrated by God to show off His sense of humor and to let me know He was in the midst of this book.

You also may not have noticed that Chapter 22 occurs on September 22, again not pre-planned by me, but I believe once again orchestrated by my Heavenly Father.

And lastly, Chapter 23 occurs on September 23. Need I explain this one? I didn't think so.

I stand in awe of my Heavenly Father and I am reminded that even in the littlest details, He is still paying attention. I am so thankful for His love and His grace. He's been merciful to me. I love you, Lord!!

While walking the road with Joe, I learned a lot about the dying process, healthcare, nursing homes, and hospice. I became all too familiar with the paperwork required and all the legal mumbo jumbo. It's not as easy as it seems when dealing with all the ins and outs of the healthcare system and your loved one's sickness.

Allow me to share some of the important things I learned as I walked by my brother's side. They may not apply to your situation. Please note these may be different in your state. Research your state for specific guidelines.

HIPAA - For starters, if you are not married to the person who is ill, you have no legal rights to their medical information. It's called HIPPA. Our mother couldn't obtain information either because Joe was an adult. Joe was required to sign HIPAA forms giving permission to medical staff to release his information. We were designated as health surrogates. Normally you choose two people to receive your medical information. Two in case something happens to the other person or in case they can't be at the appointment.

In our case, my mother had been the main health surrogate until Joe removed her name and designated me as the main surrogate. I don't remember if he put her as a backup, but I also don't recall her being involved in a lot of the decisions Joe made in those last months of his life. Without this document, the doctors, nurses and whoever else has the medical information on the one sick cannot release any information to you.

Many people are living together today and are not married. I believe this rule applies to them as well. Just because you are cohabitating under the same roof, doesn't mean you automatically have access to your significant other's medical information. You will need to get the forms signed authorizing you to receive the information. Don't assume just because you live together, the medical community will automatically recognize you as eligible. Don't wait for a health crisis to occur only to find out you have no right to their medical information.

Medical Records – It is very helpful to obtain copies of all reports done, whether blood tests and any scans or films taken. Keep a file on yourself or your loved one so when you go to multiple doctors' appointments, you don't have to start from scratch explaining everything. Keep a record of all medications taken, both the name of the medication, dosage and how often it is taken to avoid complications and allergic reactions. Keep a calendar of when appointments and events take place. Also, it helps to have the information handy because we don't always remember all the dates of when medical things occurred.

Take your medical file with you to the doctor, but don't allow them to keep the originals. They can make copies and give you the file back if you don't have access to a copy machine. A good medical file is one of the keys to experiencing a little less stress than you already feel when you visit the doctor. The doctors love it too. Depending on where you have the tests done, doctors can access them electronically, but this isn't necessarily the case if the information is older or your doctor is not linked up electronically.

Having the medical information also prevents serious side effects from occurring when the medicines given to the patient conflict with treatment. This happened to my dear friend's mom.

She had to have an emergency procedure done involving her heart, and they failed to recognize she had a chemo patch on her back. When they did the procedure, she started having an adverse reaction and was struggling. They couldn't figure out what was happening.

They finally asked my friend if she knew of any other medications her mom was on and she mentioned she had been wearing a chemo patch on her back. They quickly descended on her, ripping the patch off immediately. She finally stirred. If her daughter hadn't been there, she might not have survived the procedure. The chart and the lack of information almost cost her her life.

I had this happen to another friend of mine, and he didn't make it. He had broken his neck as a result of a car accident years prior. His new injury required surgery and the hospital was unaware of his neck fusion. From what I was told, he went into cardiac arrest on the operating table, and when they tried to install a trachea in his throat, they couldn't get his neck into the proper position, and they panicked. He died in the operating room. He had gone in for a simple leg surgery.

Financial Responsibility - The next thing I learned is that unless you are fine with absorbing your loved one's debts and doctor bills, you do not sign any paperwork that designates you as being financially responsible for any outstanding debts your loved ones may incur. You only sign the document designating you as a health surrogate. You do not want to put yourself in a position where you receive bills for all remaining charges after your loved one dies.

I learned this early on and refused to sign anything accepting financial responsibility. When Joe passed, the nursing home still tried to charge me for the balance they were owed. I declined, citing I had not signed anything that held me legally responsible for his bills. There was nothing they could do to me.

If you don't want to incur the costs, don't sign anything that ties you to your loved one financially. There is a difference in the forms used for financial responsibility and health surrogate. Read the wording closely. You will also need to find out how much time is allowed between depleting your loved one's assets and going into a nursing home. If your loved one still has assets in their name and they go into a nursing home, the nursing home can take what they need to cover the costs. Always check the rules for this. Check the laws in your state.

Bank Accounts - Whenever your loved one chooses to add your name to their bank account via a signature card, whether it is a personal or business account, please be sure you make a copy of the signature card BEFORE giving it to the lovely teller at the bank for processing.

A dear friend of mine did not make a copy of the signature card her mother signed for her business account. She turned in the original to the bank, and they lost it. Her mother passed away, and my friend thought everything had been processed at the bank. What she didn't know, was the employee at the bank lost the signature card request and never processed the signature card.

It is important to follow up with the bank to be sure they processed the signature card before your loved one passes away. My friend cannot get the money out of the account to pay the outstanding bills without hiring an attorney.

The bank, while they admit it was their fault, says they cannot legally allow her access to the money without her hiring an attorney. An attorney friend of mine says she sees this happen all the time and that when it happens she recommends her clients let the money sit in the account for two years and then petition a judge to have it released. The bank has no choice but to release the funds in the account. By then, any creditors who placed a judgment against the deceased account would have been paid out.

Vehicle Titles – Depending on the state, transferring a title from your loved one requires certain wording depending on the situation. Each state is different as to the wording required, so check with your local Department of Motor Vehicles for details.

Many times, vehicles are gifted to the next of kin. If there are multiple siblings, there is specific paperwork required. If it's a gift, specific wording is required on the titled. Do your homework, so you don't incur additional tax and fees. If the vehicle is designated to someone specific, make sure it is spelled out in a will, or some other legal document. Be sure the insurance on the vehicle is transferred to the new owner of the vehicle.

Nursing Homes – Always, always, always label your loved one's items. I suggest purchasing a black trunk or something similar you can padlock and keep their valuable items locked in the trunk. Too often, personal items disappear in nursing homes whether it is via other residents, visitors, or employees. Don't leave anything valuable there you don't want to disappear.

Loved ones often leave their glasses on the food tray, and the food tray gets sent to the kitchen. Glasses disappear. Hearing aids disappear the same way. Be sure your loved ones know they need to do the best they can to keep track of their stuff.

Visit them often in the nursing home. Make surprise visits often so you can see what goes on. Pay attention to their surroundings and the care they are receiving. Be sure the staff knows who you are. Be sure they know you want phone calls no matter what happens to your loved one even if in the middle of the night. If they fall, you want the nursing home to call you.

Again, it gets back to making sure you have the proper documentation in place so you can receive those important calls. Your loved ones will not remember essential information or phone numbers, so it's up to you to remember it for them, to ask questions, and be their eyes and ears.

Property – Please be sure adequate paperwork is in place, like a will to designate who gets the home once the sick person moves out and passes away. If the home is designated to a family member, be sure it is designated accordingly. Please be sure you designate who gets the personal items. Who gets the jewelry, if any? Who gets the furniture? What do we do with the fine art hanging on the walls? Who gets the sentimental items?

As your loved one's age, encourage them to start cleaning out the stuff they haven't used in years if they will allow you. Donate it to Goodwill or give it away. Have a garage sale. Start downsizing so it's not so overwhelming later. It's very difficult to go through their stuff after they are gone.

Medicines – As I eluded to before, keep track of the medications your loved one is on. As with my brother, there were certain medications he couldn't take because of the AIDS cocktail. When loved ones are sick, they don't always remember what they took and when. It helps to get a pillbox that separates them by the days of the week and put the recommended dosage in each day.

Counseling – If it becomes too overwhelming, go to counseling. Don't be ashamed or embarrassed. It's very helpful.

Don't be afraid to bring in a spiritual counselor like a chaplain.

Some hospitals offer music therapy. Some even offer dog therapy or allow the sick one's pets to visit. Don't be afraid to call and ask them. My friend even brought in a hairdresser for her mom, and they fixed her up beautifully, and she felt like herself.

Anything you can do to assist yourself is beneficial when you are going through the process. Surround yourself with people who will lift you up in prayer and support you.

Ask for help. Don't try and be a super person. It's tough and the longer it goes on, the more it wears you down. Caretakers need respite breaks – take them when you can.

Regarding Life – There are several documents you need to consider. A great website to look at is "A Place for Mom" or "Age with Dignity." You can find both online. Both will have a copy of a very important document called, "Five Wishes." You should complete this document on yourself as well as your loved one. It is free.

This document addresses important stuff like a DNR (Do Not Resuscitate), a Living Will (health care directive), Health care proxy (durable health power-of-attorney), and Authorization to release health-care information. The document "Five Wishes" makes it very easy and you and your loved one can sit down together and review each item, and they can make the decisions on how they want each situation handled – situations like them going into cardiac arrest, or suffering a stroke. How do they want to be treated if they suffer a major trauma and go into a coma? They need to answer those questions, so you as their health surrogate know their wishes and their doctors know how far to go with the treatment.

Also be sure your loved one has a current will in place that is considered legal and binding. Make sure everyone has the appropriate copies stored in a safe place and that the doctors have their copy of the Five Wishes paperwork.

Death Certificates – You will more than likely need multiple certified copies of the death certificates. You will need them to close banks accounts, credit accounts and other important transactions involving your loved one. Check for details in your state.

Be sure the Internal Revenue Service gets notification of their death. Normally the funeral home handles this, but be sure they contacted the IRS, so their disability checks or social security checks cease.

Funerals – This is a big item too, and can be costly depending on the route you take. We learned cremation is a lot more affordable than being buried in a casket. However, it is a personal choice.

Call around. Get multiple quotes. Don't take the first price quoted. Some cremation businesses use subcontractors to do the work, hence the increase in cost. Others do it themselves.

It's the same with funeral homes. Some use subcontractors, and others don't. If it is possible to pre-plan this part, then it will be much easier on the family. All they have to do is call who was chosen to handle the deceased. If you do not have plans in place, you run the risk of being taken advantage of in your time of need. Emotions run high, tears are flowing and you are overwhelmed with grief. Something sounds good to you, but then you find out they are more expensive than the guy down the street, but you're stuck.

Do your homework in advance if possible. Let your loved ones know what you want. Tell them what songs you wish to have played or what you wish to have read. It helps make the process go smoother. Have the conversation. Keep copies of the funeral arrangements, if possible, in a safe place and let your loved ones know where you stored the paperwork so they can find it when the time comes.

What To Say – This is a very difficult thing. What do we say when someone is dying? How do we treat them? Can they hear everything we say when they are no longer responding?

My suggestion would be to get your hands on a booklet hospice gives their patient families. Inside, it covers several important pieces of information. Every person is different, but hospice has been doing this for such a long time, they have narrowed down what's best in these situations.

There is also a new book that came out recently called "Don't Sing Songs to a Heavy Heart" by

Kenneth C. Haugk. It may be some help to you. I believe loved ones can still hear everything we say in their final moments, so be sensitive in those moments and guard your thoughts and words.

And lastly, pray, pray, pray! Seek the Lord each day as you walk through the difficult days. Ask God to guide you through each step of the process. He will put people in your path to help you through one of the most difficult experiences you will ever live through.

Trust me – God's grace was abundant in Joe's life and mine. He walked with us through it all, through the fire, the tears - He never left our side. To Him be the glory!

Disclaimer – The above are things I experienced. They may or may not apply in your state, your circumstance, with your loved one or even you. They are not mandates, but suggestions to help make the process a little easier. I sought the advice of several people along the way who walked similar paths and their help and insight was very valuable to me. I thank God for sending the help my way.

Appendix

The following information is taken directly from the website, www.hiv.org. Keep in mind that this information was not available to my family or me at the time of Joe's diagnosis. What information we received then, came from the doctors he saw. What you are about to read is a synopsis of the highlights of each year since the disease was first discovered in 1981. There are some very interesting and revealing facts. As I read many of them for the first time to include them in this book, I was taken aback a bit by all the information I didn't know.

----------------------------- 1981 -----------------------------

On June 5, 1981, the U.S. Centers for Disease Control and Prevention (CDC) published a Morbidity and Mortality Weekly Report (MMWR), describing cases of a rare lung infection, Pneumocystis carinii pneumonia (PCP), in five young, previously healthy, gay men in Los Angeles. All the men have other unusual infections as well, indicating that their immune systems are not working; two have already died by the time the report is published. This edition of the MMWR marks the first official reporting of what will become known as the AIDS epidemic.

On June 5, the Associated Press and the Los Angeles Times report on the MMWR. On June 6, the San

Francisco Chronicle covers the story. Within days, doctors from across the U.S. flood CDC with reports of similar cases.

In addition to reports of cases of PCP and other opportunistic infections among gay men, CDC also receives reports of a cluster of cases of a rare, and unusually aggressive, cancer, Kaposi's sarcoma, among a group of gay men in New York and California. In response, on June 8, CDC establishes a Task Force on Kaposi's sarcoma and Opportunistic Infections (KSOI) to identify risk factors and to develop a case definition for national surveillance.

On July 3, the New York Times reports on cases of Kaposi's sarcoma affecting 41 gay men in New York and California.

By year-end, there is a cumulative total of 270 reported cases of severe immune deficiency among gay men, and 121 of those individuals have died.

---------------------------- 1982 ----------------------------

The City and County of San Francisco, working closely with the Shanti Project and the San Francisco AIDS Foundation, develop the "San Francisco Model of Care" which emphasizes home- and community-based services.

In January, the first American AIDS clinic is established in San Francisco.

Gay Men's Health Crisis, the first community-based AIDS service provider in the U.S., is founded in New York City.

On April 13, U.S. Representative Henry Waxman convenes the first congressional hearings on HIV/AIDS. The U.S. Centers for Disease Control and

Prevention (CDC) estimate that tens of thousands of people may be affected by the disease.

In September, Congressional representatives Henry Waxman and Phillip Burton introduce legislation to allocate $5 million to CDC for surveillance and $10 million to the National Institutes of Health (NIH) for AIDS research.

On September 24, CDC uses the term "AIDS" (acquired immune deficiency syndrome) for the first time, and releases the first case definition of AIDS: "a disease at least moderately predictive of a defect in cell-mediated immunity, occurring in a person with no known case for diminished resistance to that disease."

On December 10, CDC reports a case of AIDS in an infant who received blood transfusions. The following week, the MMWR reports 22 cases of unexplained immunodeficiency and opportunistic infections in infants.

---------------------------- 1983 ----------------------------

The U.S. Centers for Disease Control and Prevention (CDC) establish the National AIDS Hotline to respond to public inquiries about the disease.

On January 4, CDC hosts a national conference to determine blood bank policy for testing blood for HIV, but participants fail to reach consensus on appropriate action.

On January 7, CDC reports cases of AIDS in female sexual partners of males with AIDS.

In February, Dr. Robert Gallo, from the National Institutes of Health (NIH), suggests that a retrovirus probably causes AIDS.

In the March 4 edition of the Morbidity and Mortality

Weekly Report (MMWR), CDC notes that most cases of AIDS have been reported among gay men with multiple sexual partners, injection drug users, Haitians, and hemophiliacs. The report suggests that AIDS may be caused by an infectious agent that is transmitted sexually or through exposure to blood or blood products and issues recommendations for preventing transmission.

In May, the U.S. Congress passes the first bill that includes funding specifically targeted for AIDS research and treatment—$12 million for agencies within the U.S. Department of Health and Human Services.

On May 20, Dr. Françoise Barré-Sinoussi and her colleagues at the Pasteur Institute in France, report the discovery of a retrovirus named Lymphadenopathy Associated Virus (LAV) that could be the cause of AIDS.

In June, people living with AIDS (PLWAs) take over the plenary stage at the Second National AIDS Forum in Denver, and issue a statement on the right of PLWAs to be at the table when policy is made, to be treated with dignity, and to be called "people with AIDS," not "AIDS victims." The statement becomes known as "The Denver Principles," and it serves as the charter for the founding of the National Association of People with AIDS (NAP-WA).

On July 25, San Francisco General Hospital opens the first dedicated AIDS ward in the U.S. It is fully occupied within days.

On September 2, in response to concerns about transmission of AIDS in healthcare settings, CDC publishes the first set of occupational exposure precautions for healthcare workers and allied health professionals.

In the September 9 MMWR, CDC identifies all major routes of HIV transmission—and rules out transmission by casual contact, food, water, air, or environmental surfaces.

In October, the World Health Organization (WHO) holds its first meeting to assess the global AIDS situation and begins international surveillance.

---------------------------- 1984 ----------------------------

Community-based AIDS service organizations join together to form AIDS Action, a national organization in Washington, DC, to advocate on behalf of people and communities affected by the epidemic, to educate the Federal government, and to help shape AIDS-related policy and legislation.

On April 23, Margaret Heckler, Secretary of the U.S. Department of Health and Human Services, announces that Dr. Robert Gallo and his colleagues at the National Cancer Institute have found the cause of AIDS, the retrovirus HTLV-III. She also announces the development of a diagnostic blood test to identify HTLV-III and expresses hope that a vaccine against AIDS will be produced within two years.

In June, Dr. Gallo and Professor Luc Montagnier, from the Pasteur Institute in France, hold a joint press conference to announce that Dr. Montagnier's Lymphadenopathy Associated Virus (LAV) and Dr. Gallo's HTLV-III virus are almost certainly identical and are the likely cause of AIDS.

On July 13, the U.S. Centers for Disease Control and Prevention (CDC) state that avoiding injection drug use and reducing needle-sharing "should also be effective in preventing transmission of the virus."

In October, San Francisco officials order bathhouses

closed due to high-risk sexual activity occurring in these venues. New York and Los Angeles follow suit within the year.

-------------------------- 1985 --------------------------

The U.S. Food and Drug Administration (FDA) licenses the first commercial blood test, ELISA, to detect antibodies to HIV in the blood. Blood banks begin screening the U.S. blood supply.

The U.S. Congress allocates $70 million for AIDS research.

The Pentagon announces that it will begin testing all new military recruits for HIV infection and will reject those who test positive for the virus.

Ryan White, an Indiana teenager who contracted AIDS through contaminated blood products used to treat his hemophilia, is refused entry to his middle school. He goes on to speak publicly against AIDS stigma and discrimination.

On January 11, the U.S. Centers for Disease Control and Prevention (CDC) revise the AIDS case definition to note that AIDS is caused by a newly identified virus and issued provisional guidelines for blood screening.

On April 15-17, the U.S. Department of Health and Human Services (HHS) and the World Health Organization (WHO) host the first International AIDS Conference in Atlanta, Georgia.

On September 17, President Ronald Reagan mentions AIDS publicly for the first time, vowing in a letter to Congress to make AIDS a priority.

Actor Rock Hudson dies of AIDS-related illness on October 2. Hudson leaves $250,000 to help set up the American Foundation for AIDS Research (amfAR). Elizabeth Taylor serves as the founding National Chairman.

On December 6, the U.S. Public Health Service issues the first recommendations for preventing HIV transmission from mother to child.

At least one HIV case has been reported from each region of the world.

---------------------------- 1986 ----------------------------

The National Academy of Sciences issues a report critical of the U.S. response to a "national health crisis." The report calls for a U.S. $2 billion investment. An Institute of Medicine report calls for a national education campaign and for creating a National Commission on AIDS.

AIDS activist Cleve Jones creates the first panel of the AIDS Memorial Quilt.

In May, the International Committee on the Taxonomy of Viruses declares that the virus that causes AIDS will officially be known as Human Immunodeficiency Virus (HIV).

On October 22, U.S. Surgeon General, C. Everett Koop, issues the Surgeon General's Report on AIDS. The report urges parents and schools to start frank, open discussions about AIDS and urges education and condom use.

The Robert Wood Johnson Foundation creates the "AIDS Health Services Program," providing joint funding with the U.S. Health Resources and Services Administration (HRSA) for demonstration projects in hard-hit U.S. cities. This program serves as a precursor to the Ryan White CARE Act.

The International Steering Committee for People with HIV/AIDS is created. Six years later, this will become the Global Network of People Living with HIV/AIDS the National Minority AIDS Council (NMAC) is formed.

---------------------------- 1987 ----------------------------

In February, the World Health Organization (WHO) launches The Global Program on AIDS to: raise awareness; formulate evidence-based policies; provide technical and financial support to countries; initiate relevant social, behavioral, and biomedical research; promote participation by nongovernmental organizations; and champion the rights of those living with HIV.

Emmy-award winning pianist, Liberace, dies of AIDS-related illness on February 4.

On March 19, the U.S. Food and Drug Administration (FDA) approves the first antiretroviral drug, zidovudine (AZT). The U.S. Congress approves $30 million in emergency funding to states for AZT— laying the groundwork for what will be the AIDS Drug Assistance Program (ADAP), authorized by the Ryan White CARE Act in 1990.

In March, playwright and AIDS activist Larry Kramer founded the AIDS Coalition to Unleash Power (ACT UP) in New York City.

In April, FDA approves the Western Blot blood test kit, a more specific test for HIV antibodies.

In May, FDA creates a new class of experimental drugs, Treatment Investigational New Drugs, which accelerates drug approval by 2-3 years.

On May 16, the U.S. Public Health Service adds HIV as a "dangerous contagious disease" to its immigration exclusion list and mandates testing for all visa applicants.

On May 31, President Reagan makes his first public speech about AIDS and establishes a Presidential Commission on HIV.

In July, the U.S. Congress adopts the Helms Amendment, which bans the use of Federal funds for AIDS education materials that "promote or encourage, directly or indirectly, homosexual activities."

In August, the U.S. Centers for Disease Control and Prevention (CDC) hold the first National Conference on HIV and Communities of Color in New York.

After Florida's Desoto County School Board refuses to allow HIV-positive brothers, Ricky, Robert, and Randy Ray to attend school, a Federal judge orders the board to reinstate the three hemophiliacs, who contracted HIV through contaminated blood products. After the August 5 ruling, outraged town residents refuse to allow their children to attend school, and someone sets fire to the Ray House on August 28, destroying it.

On August 14, the U.S. Centers for Disease Control and Prevention (CDC) issue Perspectives in Disease Prevention and Health Promotion Public Health Service Guidelines for Counseling and Antibody Testing to Prevent HIV Infection and AIDS.

On August 18, FDA sanctions the first human testing of a candidate vaccine against HIV.

In October, the AIDS Memorial Quilt is displayed for the first time on the National Mall in Washington, DC. The display features 1,920 4x8 panels and draws half a million visitors.

In October, AIDS becomes the first disease ever debated on the floor of the United Nations (UN)

General Assembly. The General Assembly resolves to mobilize the entire UN system in the worldwide struggle against AIDS and designates the WHO to lead the effort.

FDA declares HIV prevention as a new indication for male condoms.

Journalist Randy Shilts' book about the early years of the HIV/AIDS epidemic, and the Band Played On: Politics, People, and the AIDS Epidemic, is published.

CDC launches the first AIDS-related public service announcements, "America Responds to AIDS."

---------------------------- 1988 ----------------------------

The World Health Organization (WHO) declares December 1 to be the first World AIDS Day.

The Health Omnibus Programs Extension (HOPE) Act authorizes the use of Federal funds for AIDS prevention, education, and testing.

The National Institutes of Health (NIH) establish the Office of AIDS Research (OAR) and the AIDS Clinical Trials Group (ACTG).

The U.S. Food and Drug Administration (FDA) allows the importation of unapproved drugs for persons with life-threatening illnesses, including HIV/AIDS.

Ryan White, an HIV-positive teenager who has become a national spokesperson for AIDS education, treatment, and funding, testifies before the President's Commission on AIDS.

Elizabeth Glaser, an HIV-positive mother of two HIV-positive children, and two of her friends formed the Pediatric AIDS Foundation (later renamed the Elizabeth Glaser Pediatric AIDS Foundation to advocate for research into the care and treatment needs of children living with HIV/AIDS.

The U.S. Health Resources and Services Administration (HRSA) awards HIV Planning Grants to 11 states and ten cities to create a plan for HIV/AIDS systems of care. This lays the groundwork for the statewide programs that will later be funded under the Ryan White CARE Act.

HRSA also funds the first Pediatric AIDS Service Demonstration Grants, a program which will eventually become part of the Ryan White CARE Act.

In April, the first comprehensive needle-exchange program (NEP) in North America is established in Tacoma, WA. San Francisco then establishes what becomes the largest NEP in the nation.

On May 26, the U.S. Surgeon General, C. Everett Koop, launches the U.S.'s first coordinated HIV/ AIDS education campaign by mailing 107 million copies of a booklet, Understanding AIDS, to all American households.

On October 11, ACT UP (AIDS Coalition to Unleash Power) protests at FDA headquarters about the drug-approval process. Eight days later, FDA announces new regulations to speed up drug approvals.

UNAIDS (the Joint United Nations Programme on HIV/AIDS) reports that the number of women living with HIV/AIDS in sub-Saharan Africa exceeds that of men.

--------------------------- 1989 ---------------------------

Photographer Robert Mapplethorpe dies of AIDS-related illness on March 9.

On June 16, the U.S. Centers for Disease Control and Prevention (CDC) issued the first guidelines for preventing Pneumocystis carinii pneumonia (PCP), an AIDS-related opportunistic infection, and a major cause of illness and death for people living with AIDS.

On June 23, CDC releases the Guidelines for Prevention of Transmission of Human Immunodeficiency Virus and Hepatitis B Virus to Health-Care and Public-Safety Workers.

The U.S. Congress creates the National Commission on AIDS. The Commission meets for the first time on September 18.

Dr. Anthony Fauci, head of the National Institutes of Health's National Institute of Allergy and Infectious Diseases (NIAID), endorses giving HIV-positive people who do not qualify for clinical trials access to experimental treatments.

The U.S. Health Resources and Services Administration (HRSA) grants $20 million for HIV care and treatment through the Home-Based and Community-Based Care State Grant program. For many states, this is their first involvement in HIV care and treatment.

A CDC/HRSA initiative provides $11 million to fund seven community health centers to provide HIV counseling and testing services. This is a precursor to what will be part of the Ryan White CARE Act.

The number of reported AIDS cases in the United States reaches 100,000.

---------------------------- 1990 ----------------------------

On January 18, the U.S. Centers for Disease Control

and Prevention (CDC) report the possible transmission of HIV to a patient through a dental procedure performed by an HIV-positive dentist. This episode provokes much public debate about the safety of common dental and medical procedures.

On January 26, the U.S. Public Health Service issues a statement on managing occupational exposure to HIV, including considerations regarding the post-exposure use of the antiretroviral drug, AZT.

Pop artist Keith Haring dies of AIDS-related illness on February 16.

On April 8, Ryan White dies of AIDS-related illness at the age of 18.

On May 21, ACT UP (AIDS Coalition to Unleash Power) protests at the National Institutes of Health (NIH), demanding more HIV treatments and the expansion of clinical trials to include more women and people of color.

In June, the 6th International AIDS Conference meets in San Francisco. To protest U.S. immigration policy that bars people with HIV from entering the country, domestic and international nongovernmental groups boycott the conference.

In July, the U.S. Congress enacts the Americans with Disabilities Act (ADA). The Act prohibits discrimination against individuals with disabilities, including people living with HIV/AIDS.

In August, the U.S. Congress enacts the Ryan White Comprehensive AIDS Resources Emergency (CARE) Act of 1990, which provides $220.5 million in Federal funds for HIV community-based care and treatment services in its first year. The U.S. Health Resources and Services Administration (HRSA) manages the program, which is the nation's largest HIV-specific Federal grant program.

On October 26, the U.S. Food and Drug Administration (FDA) approves the use of zidovudine (AZT) for pediatric AIDS.

CDC adopts the HIV-prevention counseling model, a "client-centered" approach that focuses on the patient, rather than the disease.

---------------------------- 1991 ----------------------------

The Visual AIDS Artists Caucus launches the Red Ribbon Project to create a visual symbol to demonstrate compassion for people living with AIDS and their caregivers. The red ribbon becomes the international symbol of AIDS awareness.

The U.S. Congress enacts the Housing Opportunities for People with AIDS (HOPWA) Act of 1991. Administered by the U.S. Department of Housing and Urban Development (HUD), HOPWA grants to states and local communities provide housing assistance to people living with AIDS.

On July 21, the U.S. Centers for Disease Control and Prevention (CDC) recommend restrictions on the practice of HIV-positive healthcare workers and Congress enacts a law requiring states to adopt the CDC restrictions or to develop and adopt their own.

In August, the U.S. Congress passes the Terry Beirn Community-Based Clinical Trials Program Act to establish a network of community-based clinical trials for HIV treatment.

The National Minority AIDS Council (NMAC), in cooperation with the National Association of People with AIDS (NAPWA) and the National AIDS Interfaith Network, holds the first annual National Skills Building Conference, which will later become the United States Conference on AIDS.

On November 7, American basketball star Earvin "Magic" Johnson announces that he is HIV-positive.

On November 24, Freddie Mercury, lead singer/songwriter of the rock band Queen, dies of bronchial pneumonia resulting from AIDS.

---------------------------- 1992 ----------------------------

The 8th International AIDS Conference is originally scheduled to be held in Boston, but is moved to Amsterdam due to U.S. immigration restrictions on people living with HIV/AIDS.

AIDS becomes the number one cause of death for U.S. men ages 25 to 44.

On May 27, the U.S. Food and Drug Administration (FDA) licenses a 10-minute diagnostic test kit which can be used by health professionals to detect the presence of HIV-1.

On December 1, the U.S. Centers for Disease Control and Prevention (CDC) launch the Business Responds to AIDS program to help large and small businesses meet the challenges of HIV/AIDS in the workplace and the community. (CDC will start the Labor Responds to AIDS program in 1995.)

Florida teenager Ricky Ray dies of AIDS-related illness on December 13. The 15-year-old hemophiliac and his two younger brothers sparked a national conversation on AIDS after their court battle to attend school led to boycotts by local residents and the torching of their home.

---------------------------- 1993 ----------------------------

President Clinton establishes the White House

Office of National AIDS Policy (ONAP).

World-renowned ballet dancer Rudolf Nureyev dies of AIDS-related illness on January 6, and tennis star Arthur Ashe dies on February 3.

On May 7, the U.S. Food and Drug Administration (FDA) approves the female condom.

In June, the U.S. Congress enacts the NIH (National Institutes of Health) Revitalization Act, giving the Office of AIDS Research primary oversight of all NIH AIDS research. The Act requires NIH and other research agencies to expand the involvement of women and minorities in all research.

The same act codifies the U.S. HIV immigration exclusion policy into law; President Clinton signs it on June 10.

In August, the Women's Interagency HIV Study and HIV Epidemiology Study begin; both are major U.S. Federally funded research studies on women and HIV/AIDS.

On December 18, the U.S. Centers for Disease Control and Prevention (CDC) expand the case definition of AIDS, declaring those with CD4 counts below 200 to have AIDS.

In that same MMWR, CDC adds three new conditions—pulmonary tuberculosis, recurrent pneumonia, and invasive cervical cancer—to the list of clinical indicators of AIDS. These new conditions mean that more women and injection drug users will be diagnosed with AIDS.

CDC institutes the community-planning process to better target local prevention efforts.

The National Association of People with AIDS (NAPWA) convenes the first annual "AIDS Watch." Hundreds of community members from across the

U.S. come to Washington, DC to lobby Congress for increased funding.

The film "Philadelphia" starring Tom Hanks as a lawyer with AIDS, opens in theaters. Based on a true story, it is the first major Hollywood film on AIDS.

Angels in America, Tony Kushner's play about AIDS, wins the Tony Award for Best Play and the 1993 Pulitzer Prize for Drama.

---------------------------- 1994 ----------------------------

AIDS becomes the leading cause of death for all Americans ages 25 to 44.

On February 17, Randy Shilts, a U.S. journalist who covered the AIDS epidemic and who authored And the Band Played On: Politics, People, and the AIDS Epidemic dies of AIDS-related illness at age 42.

On May 20, the U.S. Centers for Disease Control and Prevention (CDC) publishes Guidelines for Preventing Transmission of Human Immunodeficiency Virus Through Transplantation of Human Tissue and Organs.

On August 5, the U.S. Public Health Service recommends that pregnant women be given the antiretroviral drug AZT to reduce the risk of perinatal transmission of HIV.

Pedro Zamora, a young gay man, living with HIV, appears on the cast of MTV's popular show, "The Real World." He dies on November 11 at age 22.

On December 23, the U.S. Food and Drug Administration (FDA) approves an oral HIV test, the first non-blood-based antibody test for HIV.

The U.S. Department of Health and Human Services (HHS) issues guidelines requiring applicants for grants from the National Institutes of Health (NIH) to address "the appropriate inclusion of women and minorities in clinical research."

---------------------------- 1995 ----------------------------

On February 23, Greg Louganis, Olympic gold medal diver, discloses that he is HIV-positive.

In June, the U.S. Food and Drug Administration (FDA) approves the first protease inhibitor. This ushered in a new era of highly active antiretroviral therapy (HAART).

Eric Lynn Wright, a.k.a. Rapper Eazy-E died on March 26 from an AIDS-related illness one month after being diagnosed.

On June 27, the National Association of People with AIDS (NAPWA) launches the first National HIV Testing Day.

On July 14, the U.S. Centers for Disease Control and Prevention (CDC) issued the first guidelines to help healthcare providers prevent opportunistic infections in people infected with HIV.

President Clinton establishes his Presidential Advisory Council on HIV/AIDS (PACHA). The Council meets for the first time on July 28.

On September 22, CDC reviews Syringe Exchange Programs -- the United States, 1994-1995. The National Academy of Sciences concludes that syringe exchange programs should be regarded as an effective component of a comprehensive strategy to prevent infectious disease.

By October 31, 500,000 cases of AIDS have been reported in the US.

President Clinton hosts the first White House Conference on HIV/AIDS on December 6.

-------------------------- 1996 --------------------------

In Vancouver, the 11th International AIDS Conference highlights the effectiveness of highly active antiretroviral therapy (HAART), creating a period of optimism.

The number of new AIDS cases diagnosed in the U.S. declines for the first time since the beginning of the epidemic.

AIDS is no longer leading cause of death for all Americans ages 25-44, although it remains the leading cause of death for African-Americans in this age group.

UNAIDS (the Joint United Nations Programme on HIV/AIDS) begins operations. It is established to advocate for global action on the epidemic and to coordinate HIV/AIDS efforts across the UN system.

The U.S. Food and Drug Administration (FDA) approves: the first HIV home testing and collection kit (May 14) a viral load test, which measures the level of HIV in the blood (June 3) the first non-nucleoside reverse transcriptase inhibitor (NNRTI) drug, nevirapine (June 21) the first HIV urine test (August 6) The U.S. Congress reauthorizes the Ryan White CARE Act on May 20.

In October, the AIDS Memorial Quilt is displayed in its entirety for the last time. It covers the entire National Mall in Washington, DC.

HIV/AIDS researcher Dr. David Ho advocates for a new strategy for treating HIV – "hit early, hit hard," in which patients are placed on new, more aggressive treatment regimens earlier in the course of their infection in hopes of keeping them healthier longer. He is subsequently named TIME Magazine's "Man of the Year."

The International AIDS Vaccine Initiative (IAVI) forms to speed the search for an effective HIV vaccine.

---------------------------- 1997 ----------------------------

In response to the call to "hit early, hit hard," highly active antiretroviral therapy (HAART) becomes the new standard of HIV care.

The U.S. Centers for Disease Control and Prevention (CDC) report the first substantial decline in AIDS deaths in the United States. Due largely to the use of HAART, AIDS-related deaths in the U.S. declined by 47% compared with the previous year.

On May 18, President Clinton announces that the goal of finding an effective vaccine for HIV in 10 years will be a top national priority, and calls for the creation of an AIDS vaccine research center at the National Institutes of Health (NIH). (He dedicated the Dale and Betty Bumpers Vaccine Research Center on June 9, 1999.)

On September 26, the U.S. Food and Drug Administration (FDA) approves Combivir, a combination of two antiretroviral drugs in one tablet, which makes it easier for people living with HIV to take their medications.

On November 21, the U.S. Congress enacts the Food and Drug Administration Modernization Act (FDAMA) of 1997, codifying an accelerated drug approval process and allowing dissemination of information about off-label uses of drugs.

UNAIDS (the Joint United Nations Programme

on AIDS) estimates that 30 million adults and children worldwide have HIV, and that, each day, 16,000 people are newly infected with the virus.

As a greater number of people begin taking protease inhibitors, resistance to the drugs becomes more common, and drug resistance emerges as an area of grave concern within the AIDS community.

-------------------------- 1998 --------------------------

The U.S. Centers for Disease Control and Prevention (CDC) report that African Americans account for 49% of U.S. AIDS-related deaths. AIDS-related mortality for African Americans is almost 10 times that of Whites and three times that of Hispanics.

In March, African American leaders, including members of the Congressional Black Caucus (CBC), are briefed on the highly disproportionate impact of HIV and AIDS in their communities. They develop a "Call to Action," requesting that the President and Surgeon General declare HIV/AIDS a "State of Emergency" in the African American community.

In October, President Clinton declares AIDS to be a "severe and ongoing health crisis" in African American and Hispanic communities in the United States and announces a special package of initiatives aimed at reducing the impact of HIV/AIDS on racial and ethnic minorities.

With the leadership of the CBC, Congress funds the Minority AIDS Initiative. An unprecedented $156 million is invested in improving the nation's effectiveness in preventing and treating HIV/AIDS in African American, Hispanic, and other minority communities.

On April 20, Donna Shalala, Secretary of the U.S. Department of Health and Human Services, determines that needle-exchange programs (NEPs) are effective and do not encourage the use of illegal drugs, but the Clinton Administration does not lift the ban on the use of Federal funds for NEPs.

On April 24, CDC issues the first national treatment guidelines for the use of antiretroviral therapy in adults and adolescents with HIV.

On June 25, the U.S. Supreme Court rules that the Americans with Disabilities Act (ADA) covers those in earlier stages of HIV disease, not just those who have developed AIDS.

On November 12, the U.S. Congress enacts the Ricky Ray Hemophilia Relief Fund Act, honoring the Florida teenager who was infected with HIV through contaminated blood products. The Act authorizes payments to individuals with hemophilia and other blood clotting disorders who were infected with HIV by unscreened blood-clotting agents between 1982 and 1987.

---------------------------- 1999 ----------------------------

The Congressional Hispanic Caucus, with the Congressional Hispanic Caucus Institute, convenes Congressional hearings on the impact of HIV/AIDS on the Latino community.

The World Health Organization (WHO) announces that HIV/AIDS has become the fourth biggest killer worldwide and the number one killer in Africa. WHO estimates that 33 million people are living with HIV worldwide and that 14 million have died of AIDS.

In March, VaxGen, a San Francisco-based biotechnology company, begins conducting the first human vaccine trials in a developing country—Thailand.

On July 19, President Clinton announces the formation of the "Leadership and Investment in Fighting an Epidemic" (LIFE) Initiative, which will provide funding to address the global HIV epidemic.

On December 10, the U.S. Centers for Disease Control and Prevention (CDC) release a new HIV case definition to help state health departments expand their HIV surveillance efforts and more accurately track the changing course of the epidemic.

---------------------------- 2000 ----------------------------

On January 10, the United Nations Security Council meets to discuss the impact of AIDS on peace and security in Africa. This marks the first time that the council discusses a health issue as a threat to peace and security.

In his State of the Union address on January 27, President Clinton announces the launch of the Millennium Vaccine Initiative to create incentives for developing and distributing vaccines against HIV, TB, and malaria.

On April 30, President Clinton declares that HIV/AIDS is a threat to U.S. national security.

On May 10, President Clinton issues an Executive Order to assist developing countries in importing and producing generic HIV treatments.

In July, UNAIDS (the Joint United Nations Programme on HIV/AIDS), the World Health Organization (WHO), and other global health groups announce a joint initiative with five major pharmaceutical manufacturers to negotiate reduced prices for HIV/AIDS drugs in developing countries.

On July 23, the leaders of the "Group of Eight" (G8) Summit release a statement acknowledging the need for additional HIV/AIDS resources. G8 members make up most of the world's largest economies and include Canada, France, Germany, Italy, Japan, Russia, the United Kingdom, and the United States.

In August, the U.S. Congress enacts the Global AIDS and Tuberculosis Relief Act of 2000.

In September, as part of its Millennium Declaration, the United Nations adopts the Millennium Development Goals, which include a specific goal of reversing the spread of HIV/AIDS, malaria, and TB.

In October, the U.S. Congress reauthorizes the Ryan White CARE Act for the second time.

---------------------------- 2001 ----------------------------

February 7 marks the first annual National Black HIV/AIDS Awareness Day in the U.S.

May 18 is the first annual observance of HIV Vaccine Awareness Day.

On June 25-27, the United Nations (UN) General Assembly holds its first Special Session on AIDS (UNGASS) and passes the UNGASS Declaration of Commitment and the ILO (International Labor Organization) Code of Practice on HIV/AIDS in the Workplace. The meeting also calls for the creation of an international "global fund" to support efforts by countries and organizations to combat the spread of HIV through prevention, care, and treatment, including the purchase of HIV medications.

Newly appointed U.S. Secretary of State, Colin Powell, reaffirms the U.S. statement that HIV/AIDS is a national security threat.

After generic drug manufacturers offer to produce discounted, generic forms of HIV/AIDS drugs for developing countries; several major pharmaceutical manufacturers agree to offer further reduced drug prices to those countries.

On November 14, the World Trade Organization (WTO) announces the Doha Declaration, which affirms the rights of developing countries to buy or manufacture generic medications to meet public health crises such as HIV/AIDS.

The U.S. Health Resources and Services Administration (HRSA) begins focusing on individuals with HIV disease who know their status and are not receiving HIV-related services. HRSA instructs its grantees to address this population's "unmet need" for services.

The U.S. Centers for Disease Control and Prevention (CDC) announce a new HIV Prevention Strategic Plan to cut annual HIV infections in the U.S. by half within five years.

---------------------------- 2002 ----------------------------

In January, the Global Fund to Fight AIDS, Tuberculosis and Malaria, a partnership between governments, civil society organizations, the private sector, and affected communities, is established.

On April 25, the Global Fund approves its first round of grants to governments and private-sector organizations in the developing world. The grants total $600 million for two-year projects.

On June 25, the United States announces a framework that will allow developing countries unable to produce pharmaceuticals to gain greater access to drugs needed to combat HIV/AIDS, malaria, and other public health crises.

In July, UNAIDS (the Joint United Nations Programme on AIDS) reports that HIV/AIDS is now by far the leading cause of death in sub-Saharan Africa and the fourth biggest global killer. Average life expectancy in sub-Saharan Africa falls from 62 years to 47 years as a result of AIDS.

The 14th International AIDS Conference is held in Barcelona, Spain from July 7-12. Dozens of countries report they are experiencing serious HIV/AIDS epidemics, and much more are on the brink.

In September, the U.S. National Intelligence Council releases Next Wave of the Epidemic, a report focusing on HIV in India, China, Russia, Nigeria, and Ethiopia.

On November 7, the U.S. Food and Drug Administration (FDA) approves the first rapid HIV diagnostic test kit for use in the United States that provides results with 99.6 percent accuracy in as little as 20 minutes. Unlike other antibody tests for HIV, this blood test can be stored at room temperature, requires no specialized equipment, and may be used outside of traditional laboratory or clinical settings, allowing more widespread use of HIV testing. Worldwide, 10 million young people, aged 15-24, and almost 3 million children under 15 are living with HIV. During this year, approximately 3.5 million new infections will occur in sub-Saharan Africa, and the epidemic will claim the lives of an estimated 2.4 million Africans.

Side effects and increasing evidence of drug resistance call into question the "hit early, hit hard" strategy.

---------------------------- 2003 ----------------------------

The U.S. Centers for Disease Control and Prevention (CDC) calculate that 27,000 of the estimated 40,000 new infections that occur each year in the U.S. result from transmission by individuals who do not know they are infected.

On January 28, President George W. Bush announces the creation of the United States President's Emergency Plan for AIDS Relief (PEP-FAR) in his State of the Union address. PEPFAR is a $15 billion, 5-year plan to combat AIDS, primarily in countries with a high burden of infections.

On February 24, VaxGen, a San Francisco-based biotechnology company, announces that its AIDS-VAX vaccine trial failed to reduce overall HIV infection rates among those who were vaccinated.

On March 31, the Bill and Melinda Gates Foundation awards a $60 million grant to the International Partnership for Microbicides to support research and development of microbicides to prevent transmission of HIV.

On April 18, CDC announces Advancing HIV Prevention: New Strategies for a Changing Epidemic, a new prevention initiative that aims to reduce barriers to early diagnosis and increase access to, and utilization of, quality medical care, treatment, and ongoing prevention services for those living with HIV.

In early June, the "Group of Eight" (G8) Summit includes a special focus on HIV/AIDS and announcements of new commitments to the Global Fund. G8 members make up most of the world's largest economies and include Canada, France, Germany, Italy, Japan, Russia, the United Kingdom, and the United States.

October 15 marks the first annual National Latino AIDS Awareness Day in the U.S.

On October 23, the William J. Clinton Foundation secures price reductions for HIV/AIDS drugs from generic manufacturers, to benefit developing nations.

On December 1, the World Health Organization (WHO) announces the "3 by 5" initiative, to bring treatment to 3 million people by 2005.

---------------------------- 2004 ----------------------------

In January, the U.S. Congress authorizes the first $350 million for the United States President's Emergency Program for AIDS Relief (PEPFAR).

In February, UNAIDS (the Joint United Nations Programme on AIDS) launches The Global Coalition on Women and AIDS to raise the visibility of the epidemic's impact on women and girls around the world.

On March 26, the U.S. Food and Drug Administration (FDA) approves the use of oral fluid samples with a rapid HIV diagnostic test kit that provides the result in approximately 20 minutes.

On May 17, FDA issues a guidance document for expedited approval of low-cost, safe, and effective co-packaged and fixed-dose combination HIV therapies so that high-quality drugs can be made available in Africa and developing countries around the world under PEPFAR.

On June 10, leaders of the "Group of Eight" (G8) Summit (Canada, France, Germany, Italy, Japan, Russia, the United Kingdom, and the United States) call for the creation of a "Global HIV Vaccine Enterprise ," a consortium of government and private-sector groups designed to coordinate and accelerate research efforts to find an effective HIV vaccine.

-------------------------- 2005 --------------------------

During its annual meeting in January, the World Economic Forum approves a set of new priorities, including one with a focus on addressing HIV/AIDS in Africa and other hard-hit regions.

On January 26, the World Health Organization (WHO), UNAIDS (the Joint United Nations Programme on HIV/AIDS), the U.S. Government, and the Global Fund to Fight AIDS, Tuberculosis, and Malaria announce results of joint efforts to increase the availability of antiretroviral drugs in developing countries. An estimated 700,000 people have been reached by the end of 2004.

Also on January 26, the U.S. Food and Drug Administration (FDA) grants tentative approval to a generic copackaged antiretroviral drug regimen for use under the United States President's Emergency Plan for AIDS Relief (PEPFAR).

May 19 is the first annual National Asian and Pacific Islander HIV/AIDS Awareness Day in the U.S.

On June 2, the United Nations (U.N.) General Assembly High-Level Meeting on HIV/AIDS meets to review progress on targets set at the 2001 U.N. General Assembly Special Session on HIV/AIDS (UNGASS).

On July 6-8, the "Group of Eight" (G8) Summit focuses on development in Africa, including HIV/AIDS. G8 members make up most of the world's largest economies and include: Canada, France, Germany, Italy, Japan, Russia, the United Kingdom, and the United States.

-------------------------- 2006 --------------------------

June 5 marks 25 years since the first AIDS cases were reported.

March 10 is the first annual National Women and Girls HIV/AIDS Awareness Day in the U.S.

March 20 is the first annual observance of National Native HIV/AIDS Awareness Day in the U.S.

On May 3-6, the Office of AIDS Research, in the National Institutes of Health (NIH), sponsors Embracing Our Traditions, Values, and Teachings: Native Peoples of North America HIV/AIDS Conference, in Anchorage, Alaska. The conference involves nearly 1,000 participants from the American Indian, Alaska Native, Native Hawaiian, First Nations, and U.S. Territorial Pacific Islander communities.

On May 31, the United Nations convenes a followup meeting and issues a progress report on the implementation of the Declaration of Commitment on HIV/AIDS.

On September 22, the U.S. Centers for Disease Control and Prevention (CDC) released revised HIV testing recommendations for health care settings, recommending routine HIV screening for all adults, aged 13-64, and yearly screening for those at high risk.

In December, a University of Illinois at Chicago study indicates that medical circumcision of men reduces their risk of acquiring HIV during heterosexual intercourse by 53 percent. The clinical trial of Kenyan men is supported by the U.S. National Institute for Allergy and Infectious Diseases and the Canadian Institute of Health Research.

On December 19, the U.S. Congress reauthorizes the Ryan White CARE Act for the third time.

------------------------ 2007 ------------------------

In an attempt to increase the number of people taking HIV tests, on May 30, the World Health Organization (WHO) and UNAIDS (the Joint United Nations Programme on HIV/AIDS) issue new guidance recommending "provider-initiated" HIV testing in healthcare settings.

In June, the Rwandan Government hosts the International HIV/AIDS Implementers Meeting. Over 1,500 delegates share lessons on HIV prevention, treatment, and care. Cosponsors include WHO, UNAIDS, the United States President's Emergency Plan for AIDS Relief (PEPFAR), The Global Fund to Fight AIDS, Tuberculosis, and Malaria, the United Nations Children's Fund (UNICEF), the World Bank, and GNP+ (the Global Network of People Living with HIV).

In October, the U.S. Centers for Disease Control and Prevention (CDC) launch Prevention IS Care (PIC), a social marketing campaign designed for healthcare providers who deliver care to people living with HIV.

CDC reports over 565,000 people have died of AIDS in the U.S. since 1981.

------------------------ 2008 ------------------------

In June, the International HIV/AIDS Implementers Meeting is hosted by the Ugandan Government. Cosponsors include the United States President's Emergency Plan for AIDS Relief (PEPFAR), The Global Fund to Fight AIDS, Tuberculosis, and Malaria, UNAIDS (the Joint United Nations Programme on HIV/AIDS), the World Health Organization (WHO), the United Nations Children's Fund (UNICEF), the World Bank, and GNP+

(the Global Network of People Living with HIV).

On July 31, President Bush signs legislation reauthorizing PEPFAR for an additional five years for up to $48 billion. The bill contains a rider that lifts the blanket ban on HIV-positive travelers to the U.S. and gives the U.S. Department of Health and Human Services the authority to admit people living with HIV/AIDS on a case-by-case basis.

On August 6, the U.S. Centers for Disease Control and Prevention (CDC) released new domestic HIV incidence estimates that are substantially higher than previous estimates (56,300 new infections per year vs. 40,000). The new estimates do not represent an actual increase in the numbers of HIV infections but reflect a more accurate way of measuring new infections. A separate analysis suggests that the annual number of new infections was never as low as 40,000 and that it has been roughly stable since the late 1990s.

September 18 is the first observance of National HIV/AIDS and Aging Awareness Day.

National Gay Men's HIV/AIDS Awareness Day is first recognized on September 27.

---------------------------- 2009 ----------------------------

Newly elected President Barack Obama calls for the development of the first National HIV/AIDS Strategy for the United States.

In February, the District of Columbia Health Department's HIV/AIDS, Hepatitis, STD, and TB Administration reports that Washington, DC has a higher rate of HIV (3% prevalence) than West Africa– enough to describe it as a "severe and generalized epidemic."

On April 7, the White House and the U.S. Centers for Disease Control and Prevention (CDC) launch the Act Against AIDS campaign, a multiyear, multi faceted communication campaign designed to reduce HIV incidence in the United States. CDC also launches the Act Against AIDS Leadership Initiative (AAALI), to harness the collective strength and reach of traditional, longstanding African American institutions to increase HIV-related awareness, knowledge, and action within Black communities across the U.S.

On May 5, President Obama launches the Global Health Initiative (GHI), a six-year, U.S. $63 billion effort to develop a comprehensive approach to addressing global health in low- and middle-income countries. The United States President's Emergency Plan for AIDS Relief (PEPFAR) will serve as a core component.

June 8 marks the first annual recognition of Caribbean-American HIV/AIDS Awareness Day.

On August 17, the Department of Veterans Affairs (VA) moves to increase the number of veterans getting HIV tests by dropping the requirement for written consent (verbal consent is still required).

On October 6, the U.S. Food and Drug Administration (FDA), in association with the PEPFAR program, approves the 100th antiretroviral drug.

On October 30, President Obama announces that his administration will officially lift the HIV travel and immigration ban in January 2010 by removing the final regulatory barriers to entry. The lifting of the travel ban occurs in conjunction with the announcement that the International AIDS Conference will return to the United States for the first time in more than 20 years. The conference will be held in Washington, DC in 2012.

On November 24, UNAIDS (the Joint United Nations Programme on HIV/AIDS) reports that there has been a significant decline (-17%) in new HIV infections in the past decade. East Asia, however, has seen a dramatic 25% increase in infections over the same period.

In December, President Obama signs the Consolidated Appropriations Act, 2010, modifying the ban on the use of Federal funds for needle exchange programs. When applicable, Federal funds may be used for personnel, equipment, syringe disposal services, educational materials, communication and marketing activities and evaluation activities, and evaluation. Some HHS programs may still contain partial or complete bans on the use of funds for needle exchange programs.

---------------------------- 2010 ----------------------------

On January 4, the U.S. Government officially lifts the HIV travel and immigration ban.

On March 23, President Obama signs the Patient Protection and Affordable Care Act, which expands access to care and prevention for all Americans—but offers special protections for those living with chronic illnesses, like HIV, which makes it difficult for them to access or afford health care.

On July 13, the Obama Administration releases the first comprehensive National HIV/AIDS Strategy for the United States.

The 18th International AIDS Conference takes place in Vienna, Austria from July 18-23. The biggest outcomes from the conference include: The results of the Centre for the AIDS Programme of Research in South Africa's (CAPRISA) 004 study of antiretroviral-based vaginal microbicides are released on

July 19. The study shows the microbicides to be safe and effective in reducing risks of new HIV infections among women by 39%. Women who use the microbicides as directed have even higher rates of protection (54%) against HIV infection.

The National Institutes of Health (NIH) announce the results of the iPrEx study, showing that a daily dose of HIV drugs reduced the risk of HIV infection among HIV-negative men who have sex with men by 44%, supporting the concept of pre-exposure prophylaxis (PrEP) in a targeted population.

On September 20-22, the United Nations (UN) convenes a summit to accelerate progress toward the 2015 Millennium Development Goals.

Also in September, the World Health Organization (WHO), UNAIDS (the Joint United Nations Programme on HIV/AIDS), and the United Nations Children's Fund (UNICEF) publish their annual Universal Access report for low- and middle-income countries. The report shows an estimated 5.25 million people were receiving antiretroviral therapy in 2009, and an estimated 1.2 million people started treatment that same year – the largest annual increase yet recorded.

AIDS Action merges with the National AIDS Fund to form AIDS United.

---------------------------- 2011 ----------------------------

Public debate begins on whether the longstanding ban on transplants of HIV-infected organs should be dropped.

Lead Federal agencies release implementation plans in support of the U.S. National HIV/AIDS Strategy.

The U.S. Department of Health and Human Services (HHS) launches the 12 Cities Project, an HHS-wide project that supports and accelerates comprehensive HIV/AIDS planning and cross-agency response in the 12 U.S. jurisdictions that bear the highest AIDS burden in the country.

AIDS activist and award-winning actress Elizabeth Taylor dies on March 23. One of the first celebrities to advocate on behalf of people living with HIV and AIDS, Taylor was the founding national chairman of amfAR (American Foundation for AIDS Research), a nonprofit organization that supports AIDS research, HIV prevention, treatment education, and advocates for AIDS-related public policy.

On June 8, HHS Secretary Sebelius hosted "Commemorating 30 Years of Leadership in the Fight against HIV/AIDS".

Over 3,000 people participate in the United Nation's (UN) High-Level Meeting on HIV/AIDS in New York from June 8–10. The session recognizes critical milestones, including three decades of the pandemic and the 10-year anniversary of the 2001 UN General Assembly Special Session on HIV/AIDS and the resulting Declaration of Commitment. At the Meeting, the U.S. joined with other partners in launching a global plan to eliminate mother-to-child transmission of HIV and keep mothers alive.

July 13 marks the one-year anniversary of the White House National HIV/AIDS Strategy. The White House released a video: "President Obama's National HIV/AIDS Strategy "and the "National HIV/AIDS Strategy: Implementation Plan Update."

On July 13, a new CDC study (TDF2) and a separate trial (the Partners PrEP study) provide the first evidence that a daily oral dose of antiretroviral drugs used to treat HIV infection can also reduce HIV acquisition among uninfected individuals exposed to the virus through heterosexual sex.

At the International AIDS Society's Conference on HIV Pathogenesis, Treatment, and Prevention in Rome (July 17-20), scientists announce that two studies have confirmed that individuals taking daily antiretroviral drugs experienced infection rates more than 60 percent lower than those on a placebo.

In September, the Office of National AIDS Policy begins to convene a series of five regional dialogues to focus attention on critical implementation issues for the National HIV/AIDS Strategy.

On September 30, the first Road to AIDS 2012 Town Hall meeting kicks off in San Francisco. This is the first of 15 meetings to be held across the country, leading up to the XIX International AIDS Conference (AIDS 2012), to be held July 22-27, 2012, in Washington, DC.

On November 8, Secretary of State Hillary Rodham Clinton shares the U.S. Government's bold new vision of creating an AIDS-free generation and speaks about the remarkable progress made in 30 years of fighting AIDS.

On December 1 (World AIDS Day), at the ONE Campaign and (RED) event in Washington, DC, President Obama announces accelerated efforts to increase the availability of treatment to people living with HIV/AIDS in the United States. He challenges the global community to deliver funds to The Global Fund to Fight AIDS, Tuberculosis, and Malaria and calls on Congress to keep its past commitments intact. He calls on all Americans to keep fighting to end the epidemic.

On December 23, the journal Science announces that it has chosen the HPTN 052 study as its 2011 Breakthrough of the Year.

-------------------------- 2012 --------------------------

March 13: Researchers from the University of New South Wales in Australia find that people living with HIV who are taking antiretroviral therapy (ART) have an increased risk of cardiovascular disease.

March 27: The U.S. Department of Health and Human Services issues new HIV treatment guidelines recommending treatment for all HIV-infected adults and adolescents, regardless of CD4 count or viral load.

July 1: The Kaiser Family Foundation and the Washington Post released a joint survey of the American public's attitudes, awareness, and experiences related to HIV and AIDS. The survey finds that roughly a quarter of Americans do not know that HIV cannot be transmitted by sharing a drinking glass—almost exactly the same share as in 1987.

July 3: The FDA approves the first at-home HIV test that will let users learn their HIV status right away.

July 16: The FDA approves the use of Truvada® for pre-exposure prophylaxis (PrEP). Adults who do not have HIV, but who are at risk for infection, can now take this medication to reduce their risk of getting the virus through sexual activity.

July 22-27: The XIX International AIDS Conference (AIDS 2012) is held in Washington, DC—the first time since 1990 that the conference has been held in the United States. Conference organizers had refused to convene the event in the U.S. until the Federal government lifted the ban on HIV-positive travelers entering the country.

During AIDS 2012, the AIDS Memorial Quilt is

displayed in its entirety in Washington, DC, for the first time since 1996. Volunteers have to rotate nearly 50,000 panels to ensure that the entire work is displayed. Microsoft Research, the University of Southern California, the NAMES Project Foundation, and a handful of other institutions collaborate to create a zoomable "map" of the Quilt.

---------------------------- 2013 ----------------------------

The U.S. President's Emergency Plan for AIDS Relief (PEPFAR) celebrates its 10th anniversary.

March 4: NIH-funded scientists announce the first well-documented case of an HIV-infected child, designated as "the Mississippi Baby," who appears to have been functionally cured of HIV infection (i.e., no detectable levels of virus or signs of disease, even without antiretroviral therapy.

June 2: The New York Times runs two articles which focus on middle-aged people living with HIV: The Faces of H.I.V. in New York in 2013 and 'People Think It's Over': Spared Death, Aging People With H.I.V. Struggle to Live.

June 5: The National Minority AIDS Council (NMAC) releases RISE Proud: Combating HIV among Black Gay and Bisexual Men, an action plan to mitigate the impact of HIV on black gay and bisexual men.

June 18: Secretary of State John Kerry announces that thanks to direct PEPFAR support, more than 1 million infants have been born HIV-free since 2003.

July 3: Researchers report that two HIV-positive patients in Boston who had bone-marrow transplants for blood cancers have apparently been virus-free for weeks since their antiretroviral drugs were stopped.

July 13: President Obama issues an Executive Order directing Federal agencies to prioritize supporting the HIV care continuum as a means of implementing the National HIV/AIDS Strategy. The HIV Care Continuum Initiative aims to accelerate efforts to improve the percentage of people living with HIV who move from testing to treatment and—ultimately—to viral suppression.

October: The National Latino AIDS Action Network (NLAAN)—a diverse coalition of community-based organizations, national organizations, state and local health departments, researchers and concerned individuals—publishes the National Latino/Hispanic HIV/AIDS Action Agenda to raise awareness, identify priorities, and issue specific recommendations to address the impact of the epidemic in Hispanic/Latino communities.

November 21: President Obama signs the HIV Organ Policy Equity (HOPE) Act, which will allow people living with HIV to receive organs from other infected donors. The HOPE Act has the potential to save the lives of about 1,000 HIV-infected patients with liver and kidney failure annually.

December 5: Nelson Mandela —South African anti-apartheid leader, political prisoner, and national President from 1994 to 1999—dies at the age of 95. After his son, Makgatho, died of AIDS-related causes in 2005, Mandela spent the remainder of his post-presidential career working to address the AIDS epidemic in South Africa, which is home to the largest number of people living with HIV (~6.8 million) in the world.

At the end of 2012, UNAIDS estimates that, worldwide, 2.3 million people were newly infected with HIV during the year, and 1.6 million people died of AIDS. Approximately 35.3 million people around the world are now living with HIV, including more than 1.2 million Americans.

UNAIDS also announces that new HIV infections have dropped more than 50% in 25 low- and middle-income countries, and the number of people getting antiretroviral treatment has increased 63% in the past two years.

---------------------------- 2014 ----------------------------

January 1: Major provisions of the Affordable Care Act (ACA) designed to protect consumers go into effect. Insurers are now barred from discriminating against customers with pre-existing conditions, and they can no longer impose annual limits on coverage—both key advances for people living with HIV/AIDS.

January 2: News sources report that the two Boston patients believed to have been cured of HIV after undergoing treatment for cancer have relapsed.

February 3: amfAR announces the launch of Countdown to a Cure for AIDS, a $100 million research initiative aimed at finding a broadly applicable cure for HIV by 2020.

March 4: European researchers announced the results of the first phase of the PARTNER Study, an observational study focusing on the risk of sexual HIV transmission when an HIV-positive person is on treatment. The study found that no HIV-positive partner who was undergoing antiretroviral therapy and had an undetectable viral load had transmitted HIV.

March—The United Nations Commission on the Status of Women releases a report on the challenges and achievements of implementing the MDGs for women and girls. The Commission concludes that progress on MDG6 (Combating HIV/AIDS, Malaria, and Other Diseases) has been limited, given that the number of women living with HIV globally continues to increase. The report notes several key challenges: adolescent/young women's particular vulnerability to HIV; the need to increase access to healthcare services; and the challenges of structural gender inequalities, stigma, discrimination, and violence.

March 24—Douglas Brooks is appointed as the new Director of the White House Office of National AIDS Policy (ONAP). He is the first African-American and the first HIV-positive person to hold the position.

April 4: Dr. Deborah Birx is sworn in as Ambassador at Large and U.S. Global AIDS Coordinator to oversee the President's Emergency Plan for AIDS Relief (PEPFAR). She replaces Dr. Eric Goosby.

July 10: The National Institutes of Health announced that the "Mississippi baby" now has detectable levels of HIV after more than two years of showing no evidence of the virus.

July 17: Flight MH17, en route from Amsterdam to Kuala Lumpur, is shot down over conflict-ridden Ukraine, killing all 298 people aboard, including six prominent scientists and AIDS activists on their way to the 20th International AIDS Conference (AIDS 2014) in Melbourne, Australia.

July 20-25: AIDS 2014 draws nearly 14,000 delegates from over 200 nations. One key message of the conference is that a one-size-fits-all approach may not be suitable for all settings, especially given the diversity of the epidemic's geographical hotspots and key populations. Interventions and policies will require target-based strategies and greater support of key populations, especially in countries where discriminatory policies and legislation are hindering prevention and treatment efforts.

September 9: The Pew Charitable Trust publishes Southern States Are Now Epicenter of HIV/AIDS in the U.S.

October 9: CDC releases a new report that finds gaps in care and treatment among Latinos diagnosed with HIV.

November 25: CDC announces that only 30% of Americans with HIV had the virus under control in 2011, and approximately two-thirds of those whose virus was out of control had been diagnosed but were no longer in care.

December 23: FDA announces it will recommend changing the blood donor deferral guidelines for men who have sex with men from permanent deferral to one year since the last sexual contact. In 1983, the agency imposed a lifetime ban on donating blood for all men who have ever had sex with another man.

--------------------------- 2015 ---------------------------

January 8: A review of multiple studies of South African women indicates that using Depo Provera, an injectable contraceptive, may increase women's chances of contracting HIV by 40 percent.

February 5: HHS announces the launch of a new, 4-year demonstration project to address HIV disparities among MSM of color. The cross-agency project, "Developing Comprehensive Models of HIV Prevention and Care Services for MSM of Color," will support community-based models for HIV prevention and treatment.

February 23: CDC's annual HIV Surveillance Report, indicates that HIV diagnosis rates in the U.S. remained stable between 2009-2013, but men who have sex with men, young adults, racial/ethnic minorities, and individuals living in the South continue to bear a disproportionate burden of HIV.

February 23: CDC announces that more than 90% of new HIV infections in the United States could be prevented by diagnosing people living with HIV and ensuring they receive prompt ongoing care and treatment.

February 25: Indiana state health officials announced an HIV outbreak linked to injection drug use in the southeastern portion of the state. By the end of the year, Indiana will confirm 184 new cases of HIV linked to the outbreak.

April 15: NIH launches a large, multicenter, international clinical trial to study heart disease in people living with HIV, who are up to twice as likely as HIV-negative individuals to have heart attacks and other forms of cardiovascular disease.

May 8: The U.S. Department of Health and Human Services announces on May 8 that it will amend the Federal rules covering organ transplants to allow the recovery of transplantable organs from HIV-positive donors. The new regulations will provide a framework for clinical studies on transplanting organs from HIV-positive donors to HIV-positive recipients.

May 27: Results from the Strategic Timing of AntiRetroviral Treatment (START) study indicate that HIV-positive individuals who start taking antiretroviral drugs before their CD4+ cell counts decrease to have a considerably lower risk of developing AIDS or other serious illnesses. Subsequent data releases show that early therapy for people living with HIV also prevents the onset of cancer, cardiovascular disease, and other non-AIDS-related diseases.

June 30: The World Health Organization certifies that Cuba is the first nation to eliminate mother-to-child transmission of both HIV and syphilis.

July 14: UNAIDS announces that the targets for Millennium Development Goal #6—halting and reversing the spread of HIV—have been achieved and exceeded nine months ahead of schedule set in 2000.

July 20: Researchers report that antiretroviral therapy is highly effective at preventing sexual transmission of HIV from a person living with HIV to an uninfected heterosexual partner when the HIV-positive partner is virally suppressed. The finding comes from the decade-long HPTN 052 clinical trial.

July 23: The U.S. Food and Drug Administration approves the first diagnostic test that differentiates between different types of HIV infections (HIV-1 and HIV-2). The test can also differentiate between acute and established HIV infections.

July 30: The White House launches the National HIV/AIDS Strategy: Updated to 2020. The updated Strategy retains the vision and goals of the original but reflects scientific advances, transformations in healthcare access as a result of the Affordable Care Act, and a renewed emphasis on key populations, geographic areas, and practices necessary to end the domestic HIV epidemic.

September 18: The U.S. Departments of Housing and Urban Development and Justice announced they will collaborate on a demonstration project to provide housing assistance and supportive services to low-income persons living with HIV/AIDS who are victims of sexual assault, domestic violence, dating violence, or stalking.

September 26: At a United Nations summit on the Sustainable Development Goals, the United States announces new PEPFAR prevention and treatment targets for 2016–2017. By the end of 2017, the U.S. will commit sufficient resources to support antiretroviral therapy for 12.9 million people, provide 13 million male circumcisions for HIV prevention, and reduce HIV incidence by 40% among adolescent girls and young women within the highest burdened areas of 10 sub-Saharan African countries.

September 30: The World Health Organization announces new treatment recommendations that call for all people living with HIV to begin antiretroviral therapy as soon after diagnosis as possible. WHO also recommends daily oral PrEP as an additional prevention choice for those at substantial risk for contracting HIV. WHO estimates the new policies could help avert more than 21 million deaths and 28 million new infections by 2030.

October 20: Greater than AIDS launches a new campaign, Empowered: Women, HIV, and Intimate Partner Violence, to bring more attention to issues of relationship violence and provide resources for women who may be at risk of, or dealing with, abuse and HIV.

November 17: Actor Charlie Sheen announces his HIV-positive status in a nationally televised interview. The significant public conversation about HIV follows his disclosure. Earlier in the year, rapper, performance artist, and poet Mykki Blanco took to Facebook to disclose his HIV status, and former child TV star Danny Pintauro told Oprah that he is living with HIV.

November 24: UNAIDS releases its 2015 World

AIDS Day report, which finds that 15.8 million people were accessing antiretroviral treatment as of June 2015—more than doubling the number of people who were on treatment in 2010.

November 30: amfAR, The Foundation for AIDS Research, announces its plan to establish the amfAR Institute for HIV Cure Research at the University of California, San Francisco. As the cornerstone of amfAR's $100 million investment in cure research, the Institute will work to develop the scientific basis for an HIV cure by the end of 2020.

December 1: The White House releases a Federal Action Plan to accompany the updated National HIV/AIDS Strategy. The plan was developed by 10 Federal agencies and the Equal Employment Opportunity Commission and contains 170 action items that the agencies will undertake to achieve the goals of the Strategy.

December 6: CDC announces that annual HIV diagnoses in the U.S. fell by 19% from 2005 to 2014. There were steep declines among heterosexuals, people who inject drugs, and African Americans (especially black women), but trends for gay/bisexual men varied by race/ethnicity. Diagnoses among white gay/bisexual men decreased by 18%, but they continued to rise among Latino gay/bisexual men and were up 24%. Diagnoses among black gay/bisexual men also increased (22%), but the increase has leveled off since 2010.

December 19: Partly in response to the HIV outbreak in Indiana, which is linked to people injecting drugs, Congress lifts restrictions that prevented states and localities from spending Federal funds for needle exchange programs.

December 21: The U.S. Food and Drug Administration

announces it will lift its 30-year-old ban on all blood donations by men who have sex with men and institute a policy that allows them to donate blood if they have not had sexual contact with another man in the previous 12 months.

---------------------------- 2016 ----------------------------

January 19: The U.S. Centers for Disease Control and Prevention report that only 1 in 5 sexually active high school students has been tested for HIV. An estimated 50% of young Americans who are living with HIV do not know they are infected.

January 28: Researchers announce that an international study of over 1,900 patients with HIV who failed to respond to the antiretroviral drug tenofovir— a key HIV treatment medication—indicates that HIV resistance to the medication is becoming increasingly common.

February 25: At the annual Conference on Retroviruses and Opportunistic Infections (CROI), researchers report that a man taking the HIV-prevention pill Truvada® has contracted HIV— marking the first reported infection of someone regularly taking the drug.

March 3: The White House Office of National AIDS Policy, the NIH Office of AIDS Research, and the National Institute of Mental Health co-host a meeting to address the issue of HIV stigma: Translating Research to Action: Reducing HIV Stigma to Optimize HIV Outcomes. Participants include researchers, policymakers, legal scholars, faith leaders, advocates, and people living with HIV.

March 3: Pharmacy researchers report finding that women need daily doses of the antiviral medication Truvada® to prevent HIV infection, while men only need two doses per week due to differences in the way the drug accumulates in vaginal, cervical and rectal tissue.

March 29: The U.S. Department of Health and Human Services releases new guidance for state, local, tribal, and territorial health departments that will allow them to request permission to use federal funds to support syringe services programs (SSPs). The funds can now be used to support a comprehensive set of services, but they cannot be used to purchase sterile needles or syringes for illegal drug injection.

May 24: The National Institutes of Health and partners announce they will launch a large HIV vaccine trial in South Africa in November 2016, pending regulatory approval. This represents the first time since 2009 that the scientific community has embarked on an HIV vaccine clinical trial of this size.

June 8-10: The United Nations holds its 2016 High-Level Meeting on Ending AIDS. UN member states pledge to end the AIDS epidemic by 2030, but the meeting is marked by controversy after more than 50 nations block the participation of groups representing LGBT people from the meeting. The final resolution barely mentions those most at risk for contracting HIV/AIDS: men who have sex with men, sex workers, transgender people and people who inject drugs.

Disclaimer and Acknowledgements

The information contained in this timeline has been drawn from numerous sources, including (but not limited to) the Kaiser Family Foundation, Australia's Albion Center, and the National Minority AIDS Council (NMAC).

We have also relied on material provided by the U.S. Centers for Disease Control and Prevention (CDC), the National Institutes of Health (NIH), the U.S. Food and Drug Administration (FDA), and the

U.S. Health Resources and Services Administration (HRSA).

The timeline is presented for informational purposes only. HIV.gov does not endorse any organization or viewpoint represented in entries drawn from non-Federal sources.

Where possible, specific dates have been provided, and events have been listed in chronological order. Entries without specific dates occurred in the year in which they are listed, but the order of those entries may not reflect the actual chronology of events.

Every attempt has been made to ensure that the information contained in the timeline is accurate. Please send any corrections to contact@AIDS.gov.

I hope you found the above information helpful and interesting. Certainly, a lot is being done to try and eradicate AIDS permanently, but more needs to be done. One way we can slow the spread of the disease is to abstain from sexual activity, illegal drug use, rape and sexual abuse by infected people.

My brother is now a statistic of a disease known worldwide.

One of the highlights most interesting to me was the reference to the youth in America. In today's society, sexual activity is at an all-time high among young people. Young people need to take this seriously. My brother was young when he was first diagnosed, and as you read, it changed the course of his life forever. Young people cannot afford to be complacent. They cannot afford to be as careless as the young man who expressed his incorrect opinion about AIDS to my brother.

If you have children old enough to understand sex, talk with them about HIV/AIDS and be sure they understand it is a very serious disease.

Exhort them to abstain from sex until marriage. Their ability to understand the risks associated with this life changing disease as well as other sexually trasmitted diseases can help save their lives and save your family from the life altering pain it caused my brother and our family.

Bibliography

Chapter 1:

    1.   HIV/AIDS Definition from https://www.hiv.org

Chapter 2:

    1.   Romans 13:13-14

    2.   Jeremiah 29:11

    3.   Psalm 139:13

Chapter 5:

    1.   Exodus 20:15

Chapter 6:

    1.   Proverbs 17:25

    2.   1 John 1:9

    3.   Acts 3:19

    4.   Proverbs 16:9

Chapter 7:

    1.   James 1:19-20

    2.   Psalm 103:13

    3.   1 Corinthians 13:13

    4.   John 3:16

    5.   1 Peter 5:8

    6.   John 8:12

Chapter 8:

1. Psalm 103:8

Chapter 9:

1. Proverbs 15:3

2. Proverbs 3:7

3. 2 Corinthians 3:16

Chapter 10:

1. Romans 3:23

2. 2 Peter 3:9

3. "I Have Decided to Follow Jesus – Lyrics by Sanhu Sundar

Chapter 11:

1. Matthew 9:20

Chapter 12:

1. James 1:2-5

2. James 1:5

3. James 1:12

Chapter 13:

1. The Lord's Place; https://theLordsplace.org

2. Proverbs 3:5-6

Chapter 14:

1. 2 Corinthians 12:9

2. "Thy Will" lyrics by Hillary Scott

Chapter 16:

1. Hebrews 2-4:14-16

2. Hebrews 9:14

3. John 14:21

4. Psalm 119:11; Romans 12:4-5; Galatians 5:16; 22-23;

Philippians 1:6; 1 Corinthians 2:14

5. 2 Timothy 3:16; Philippians 4:6; Matthew 28:18-20

6. "How He Loves" lyrics by John Mark McMillian

7. Romans 12:2

8. Matthew 22:37-39

9. Hebrews 10:35-39

10. Psalm 1:2-3

11. Psalm 51:16-17

12. Hebrews 11

13. Hebrews 13

14. James 1:2

15. James 1:12

16. James 3

Chapter 17:

1. "Dear Younger Me" Lyrics by Mercy Me

2. Ephesians 4:31

3. Ephesians 4:32

Chapter 18:

1. Would You Like to Know God Personally – Campus Crusade for Christ, Bright Media Foundation

2. Psalm 25:7

Chapter 19:

1. Matthew 5:4

2. Romans 8:28

3. Psalm 86:12

Chapter 20:

1. Psalm 25:4

2. Psalm 37:5

3. Psalm 19:14

Chapter 22:

1. CAP – Comprehensive AIDS Program – Found Care; www.foundcare.org/hiv-services

2. John 6:1-15

3. John 5:24

4. Romans 8:16-17

5. Philippians 4:19

Chapter 23

1. James 5

2. 1 Peter 4

3. 1 Peter 5

4. James 5:19-20

5. Matthew 11:28-30

Postlude

1. "A Place for Mom" www.aplaceformom.com › Assisted Living

2. "Age with Dignity" www.agingwithdignity.org

3. "Don't Sing Songs to a Heavy Heart" by Kenneth C. Haugk

Appendix:

1. The Federal Response to HIV/AIDS Epidemic; https:www.hiv.gov

Other Works
Written by
Jeanette Duby

The Fruit Wars © 2012
The Fruit Wars 2 © 2013
Purchase on Amazon.com

You can follow Jeanette Duby on
Facebook, Twitter, Instagram or her blog
at http://www.jeanetteduby.com.

www.ingramcontent.com/pod-product-compliance
Lightning Source LLC
LaVergne TN
LVHW041151080426
835511LV00006B/547